D0214573

DAILY LIFE DURING THE

SALEM WITCH TRIALS

DAILY LIFE DURING THE

SALEM WITCH TRIALS

K. DAVID GOSS

The Greenwood Press Daily Life Through History Series

 GREENWOOD

AN IMPRINT OF ABC-CLIO, LLC
Santa Barbara, California • Denver, Colorado • Oxford, England

Library of Congress Cataloging-in-Publication Data

Goss, K. David, 1952–
    Daily life during the Salem witch trials / K. David Goss.
        p. cm. — (The Greenwood Press daily life through history series)
    Includes bibliographical references and index.
    ISBN 978–0–313–37458–6 (hard copy : acid-free paper) — ISBN 978–0–313–37459–3 (ebook) 1. New England—History—Colonial period, ca. 1600–1775. 2. Massachusetts—History—Colonial period, ca. 1600–1775. 3. Salem (Mass.)—History—17th century. 4. New England—Social conditions—17th century. 5. Massachusetts—Social conditions—17th century. 6. Salem (Mass.)—Social conditions—17th century. 7. Witchcraft—Massachusetts—Salem—History—17th century. 8. Trials (Witchcraft)—Massachusetts—Salem—History—17th century. 9. Witchcraft—Social aspects—Massachusetts—History—17th century. 10. Trials (Witchcraft)—Social aspects—Massachusetts—History. I. Title.
    F7.G695   2012
    974.4′02—dc23   2012000202

ISBN: 978–0–313–37458–6
EISBN: 978–0–313–37459–3

16 15 14 13 12   1 2 3 4 5

This book is also available on the World Wide Web as an eBook.
Visit www.abc-clio.com for details.

Greenwood
An Imprint of ABC-CLIO, LLC

ABC-CLIO, LLC
130 Cremona Drive, P.O. Box 1911
Santa Barbara, California 93116-1911

This book is printed on acid-free paper ∞

Manufactured in the United States of America

This book is dedicated to my parents-in-law,
David and Doris Franz.

CONTENTS

ACKNOWLEDGMENTS

It is with deep appreciation that I must recognize the support and assistance I have received in the production of this book. For exhaustive work on researching images and illustrations, I would like to thank my colleague and research assistant, Mary-Ellen Smiley who greatly facilitated the organization and coordination of all sources. In addition, I must recognize the support and advice of my colleagues at Gordon College, particularly Dr. Steve Alter, Dr. Myron Schirer-Suter, and Dr. Mark Sargent, as well as the help and cooperation of Dr. Emerson Baker of Salem State University's history department, who kindly offered his assistance with sources and illustrations from his own research into the area surrounding Sir William Phips. Also, I am indebted to the Board of Trustees of Gordon College for granting me a semester sabbatical allowing me the time to research and write the book without the burden of teaching responsibilities. Moreover, I wish to thank Christine Bertoni, the assistant registrar for collection image services of the Peabody-Essex Museum and my long-time colleague, Richard Trask, director of the Danvers Archival Center for their assistance in locating some wonderful images to enrich the study of late seventeenth-century life. For some fascinating insights into several areas of study that enriched the text significantly, I wish to thank my son-in-law, and Harvard classics scholar, Alexei Grishin. For his work in transcribing several lengthy primary sources, I want to thank my son, David Andrew Goss as well as my daughter, Jennifer Anne Goss who assisted me with the development of the bibliography. Finally, for her patience, support, and encouragement in helping see the project through to a successful conclusion, I wish to thank my dear wife and best friend, Rebecca Joy Goss.

INTRODUCTION

The era of the Salem witch trials of 1692 has been the subject of intense scholarly interest for many years. Since the first published works were produced by contemporary observers such as Rev. Cotton Mather and Robert Calef to the present, the trials and the events surrounding them have fascinated both writers and their readers. In particular, numerous studies have focused upon the afflicted children and their possible motives for accusing nearly 200 individuals of witchcraft.

Narrative historians such as Marion Starkey have tried to explain the event as the result of excited young women seeking attention from their elders. Demographic historians, such as Paul Boyer and Stephen Nissenbaum have examined community conflict and the economic conditions prevailing in Salem Village in their search for motivation. Social historians such as Richard Godbeer, John Putnam Demos, and David D. Hall have explored the historical context which produced numerous incidences of trials and executions in New England from the 1640s to the 1690s. Sociologists and anthropologists, such as Chadwick Hansen have explored the dominant and underlying belief systems of the Salem community as a whole. Were the children consciously accusing innocent people, or were they the product of a repressive environment which preconditioned them to believe themselves to be under the power of satanic forces? Feminist historians have examined the dynamic tensions that existed between the patriarchal Puritan society and those women who sought to assert themselves, or simply resisted the norms that dominated and rigidly controlled female behavior. Others more recently have introduced the impact of psychological tensions prevalent in life on the frontier facing the constant threat of destruction with the sudden attack of native people as a contributing factor.

All of these studies have touched upon New England Puritan society in a tangential manner, but none have examined in detail the common daily lives of those who lived through this troublesome period in American colonial history.

The purpose of this book is to examine the daily lives of those people who lived in New England during the last decade of the seventeenth century. It will explore who they were, how they came to be in New England, their domestic life, prevailing customs, attitudes concerning the roles of men and women, and the importance of children and childrearing. Beyond the Puritan family, this book will examine prevailing Puritan attitudes concerning work, education, economy, business, politics, war, and religion. In exploring these various facets of life during the Salem witch trial period, it is hoped that a clearer image will emerge of New England's Puritan culture, enabling the student of that era to better understand the unique colonial society that existed in the late-seventeenth-century Massachusetts.

CHRONOLOGY: KEY EVENTS IN THE DEVELOPMENT OF NEW ENGLAND FROM 1620 TO 1700

1624–1626	The Dorchester Company establishes a short-lived fishing station on Cape Anne, Massachusetts and places it under the resident governorship of Roger Conant.
1626	After the dissolution of the Dorchester Company, the Cape Ann fishing station is disbanded and colonists remove themselves to Virginia Colony or return to England, while a small remnant of so-called "Old Planters" remain under the leadership of Roger Conant. Conant moves his group of followers to a new location which he calls "Naumkeag" located along the southern shore of the North River of present-day Salem Harbor.
1628	The Dorchester Company's claim to Massachusetts is purchased and transferred to the Massachusetts Bay Company based in London, England. In September, more settlers under the leadership of John Endicott arrive at Naumkeag (Salem) on

board the *Abigail*, revitalizing the colony and preparing the community for greater numbers of colonists.

1629   A vessel, the *Talbot*, carrying two ministers and more settlers arrive at Naumkeag. The name of the settlement is changed to "Salem," the place of peace. Upon their arrival, a new church was established at Salem, the first in Massachusetts Bay Colony.

1630   On June 12, 1630, the flagship, *Arbella*, a fleet of nine other vessels, and nearly 1,000 colonists arrive at Salem under the leadership of the newly appointed governor of the Massachusetts Bay Company, John Winthrop. Within three months of arrival, Governor Winthrop has established several other settlements including Charlestown, Boston, and Cambridge, Massachusetts.

October 19, 1630   First meeting of the Great and General Court, the governing body of Massachusetts Bay Colony.

1631   The right to vote in colonial elections extended to all male church members.

1632   The Massachusetts Great and General Court vote that the governor will be elected by the freemen of the colony.

1632   Rev. Thomas Hooker and his Cambridge congregation seek permission to migrate to the Connecticut River Valley.

1634   Rev. Roger Williams becomes the center of a lengthy controversy involving issues of landownership, qualifications for church membership, and the question of whether Puritans in New England should openly declare their separation from the Church of England.

1635–1638	Anne Hutchinson begins to hold meetings in her home to discuss Sabbath sermons and becomes involved in the Antinomian controversy which ultimately results in her expulsion from Massachusetts Bay Colony.
1636	Rev. Roger Williams is banished from Massachusetts Bay Colony and establishes the colony of Providence, later Rhode Island. This settlement will support a position of religious toleration under Williams's leadership.
1636–1637	The Pequot War breaks out between the Pequot and the colonists of Massachusetts, Connecticut, and Plymouth, resulting in the virtual destruction of the Pequot. This is the first major conflict between Puritan colonists and the Native American population.
1636	Rev. Hugh Peters replaces Roger Williams at Salem as pastor of the Salem congregation. He reunifies the community and establishes Winter Island as Salem's center for the fishing industry. Surplus salt cod becomes the town's principal export cargo, the foundation of the local economy.
1636	Newly arrived gentleman, Sir Henry Vane is elected governor of Massachusetts Bay Colony, replacing John Winthrop.
1636	Harvard College is established to train clergy for the pulpits of Massachusetts Bay Colony.
1637	John Winthrop is reelected governor of Massachusetts, defeating Sir Henry Vane.
1638	The vessel *Desire* arrives in Salem from the West Indies bearing Salem's first cargo of cotton, tobacco, and African slaves. This establishes Salem's essential West Indies Trade, the mainstay of the town's economy until the opening of trade with the Far East after the American Revolution.

1638	First American printing press is established at Cambridge by Stephen Daye.
1638	Rev. John Wheelwright is banished from Boston due to his support of Anne Hutchinson's position in the Antinomian controversy and establishes the town of Exeter, New Hampshire. Anne and her husband William Hutchinson establish the town of Portsmouth, Rhode Island.
1641	*Massachusetts Bay Psalm Book*, the first book to be published in America, is printed.
1641	The *Massachusetts Body of Liberties* is produced consisting of 100 liberties intended for use as guidance for the Massachusetts General Court of the time. It is considered by some legal experts as the precursor to the *General Laws of Massachusetts* and the *Massachusetts Constitution*. It incorporates English legal tradition into a colonial legal system—including the notion of equal justice for all citizens, the right of appeal, prohibitions against double jeopardy, and banned cruel punishment. The right to counsel and jury trial for all citizens is affirmed. The man responsible for compiling and editing this body of law was Nathaniel Ward (1578–1652) of Ipswich.
1643–1646	The first ironworks in America are established at Saugus and operated by indentured Scottish prisoners of war from Cromwell's war with Scotland.
1644	Massachusetts Great and General Court divides into an upper and lower house, the Court of Assistants (upper) and the General Assembly (lower house). The Court of Assistants retained veto authority over all lower-house activities.

1647	Alice Young of Windsor, Connecticut is tried and hanged at Hartford, Connecticut, becoming the first person executed for witchcraft in New England.
1648	Margaret Jones of Charlestown is hanged in Boston for witchcraft, becoming the first person in Massachusetts Bay Colony executed for witchcraft.
1648	Mary Johnson hanged for witchcraft at Hartford, Connecticut.
1648	*The Cambridge Platform* is announced to the residents of Massachusetts Bay Colony. This document, the result of two years of discussion and debate, clearly defines the religious way of life in Puritan New England. It outlines the Congregational method of church government and endorses the Westminster *Confession of Faith*.
1650	Mrs. Kendall of Cambridge hanged at Boston for witchcraft.
1651	Alice Lake, wife of Henry Lake of Dorchester is hanged for witchcraft at Boston.
1651	Mary Parsons of Springfield hanged at Boston for witchcraft.
1651	Goodwife Basset hanged for witchcraft at Fairfield, Connecticut.
1653	Goodwife Knapp hanged for witchcraft at Hartford, Connecticut.
1653	The first American public library established in Boston.
1656	Ann Hibbins hanged for witchcraft at Boston.
1656	The first group of Quakers arrive in Massachusetts Bay Colony, and are banished to Rhode Island.

1657–1662	The "Halfway Covenant" is instituted throughout the churches of Puritan New England allowing for partial church membership for those unable to testify publicly to a conversion experience. Those who accepted the Covenant and agreed to follow the essential principles of the Puritan faith would be allowed to become church members and partake of Communion with other church members.
1663	Goodman and Goodwife Greensmith are executed for witchcraft in Hartford, Connecticut.
1675–1676	"King Philip's War"—primarily between the New England Puritans and the Native American tribes of Massachusetts and Connecticut results in the destruction of dozens of colonial towns and villages and devastating casualties for both sides.
1684	Under the command of King Charles II, the Massachusetts Bay Charter is annulled and the rights of citizens to elect a colonial governor are revoked.
1686–1689	The Dominion of New England is created incorporating the colonies of Massachusetts, Connecticut, Rhode Island, New Hampshire, New York, and New Jersey under the governorship of Sir Edmund Andros.
1688	Boston experiences its final bout of witchcraft hysteria in a case involving the children of John Goodwin and Goody Glover, an elderly laundress who is hanged for witchcraft. Rev. Cotton Mather is involved in the case and writes a narrative, *Memorable Providences Relating to Witchcrafts and Possessions*, which is published and widely circulated.

1689   Governor Edmund Andros is arrested during the Boston Revolt and in 1690 is sent to England as a result of the Glorious Revolution in England and the removal of King James II. The Dominion of New England is ended and all its colonies return to their previous statuses.

1689   Rev. Samuel Parris is invited by the majority of residents of Salem Village to serve as pastor of their congregation which immediately splits into pro- and anti-Parris factions.

February 1691–1692   Tituba, the West Indian slave of Reverend Parris, begins her afternoon sessions with Elizabeth Parris and her cousin, Abigail Williams resulting in an outbreak of witchcraft accusations at Salem Village.

May 1692   Rev. Increase Mather and newly appointed royal governor Sir William Phips return to Boston from London bringing with them the new Massachusetts Colonial Charter issued by King William and Queen Mary.

1

THE CREATION OF PURITAN NEW ENGLAND, 1623–1692

Puritan New England has its true beginnings in 1620 when a small contingent of separatist exiles made their way from Holland via Plymouth, England to Cape Cod, settling along the inside arm of the Cape at a place called Plymouth. Although technically these people had abandoned the Church of England in favor of an independent, separate, and reformed Protestant faith, they nonetheless upheld those essential Calvinist principles which all Puritans espoused such as predestination (God chooses who will be saved), justification by faith (salvation is the gift of God through faith alone), and sanctification (all who are saved are spiritually transformed). In this way, separatists must be understood as the more radical spiritual kindred of the Puritans that would soon settle at Massachusetts Bay Colony.

But how did such an independent and reformed faith come into existence in the face of the power of Roman Catholicism? Simply put, a German monk by the name of Martin Luther (1483–1546), while teaching at the University of Wittenburg, Germany nailed a protest listing 95 disagreements he had with the Roman Catholic faith onto the door of the university church in 1517. He strongly protested the sale of indulgences which were licenses bought from the Roman Catholic Church to get relatives out of hell or purgatory. As a result of Luther's unwillingness to back down when confronted

Pilgrims arriving. (From *The History and Antiquities of New England* by John Barber [1844]. Private collection.)

by church authorities, he was excommunicated and fled into hiding, protected by the powerful elector of Saxony. Over time, he gathered thousands of followers who were likewise alienated from the Roman Catholic Church, and established the first Protestant sect, the Lutheran Church, in northern Germany.

From this point onward, thousands of European people converted to the new and independent protestant faith, among them a French priest named John Calvin who established a center for his particular brand of Protestantism in Geneva, Switzerland. Calvin took the ideas of Luther, and built a complex theology on top of them, gaining followers from all over Europe. Among his most devoted followers were England's small minority of "Puritans" who sought to truly reform the Church of England by purifying it of all vestiges of the Roman Catholic faith.

THE ORIGINS OF PURITANISM

Who were these Puritans and why did they come to New England in the seventeenth century? The answer to this question is long and complex—well beyond the scope of this work. In brief, the story of the Puritans of New England begins in 1534 when King Henry VIII broke from the Roman Catholic Church by the Act of Supremacy, making the monarch of England the supreme head of the Church of England.

This break with Rome took place at the height of the Protestant Reformation in Europe, sparking the creation of several denominations of reformed Protestantism including that of the Lutherans and Presbyterians. A small minority of reformed English Protestants hoped that King Henry's break with Rome would result in the creation of a truly reformed English Church as well—cleansed of all vestiges of Roman Catholicism. This purification included such changes as a complete transformation of worship practices including no use of Latin, no praying to saints, the removal of ceremonial clerical vestments, and the elimination of burning incense, candles, depictions of saint's images, stained-glass windows, crosses, and other imagery.

Clearly such changes were not what King Henry had in mind for the Church of England when he broke with Rome since he intended to keep the churches and services essentially the same, but without allegiance to Rome. The English Church, therefore, remained essentially Roman Catholic in its theology, ceremony, and litany only outside the control of the papacy. In this way, King Henry was able to make the break without alienating his many subjects who still felt the need to worship in the same way they had for centuries. The Puritans did not share this sentiment and wanted every last tradition and vestige of Roman Catholicism to be driven out of the Church of England. Thus, from the mid-sixteenth century onward, England supported an independent church, but with little evidence of reformed Protestant influence. At the same time, a minority of English Christians sought to "purify" the Church of England without success. These were the first "Puritans."

There were very good reasons for the reluctance of the English Church to jump headlong into the Protestant Reformation with enthusiasm. Chief among these was that a large part of the English population were still, in their hearts if not otherwise, Catholics. To completely transform the manner and style of worship of so many would be to provoke unrest and possible rebellion.

After King Henry's death, his heir, Edward VI (1537–1553), might have steered England into a more reformed path had he lived, and Edward's successor, and Catholic half-sister, Mary Tudor (1516–1558), or "Bloody Mary," might have brought England back under papal control had she had the time and political skill to do so. With her death in 1558, Elizabeth I (1533–1603) was placed upon the throne, and while committed to maintaining the independent Protestant status of the Church of England, she was equally determined to keep the nation from becoming a bastion of radical Protestantism. This meant that she would never sympathize with the now fully formed and articulated Puritan political agenda, and successfully kept the Puritan movement under control until her death in 1603.[1]

Thus, throughout the long Elizabethan Age (1558–1603), England's Puritan leadership struggled in their efforts to cleanse the Church of England, running headlong into repressive policies, laws, and measures minimizing their effectiveness, and often depriving them of their power and freedom entirely. It was only with the ascension of King James I in 1603, and the advent of the Stewart dynasty, that England's Puritans began to take hope in the future of their cause. James had been raised and taught the faith of reformer, John Knox, and was therefore thought to be more sympathetic with the Reformed faith.

The Puritan hope for the future purification of the English Church was dashed in a clash between England's Puritan leaders and King James I at the Hampton Court Conference in 1604. It was the Puritans' desire to reorganize the Church of England in such a way as to place all power in the hands of the clergy, or as one commentator describes, it was "a scheme of church government as would have put the religious life of the people . . ., in the uncontrolled hands of the preachers."[2] After several days of heated discussion, King James threatened to "harry them out of the land" if the Puritan agitators persisted in being a bother to him. At this point, a small contingent of Puritans, "abandoning all hope of purifying the English Church" or bringing it into conformity with reformed Protestantism, broke away to establish an independent "Separate" church. These radical ex-Puritans, refusing to worship with the unreformed majority in the state church, decided to risk arrest and imprisonment, rather than suffer guilt by association. It is this group of "Separatists," originating in the Lincolnshire region, near Scrooby, England, that ultimately were forced to relocate to more religiously tolerant Holland, in 1609.[3]

In Holland, two distinct Puritan/Separatist congregations were established—in Amsterdam and in Leyden. In 1619, the Leyden congregation, under the leadership of Rev. John Robinson with assistance from William Bradford, decided to relocate to the New World. Their reasons for the migration revolved primarily around what was perceived as the unfortunate corrupting influence the liberal Dutch culture was having upon their children. It was generally felt that a new environment, free from persecution and from corrupting moral and cultural influences, would be preferable. This decision led to the departure of a small number of Leyden's congregation without Pastor Robinson who chose to remain with hopes of a later crossing.

After much difficulty with transportation and recruiting additional colonists, the Leyden remnant of "saints," together with a group of approximately 50 non-Separatist "strangers" sailed from England, arriving at Cape Cod in December 1620. Importantly, in his advice on the departure of his followers, Pastor Robinson strongly urged them to work and worship together with those "strangers" that were to accompany them to the new colony. Thus somewhat ironically, the group to settle in New England though originally Separatist was by circumstances compelled to integrate themselves with a group of Church of England members, similar to those from whom they fled a decade earlier. The result of their efforts was the permanent establishment of Plymouth Colony and the planting of reformed Protestantism firmly in the soil of New England. In 1691, Plymouth Colony would be joined with Massachusetts Bay Colony, Martha's Vineyard, Nantucket Island, and what is now New Brunswick, Nova Scotia, and Maine to form the Province of Massachusetts Bay.

Massachusetts Bay Colony has its origins in the efforts of Rev. John White (1575–1648) and a small group of merchant-adventurers based in Dorchester, England known as the Dorchester Company. In 1624, this group, under the authority of the Plymouth Council for New England and the leadership of overseer Thomas Gardner (c. 1592–1674), established a small fishing station on Cape Ann, near present-day Gloucester. The overriding economic purpose of this settlement was to provide a regular, year-round supply of salt codfish to the markets of England. This would have the two-fold benefit of providing dividends to the merchant-adventurers, while helping to make the colony self-supporting. Secondarily, the vision of Rev. John White, one of the prime movers in this venture, was to create a religious sanctuary for England's nonconforming Puritans where a truly reformed English Church might flourish without the direct interference of archbishop of Canterbury or the king.

In 1625, the members of the Cape Ann settlement recruited a new overseer and minister, Roger Conant (1592–1679) and Rev. John Lyford (1580–1634) respectively, from the struggling South Shore fishing station of Nantasket (a Plymouth Colony trading post), located near present-day Hull. Roger Conant, a "salter" by profession, and his colleague, Rev. John Lyford were recent exiles from the Separatist colony at Plymouth—having been banished the previous year by Plymouth's governor William Bradford (1590–1657). Although no longer a Plymouth resident, Conant was an able negotiator and successfully resolved a dispute between the Plymouth

Colony and the settlers of the Cape Ann fishing station. In 1626, the Cape Ann settlement disbanded—some returning to England, others with Rev. Lyford, heading for Virginia, and a small remnant known colloquially as "The Old Planters" relocating with Conant to a site on the shore of present-day Salem Harbor known as "Naumkeag" from the Algonkian *namaas* (fish) *ki* (place) or "the fishing place."

Here, Conant and his followers would establish the first permanent settlement of what would soon become Massachusetts Bay Colony. Unfortunately for them, after 1626, the Dorchester Company was unable to provide any further economic support, and out of necessity a new and better funded company was formed upon the ruins of the old, with some of the same leadership. By 1628, partly due to the efforts of Rev. White, this new London-based group of merchants under the title "The New England Company for a Plantation in Massachusetts Bay," now under the leadership of their newly-elected governor, Matthew Craddock (?–1641) took up the challenge. In June 1628, this new company dispatched another shipload of colonists to Massachusetts under the direction of resident governor John Endicott (1588–1665) who replaced Roger Conant as the executive authority at Naumkeag.

THE FOUNDING OF MASSACHUSETTS BAY COLONY

These colonists were sent under the authority of a new patent giving the Massachusetts Bay Company claim to the land previously held by the Dorchester Company. Under the terms of this new patent, issued by the Council for New England in March 1628, the revitalized Massachusetts colonial enterprise was granted control of "all that parte of Newe England in America" located between three miles north of "a great river there commonly called Monomack, alias Merriemack" and three miles south of "a certain other river there called Charles river, being in the bottom of a certain bay there, commonly called Massachusetts, . . . from the Atlantick and western sea on the East parte, to the South sea on the west parte."[4]

Unfortunately, these "new planters" arrived in the ship *Abigail* in September 1628, a time of year ill-suited for planting crops or building adequate winter housing. With scant food and shelter for the 100-plus new arrivals, the very survival of the enterprise was at risk. Unhealthy, non-nutritious ship's stores—hardtack, salt pork, and the like—were all the colonists had to consume during their first difficult winter. Malnutrition and sickness took a high toll

English Wigwams. (Private collection)

during this "starving time" at Naumkeag, and Governor Endicott felt compelled to ask assistance from Governor William Bradford (1590–1657) at Plymouth who kindly dispatched Dr. Samuel Fuller (1580–1633) with a boatload of provisions. As a result of this effort, the Massachusetts Bay Colony and many lives were saved.

In addition to these difficulties, trouble between the Conant group and Endicott faction reached a point of confrontation when Endicott, somewhat high-handedly demanded that the Old Planters return to their earlier settlement at Cape Ann, disassemble the house, and remove it to Naumkeag. It was his belief that this structure was now the property of the Massachusetts Bay Company and, as such, should serve as his seat of colonial government as well as a personal residence. Conant and his men complied with Endicott's request, but made it clear that they resented being treated in a subordinate manner by the new governor.

In the meanwhile, back in England, the newly established Massachusetts Bay Company of London was concerned that their patent might be challenged by others who, prior to 1628, had also claimed lands within the boundaries set by the Council for New England. Of particular concern was the claim of Sir Fernando Gorges (1565–1647) "who declared that [the (Massachusetts Bay Company] patent had been claimed surreptitiously . . . during his absence in the war with France."[5] To absolutely confirm their title to their Massachusetts colony, the Massachusetts Bay Company sought and received from King Charles I a royal charter "under the name of the Governor and Company of Massachusetts Bay in New England" on March 4, 1629. As a result, the Massachusetts Bay Charter would "serve for over fifty years as the constitution of the self-governing colony of Massachusetts Bay."[6]

A copy of the Charter had all ready been delivered to John Endicott in 1629, when a small fleet including the *Talbot*, the *Lion's Whelp*, and three other vessels arrived with the document and 300 new colonists. Among this latest group of settlers were two ministers, Rev. Francis Higginson (1588–1630) and Rev. Samuel Skelton (1584–1634), who lost no time in establishing the first church in Massachusetts Bay Colony. At about this time, it was also decided to change the name of the settlement from Naumkeag to Salem, an English derivation of the Hebrew word "shalom"—the place of peace—to acknowledge the recent resolution of conflict between Conant's Old Planters and Endicott's newer group.

An important distinction between the Massachusetts Bay Puritans and their Separatist brethren at Plymouth was confirmed at this juncture. Whereas the Plymouth colony was established by colonists who had declared their unequivocal separation from the Church of England and all its corruption, the ministers of the new church at Salem wished to publicly acknowledge their steadfast loyalty to that Church, and did so from the outset. Rev. Cotton Mather years later described this position in a narrative recounting the departure of Higginson and Skelton from England on board the ship *Talbot* in April 1629:

> And when they came to Land's End, Mr. Higginson, calling up his children and other passengers unto the stern of the ship to take their last sight of England, said, "We will not say as the Separatists were wont to say at their leaving of England, Farewell Babylon! Farewell Rome! But we will say, Farewell dear England! Farewell the Church of God in England and all the Christian friends there! We do not go to New England as Separatists from the Church of England; though we cannot but separate ourselves from the corruption in it; but we go to practice the positive part of church reformation, and propagate the gospel in America."[7]

While this official position of loyalty to the Church of England would remain in effect throughout much of the seventeenth century in Massachusetts Bay Colony, in actuality, the arrival of Rev.

Map of Salem Area, 1667. (From *The History and Antiquities of New England* by John Barber [1844]. Private collection.)

Higginson and Rev. Skelton marked a major shift in church polity and belief—first at Salem, and subsequently throughout the congregations of the Bay Colony. Whereas in England church officers were appointed by the Church of England to serve in their various capacities, in Salem on July 20, 1629, Higginson and Skelton were elected by ballot of the congregation membership to the positions of teacher and pastor, respectively. They were later presented to be ordained as ministers of the gospel by the laying on of hands of "three or four of the gravest members of the church . . . using prayer therewith." In this way, a new precedent for the creation of ministers was established without the benefit or necessity of the involvement of the Church of England or its officers. Ordination in Massachusetts would be conducted by laymen, or other recognized ministers of the gospel, a precedent that would be maintained to the present time.

This marks the start of what would become the Congregational Church in Massachusetts Bay Colony.

As if to stress the genuine nature of this "unofficial" separatism of the Salem congregation, on August 6, 1629, Governor William Bradford and Dr. Samuel Fuller of Plymouth traveled to Salem to attend the ordination ceremony of the Salem church elders and deacons, and though delayed by adverse weather, they nevertheless arrived to extend to Reverends Skelton and Higginson and their new officers the "right hand of fellowship." Ten months later, on June 12, 1630, John Winthrop (1588–1649) would arrive on board the flagship *Arbella* with nine other vessels bringing nearly 1,000 additional colonists and vast quantities of supplies and livestock. In addition, Winthrop would bring his personal copy of the Massachusetts Bay Charter, as well as his commission identifying him as the newly elected governor of Massachusetts Bay Colony— replacing Endicott. It was on the occasion of this voyage that Winthrop preached his famous sermon, "A Modell of Christian Charity" to the passengers of the *Arbella*. This sermon identified the colony of Massachusetts Bay as a "city upon a hill" serving as a witness to the world at large of the godly example of the Puritan commonwealth, warning them that failure in any respect would expose them and their experiment in godliness to public ridicule, and was therefore to be avoided at all costs.

This was the completion of a plan devised by the governor of the company, Matthew Craddock, as early as July 29, 1629, when he suggested to the Court of Assistants and freemen (stockholders), that the company's corporate administration as well as the charter should be transferred to New England where all future meetings of the company should take place. By removing the entire administrative structure of the Massachusetts Bay Company to the other side of the Atlantic and expanding the number of freemen to include the colonists themselves, they would accomplish two things. The first is that they would be effectively removed from the influence of the archbishop of Canterbury, and could therefore operate in an essentially autonomous fashion. Second, they would transform a commercial corporation into a provincial government.[8]

Upon Winthrop's arrival, Endicott would be removed from office and the new governor would immediately begin the serious business of the colony, identifying the best location for a new capital as Salem was deemed by Winthrop to be inadequate for that purpose. Charlestown, which had already been established in 1629 under John Endicott, was selected as a temporary colonial capital.

Governor John Endicott. (Engraving from a portrait. Private collection.)

A shortage of fresh water there, however, prompted Winthrop and his Court of Assistants to accept the kind offer of reclusive settler, William Blackstone, aka Blaxton (1595–1675), the first European resident of Beacon Hill, to relocate their capital settlement across the Mystic River to the Shawmut Peninsula, or "Trimountaine." On September 7, 1630, the Massachusetts Colony Court of Assistants declared that henceforth "Trimountaine shall be called Boston." In October, the first meeting of the Massachusetts Bay Colony Court of Assistants with the governor was held in Boston. It was the first gathering of that body since the Charter had been transferred to New England from London. From this point until immediately before the outbreak of the American Revolution, Boston would serve as the capital of Massachusetts Bay Colony.[9]

The following six months in Massachusetts Bay Colony were another "starving time" as the size of the population far outstripped the amount of available food and essential supplies. This period came to an abrupt end in February 1631 when the ship *Lion* arrived from England loaded with foodstuffs, grain, beer, barreled-beef, and lemon juice. This relief was acknowledged with a February thanksgiving celebration throughout the colony. Shortly following this event other vessels arrived from Ireland and Virginia with additional supplies of grain, and by planting time the colony was well stocked with necessities.

Beginning with the arrival of the Winthrop fleet in 1630, the so-called Great Migration to Massachusetts continued to gain momentum, reaching its peak during the last half of the 1630s. Two important reasons for this movement of reformed Protestants out of England were the closing of Parliament in 1629 and the appointment in 1633 of anti-Puritan William Laud (1573–1645) as archbishop of Canterbury by King Charles I. The loss of Parliament foretold an increasingly repressive regime under King Charles for nonconforming English people, while Laud's appointment confirmed in the minds of many that the Puritan way of life would be soon made intolerable at home. This prediction soon proved accurate. As a result, an estimated 20,000 Puritan immigrants made their way to the Massachusetts Bay Colony between 1630 and 1640. Thousands more made their way to Ireland and the sugar islands of the West Indies during the same period. The migration ended largely with the outbreak of the English Civil War in 1641, an event which drew many Puritans home to England to support the forces of Parliament against their king.

The growing influx of so many colonists in so short a time necessarily increased the overall size and diversity of the Massachusetts population, drawing a great variety of Puritan settlers as well as a small minority of nonconforming Protestants of nearly every sect. This created a problem since spiritual consensus, not religious diversity, was needed for Winthrop's "city upon a hill" and immediate steps were taken to control and, in some cases, eliminate some of the more controversial and divisive elements from among "God's elect." Moreover, it should be noted that despite the eventual outcome, neither Winthrop nor the Puritan leadership were lovers of democracy, and it was never their intent to create a democratic commonwealth. This was the guiding principle in place when the Massachusetts Bay Court of Assistants met for the first time in Charlestown on August 23, 1630. Indeed, concerning the inappropriateness of a democratic government, Winthrop himself rather contemptuously remarked that "there was no such government in Israel," and that "democracy is amongst civil nations, accounted the

Governor John Winthrop. (Engraving from a portrait. Private collection.)

meanest and worst of all forms of government," and to allow it
would be "a manifest breach of the Fifth Commandment."[10]

At the August meeting of the Court of Assistants in Charlestown—
the elite nine freemen in league with Governor Winthrop and Deputy
Governor Thomas Dudley (1576–1653) took immediate action to
resolve the recurring problem of the profligate Thomas Morton
(1576–1647) by having him arrested and deported from the colony a
second and final time. Morton had for some time maintained a trading post south of Boston called "Merry Mount" where he exchanged
guns, powder, and liquor with Native Americans for fur pelts. He
was also alleged by his enemies to have sponsored social events, fea-
turing maypole dancing, with his followers and Native American
women which were viewed dimly by the leaders of both Plymouth
and Massachusetts colonies. He was arrested several times and
finally exiled to England where he did his best to discredit the
Puritan experiment.

They next attacked the issue of wage and price controls by
setting maximum restrictions on each—wages at two shillings per

day—eight pence more than in England—and commodity prices at four pence above similar goods in England. In September, the assistants outlawed the selling of firearms to Native Americans.

THE CREATION OF A NEW MASSACHUSETTS
BAY COLONY GOVERNMENT

By September, pressure was building among the colonists for a greater voice in establishing government policies. In response, at the October meeting in Boston, the first careful steps were taken to adjust the new colonial government in order to maintain a measure of control on the part of the Puritan oligarchy—the governor and his nine assistants—and yet simultaneously allow a measure of limited participation on the part of the colonial population, but with certain important restrictions.[11, 12] Accordingly, the following entry in the *Colony Record* was made:

> For the establishing of the government. It was propounded if it were not the best course that the freemen should have the power of choosing Assistants when there are to be chosen, and the Assistants from amongst themselves to choose a Governor and Deputy Governor, who with the Assistants should have the power of making laws and choosing officers to execute the same. This was fully assented to by a general vote of the people, and erection of hands.[13]

At this same meeting, 106 male colonists presented themselves before the governor and his assistants to be recognized as new "freemen" of the Company, and were accepted. After this initial general acceptance of this group as freemen, Winthrop saw to it that henceforth only males who had been accepted first as church members would be given the rank of "freemen." In this way, the voting franchise in Massachusetts Bay Colony after 1631 was limited only to those who were "visible saints" and therefore recognized as members of God's elect—saved by the grace of God and able to testify to the fact. This was, as S. E. Morison observed, "a logical restriction for the Bible Commonwealth Winthrop intended to found."[14]

The rule supplied by the king's Charter required that each year a governor, deputy governor, and 18 assistants should be elected annually in the spring—on the "last Wednesday of Easter term," or as it came to be known, "Election Day." But since only nine assistants actually left England and arrived in Massachusetts, it was decided that, in spite of the Charter requirements, the number

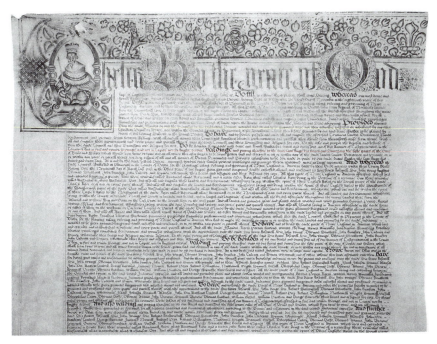

Massachusetts Bay Colony Charter. (From *Tercentenary Guide to Salem 1630, June 12–September 1, 1930*. Private collection.)

of assistants would remain at nine. Six of these nine assistants were subsequently appointed magistrates to preside "with the like power as justices of the peace hath in England," giving the assembled Court of Assistants enormous power to render verdicts—taking unto itself supreme judicial authority. Within a short time, all of the assistants came to be regarded as "magistrates" and the two terms—*assistants* and *magistrates*—became synonymous in the Bay Colony.

Another major change took place when the previous decision to allow the Court of Assistants the right to elect the governor and deputy governor from among themselves was radically altered. At the 1632 annual election, the assembled freemen of the colony demanded that they be allowed to directly elect the governor and deputy governor without the involvement of the Court of Assistants. In order that these elections remain entirely confidential, by 1635 a secret paper ballot system was introduced, a practice later changed in 1644 to grains of corn for votes in favor of a candidate and beans against a candidate.

But the newly created freemen of Massachusetts were not content with a ruling elite consisting of a governor, deputy governor, and a mere nine magistrates. In 1634, in response to a general dissatisfaction—especially from the citizens of Watertown—with how taxes were being levied by the oligarchy, Governor Winthrop offered the freemen the right to elect from each town two representatives—or deputies—to serve as an advisory committee on issues involving taxation. Receiving this welcome concession, the newly elected town representatives asked Governor Winthrop if they might read the Massachusetts Bay Charter, and were allowed to do so. Within this constitutional document the deputies found a passage allowing them the right to represent the freemen at the next meeting of the Court of Assistants. This joint meeting of assistants and town deputies was called the "Great and General Court of Massachusetts Bay Colony." On this occasion, the town representatives voted into existence three key laws:

> 1. That none but the General Court hath the power to choose and admit freemen. 2. That none but the General Court hath the power to make and establish laws, nor to elect and appoint officers ... 3. That none but the General Court hath power to raise monies and taxes and to dispose of lands.

This meant that the town deputies must now be considered a part of the ruling administration, and that their consent was required before any laws or taxes might be put into effect. It also meant that the Massachusetts colonial government now had what amounted to two distinct houses to oversee legislation. The problem was that, for a while, *these two groups would continue to meet in joint session,* the assistants claiming *a veto power* over the deputies—a claim confirmed by 1636 statute—while the deputies sought to intimidate, influence, and dominate legislation by their superiority in numbers.

Attempted Revocation of Massachusetts Bay Charter

Perhaps somewhat ironically, it was during the height of this controversy that England's King Charles I decided to rein in the Massachusetts Bay Colony's tendency toward political autonomy. He was keenly aware that in many respects the Winthrop government had extended its power well beyond what the original Charter had allowed or intended—including the creation of a representative body replacing the authority of Parliament, and the physical removal and exclusion of many non-Puritan Christian colonists. Conversely, Governor Winthrop was only willing "to acknowledge the subordination of Massachusetts to England, provided the mother country made no serious attempt to recover the powers which" in his view "the king had so freely given." King Charles took issue with Winthrop's view and challenged his authority to create an autonomous colony without royal permission to do so.[15]

There followed a series of transatlantic dispatches between the king and Massachusetts governor which were answered with evasive responses from Boston. A thoroughly exasperated King Charles finally attempted to recover the Massachusetts Bay Charter, regretting his decision issuing it to the Massachusetts Bay Company. Losing patience, the king obtained a judgment in court revoking the Massachusetts Bay Charter in 1638. But actual revocation was not possible, ruled the Court, unless the Charter itself was physically recovered from Massachusetts, and Winthrop was not about to give it up. From 1638 onward, the colony began an effort "to hasten our fortifications" in order to defend itself in the event of a royally sponsored invasion to regain the Charter. "Massachusetts was saved the necessity of outright defiance only by the recalling of the Long Parliament in 1640" whose members were willing to defend Massachusetts against the king. As a result, that body issued an order "that we (Massachusetts) should enjoy all our liberties ... according to our patent, whereby our patent, which had been condemned and called in ... was now implicitly revived and confirmed."[16]

Throughout all this, the contentious Massachusetts Great and General Court continued as a unicameral legislature until 1643 when a woman known as Goody Sherman, accused wealthy Boston merchant Captain Robert Keayne (1595–1656) of stealing her sow. The case was first brought before the Court of Assistants alone who ruled in favor of Keayne, but was later appealed to the joint "Great and General Court" of Assistants and Deputies. On the strength of this appeal, the sympathetic deputies ruled in favor of Goody Sherman. The assistants claimed the right to exercise a veto over the deputies' decision. Neither assistants nor deputies were willing to concede on the issue, and no committee was convened to resolve what Winthrop called the "sow business." Instead, the Great and General Court dissolved in June 1643, and when they reconvened in 1644, they met as a bicameral legislature—the first such in the American colonies. This meant that all provincial legislation had to be submitted to both houses before being ratified and before being sent to the governor.

Prior to the "sow business," the governor's assistants and deputies met together as one legislative body, but because of the sharp division over the Goody Sherman case, it was decided that the two groups should meet and vote on legislation separately. This created a type of Parliamentary model with an "upper house," consisting of assistants and a "lower house" consisting of town representatives, or deputies. In present-day Massachusetts, the same division is still maintained with the State Senate serving as the "upper house," and the House of Representatives serving as the "lower house." In England, an equivalent system is followed in Parliament with the "upper house" being the House of Lords and the "lower house" being the House of Commons.

Sadly, Goody Sherman received no compensation for the loss of her sow. However, the clash over her pig resulted in the division of the Great and General Court into two distinct and physically separate legislative houses, a major step in the creation of a more democratic, representative government. But two far more serious cases would shake the Puritan commonwealth in the 1630s—the conflicts over Rev. Roger Williams (1603–1683) and the irrepressible Anne Hutchinson (1591–1643).

Roger Williams

Just as the Puritan leadership struggled to achieve political consensus, so too they struggled with some notable members within their ranks on religious issues at odds with the prevailing view of the New England way. The arrival of Rev. Roger Williams in 1631 marked the beginning of one such confrontation.

Already known to Winthrop prior to his landing in the Bay Colony, Williams was regarded as a "brilliant intellect" and worthy addition to the gathering cloud of witnesses at Boston. Initially, he was offered the position of teacher at the Boston congregation, but declined the offer unless the congregation was willing to make an open break with the Church of England. The public nature of Williams's position concerning the "Separatist view" immediately drew the attention of the colony's leadership, especially after he quickly accepted the same position in Salem. (Rev. Francis Higginson, the first Salem pastor, had recently died.) The resulting inquiry on the part of the governor and General Court prompted the Salem congregation to withdraw its offer, and Williams left Massachusetts for Plymouth, where—according to Governor Bradford—his teachings were well approved.[17]

Roger Williams. (From *The History and Antiquities of New England* by John Barber [1844]. Private collection.)

However, within a short period, Williams's views began to conflict with those of his Plymouth brethren and he "fell into some strange opinions which caused some controversy between the Church and him."[18] Among these ideas were the conviction that the church at Plymouth had not declared itself publicly to be outside the jurisdiction of the Church of England, and that King James I had no legitimate claim to his North American territories, and therefore no right to dispense charters giving American land to his subjects. Consequently, Williams left Plymouth and returned to Salem in 1633.

Re-ensconced in Salem, Williams quickly assumed the role of assistant pastor to Rev. Samuel Skelton (1584–1634). He and Skelton began to jointly criticize the Massachusetts ministers for their growing tendency to meet at regular intervals to decide unilateral church policy. The New England clergy denied Williams's charge, and continued the practice of joint meetings. More significantly, Williams made a public statement to the effect that he denied the validity of the Massachusetts Bay Charter since King Charles I, like his father, had no right to dispose of lands belonging to Native Americans. He made it known that he intended to communicate his views with the crown and was promptly censured by the Great and General Court.[19]

Upon Rev. Skelton's death in 1634, Roger Williams became the pastor of the Salem congregation, prompting the Puritan leadership to express grave concern. At this juncture, he made known his strong opposition to a theocratic state, fearing the contamination of God's ordinances by the secular government, or as one historian explains, "denying the Puritan state's right to protect the true faith." To this, he added that under no circumstances should an unsaved and sinful person be permitted to join members of the elect in corporate prayer or worship. Finally, Williams expressed his objection to the use of oaths for any government purpose such as the acceptance of an elected office or trial testimony.

In the following year, Winthrop and the Court of Assistants requested an interview with Williams to examine his position concerning the use of civic oaths. Despite all efforts by several Boston ministers to persuade him to change his views, Williams was determined to hold to his heretical position—even after being brought before the Great and General Court in July 1635. His unrelenting criticism of the Puritan oligarchy finally compelled the government to take drastic action and warn the Salem congregation to turn Williams away. Not to do so, they threatened, would result in a negative vote on a Salem petition to the Great and General Court for more land. Furthermore, those supporting Williams's heretical views were threatened with deportation from the colony.

In reaction to the Court's response, Williams warned the Salem congregation that if it did not reject its affiliation with all other Massachusetts churches, he would break off his communion with the church at Salem. Not surprisingly, the people of Salem relented to the public pressure and repudiated Williams and his views withdrawing all support. By October 1635, he was called before the Great and General Court for the last time, and appealed to by noted Boston divine, Rev. Thomas Hooker, who pleaded with Williams to return to orthodoxy. Upon his refusal to relent, he was asked to leave the Bay Colony in six weeks, a deadline moved ahead to the following spring if agreed not to propagate his views. Unwilling to agree to this condition, Williams fled Salem to the area of Narragansett Bay in January 1636, to avoid being shipped back to England. There, he would finally negotiate the purchase of a parcel of land from Canonicus and Miantonomi chief sachems of the Narragansett people, and establish the independent settlement of Providence, later to become the colony of Rhode Island. Providence was, in Williams' words, to become a sanctuary for those "distressed of conscience."

Anne Hutchinson Memorial. (Library of Congress)

Anne Hutchinson

Eventually, Rhode Island would become a sanctuary for Anne Hutchinson, her family, and her followers, who, like Williams and his followers, would be warned away from Massachusetts Bay Colony following a period of internal crisis. Anne arrived in Boston with her husband William and her family in 1634, having followed her pastor, Rev. John Cotton (1585–1652) from their native Lincolnshire, England. Cotton's first assignment was to fill in the Boston pulpit of Rev. John Wilson, while he returned to England to fetch his family. The following year, while William Hutchinson busied himself establishing a merchant business, Anne established a weekday women's Bible-study group in her home where she

summarized and clarified the main points of the past Sabbath's sermon. These meetings soon became increasingly popular among
Boston's female members of the congregation, and in time, men
began to attend her sessions as well. Eventually, by the summer of
1635, Anne's Bible-study group grew large enough to require two
weekly gatherings.

Hutchinson's growing role as a teacher and self-appointed religious leader in Boston caused the professional clergy some concern, but matters did not reach the crisis stage until October 1635,
when Rev. John Wilson returned from England to resume his role
as the principal lecturer at the Boston meetinghouse—displacing
Rev. John Cotton. Whereas Cotton's sermons emphasized the free
grace of Christ as the sole means of salvation with less stress placed
upon good works, Wilson greatly emphasized the essential need to
perform good works as a means of preparing the believer to receive
God's free gift of salvation, and also as an indication of one's status
as a member of the elect. This shift of emphasis bothered Anne
Hutchinson greatly. She interpreted Wilson's doctrinal position as
one which advocated a "covenant of works," and not a "covenant
of grace." This criticism was leveled against Wilson to his parishioners at the private gatherings held in her home.

Within a brief period, Hutchinson had attended the sermons of
the greater part of the clergy in the Boston area, and arrived at the
conclusion that Rev. Wilson was only one of many clerics preaching
a "covenant of works" to their listeners. She stressed that moral
behavior was in no way related to salvation, and that assurance of
salvation "was conveyed, not by action, but by an essentially mys-
tical experience of grace—an inward conviction of the coming of
the Holy Spirit to each individual, that bore no relationship to
moral conduct."[20]

Carrying this argument to its logical conclusion, Hutchinson
insisted that the state should not legislate morality, and to do so
was to advocate a form of spiritual legalism condemned by Jesus
Christ in the Gospels of the New Testament. Her spiritual oppo-
nents countered by agreeing that, while good works could not save
a person's soul, they nonetheless represented the "fruits of the spirit," giving outward testimony to an inward spiritual transformation. Moreover, they firmly maintained that in order for a truly
Christian society to exist in this imperfect world, all citizens, saved
and unsaved, must strive to live by the moral law, and it was the
function of both church and government to compel them to do so.
By taking the opposing view that the church should have nothing

to do with the law, Hutchinson was guilty, in the opinion of her adversaries, of the heresy of antinomianism—looking inward for assurance of salvation and guidance for moral conduct instead of to the church and state.

By December 1636, the ministers of Boston had interviewed Rev. Cotton and Rev. Wheelwright to ascertain their positions concerning Mrs. Hutchinson. They also spoke to Anne herself, and were dismayed to discover an unrepentant heretic who "cast doubt upon whether the ministers themselves were saved."[21] What protected her throughout this period was the support of her following which by now included some powerful political figures including the newly elected governor, Sir Henry Vane. This would soon change as a result of the return to power of Governor Winthrop in the spring election of 1637. The losing candidate and Hutchinson supporter, Sir Henry Vane shortly departed the colony and returned to his home in England.

As in the case with the radical Roger Williams, neither side was willing to compromise since both Hutchinson and the Court were equally convinced of the absolute correctness of their position. Ultimately, it was the Boston clergy who would emerge triumphant. In August 1637, a colonywide synod was held correcting and clarifying many disputed theological issues raised by Anne Hutchinson, and concluding that all future home meetings be discouraged and criticism of clergy forbidden. At this gathering, the bounds of New England Puritan orthodoxy had been clearly redrawn and the Hutchinsonians were clearly outside the pale. Action was quickly and decisively taken. In November 1637, under the direction of the reinstated governor Winthrop, Rev. Wheelwright was first called to account by the Great and General Court, examined, found guilty of "sedition," disenfranchised, and banished from the colony. Others who had defended Hutchinson from their positions as deputies of the Great and General Court—John Coggeshall and William Aspiwall—were also confronted, convicted, relieved of their offices, disenfranchised, and banished. Finally, the newly reelected governor Winthrop and the Great and General Court called Hutchinson to stand before them in Cambridge on charges of heresy.

Throughout this confrontation, Anne confidently defended herself with "a ready wit," and Winthrop himself later admitted a grudging admiration for her intellectual skill. However, when asked how it was possible for an uneducated woman to be so certain of the correctness of her theological position in such matters when opposed by so many learned ministers, Hutchinson boldly responded by stating that she received direct personal revelations from God. This amounted to a self-confession of guilt, since all orthodox Christians—Protestants and Catholics agreed that God's last word to humanity was given in the Book of Revelation, and any claim to the contrary amounted to blasphemy.[22] Largely on the basis of her own testimony, a verdict of guilty was rendered by the Court against her, and Hutchinson was banished "for the troublesomeness of her spirit" and "the danger of her course amongst us." She took her family with her to Rhode Island along with her supporters Coddington and Coggeshall, while her exiled brother-in-law, Wheelwright travelled north to New Hampshire. By the end of November 1637, the Antinomian Controversy was over and the boundaries of religious liberty more clearly defined.[23]

THE PEQUOT WAR

While the Puritan religious establishment in Massachusetts was being torn apart by the spiritual controversy of the Hutchinsonian heresy, a simultaneous external threat presented itself, the Pequot War. The background of this conflict shifts the focus of colonial concerns to southern New England, in an area presently known as eastern Connecticut. Here, many disreputable traders carried on a brisk fur trade with the Native American population, often in exchange for firearms and liquor. On one such foray into the land of the Pequot people in 1634, a privateer and slaver named John Stone and six English crew-members were killed. On closer inspection of the circumstances surrounding the deaths and the character of the victims, the blame for the incident was unclear. Some contemporary evidence indicated that they were attempting to enslave a group of Pequot women and children. The official reaction on the part of Massachusetts authorities to Stone's death was to quickly negotiate a treaty with the Pequots to prevent further bloodshed.[24]

Unfortunately for all parties, anger and violence continued to escalate in the months following the treaty negotiations, and another incident took place in July 1636—the killing of trader John Oldham near Block Island by the Niantic. In response, Salem militia commander and former resident governor, John Endicott was dispatched by Massachusetts governor Sir Henry Vane with 90 militiamen to punish the Native Americans in the area around Block Island. Endicott attacked and burned two Niantic villages, claiming to have killed 14 Native Americans with casualties of only two wounded. Endicott carried away the tribe's entire supply of winter

The figure of the Indians fort or Palizado in
NEW ENGLAND
And the maner of the destroying
It by Captayne Vnderhill
And Captayne Mason.

Attack of a Pequot Town. (Library of Congress)

corn and destroyed what supplies his men could not carry. Endicott next moved to Fort Saybrook in Connecticut Colony, secured
guides, and proceeded to attack and burn another neighboring
Pequot village and destroy their winter supply of corn. Endicott's
heavy-handed tactics infuriated the Pequots who, in 1637, initiated
an intense campaign against all English colonists in southern New
England. Siding with the English in this conflict were the traditional enemies of the Pequots, the Mohegan and Narragansett, both
of whom wished to eliminate the Pequot competition for the fur
trade.

The Pequots attacked Fort Saybrook, placing it under siege
and killing several residents. Wethersfield, Connecticut was
attacked on April 23, 1637 with a loss of six men and three women,
and two girls taken captive along with much livestock. Total losses
in these attacks numbered in excess of 30 colonists. The towns of
the Connecticut River Valley raised a company of 90 militiamen
placing them under the command of John Mason. This force, in
conjunction with John Underhill's company of militia, plus a war
party of about 70 Mohegan warriors devastated the fortified

Indian War attack. (From *The History and Antiquities of New England* by John Barber [1844]. Private collection.)

Pequot town of Mystic (Misistuck) located on the Connecticut coast, killing between 600 and 700 men, women, and children by setting the village on fire and shooting those who attempted escape. This was the New England Native Americans' first direct encounter with European-style "total war," and it would have a negative impact upon their collective memory, resurfacing in 1675 during the King Philip's War.

The final episode of the Pequot War took place in the "Great Swamp Fight" which occurred July, 13–14, 1638, and resulted in Captains John Mason and Israel Stoughton defeating Pequot war sachem, Sassacus and his band of over 100 Pequot warriors. Noncombatants in the company of the Pequot war party were allowed to escape with their lives, but were subsequently enslaved and sold to New England households or to plantations in the West Indies. The remaining unsurrendered Pequots were systematically killed by gunfire with a small remnant together with Sassacus escaping on the second day. The result of this first war between New England Native Americans and the Puritan colonists was the virtual destruction of the Pequot people. Secondarily, it sent a clear warning to the remaining tribes of New England that the English were a force to be carefully dealt with in the years ahead.

Indian Wars Bloody Brook. (From *The History and Antiquities of New England* by John Barber [1844]. Private collection.)

FISHING AND EARLY MARITIME TRADE

By the conclusion of the conflict with the Pequots, Massachusetts was well-established in maritime industries, the primary being fishing and the secondary being trade. Salem's minister following Rev. Williams was Rev. Hugh Peters who, besides bringing the Salem congregation back together in the wake of Williams's departure, also was responsible for organizing that community's fishing industry. His innovative plan included providing common land at Winter Island, located near the harbor entrance, as a free base of operations for a growing community of fishermen.

Here in Salem, along the shoreline of Winter Island, so-called because its harbor remained unfrozen throughout the winter, fishermen were allowed to construct simple dwellings and storage sheds, build fish flakes for the drying of cod fillets, and maintain their fishing vessels without the necessity of payment to the town. The result of this policy was to attract a large number of fishermen to Salem, providing that seaport town with a ready surplus of salt cod to be used in commercial trade with Europe and the West Indies. In this way, the Massachusetts cod fisheries became, from the first decade of settlement, the essential foundation of the economy of the Massachusetts Bay Colony. Its traditional economic

Fishing and fish flakes. (From *The History and Antiquities of New England* by John Barber [1844]. Private collection.)

importance is still symbolically acknowledged by the presence of a gilded codfish suspended above the speaker's chair in the Massachusetts State House.

It should be noted that this dependence upon the sea for the colony's economic survival was not the original vision for Massachusetts Bay settlement. The original plan had been to encourage farming on freehold farms and landed estates, much like England. However, it soon became clear to the newly arrived colonists that the strength of New England, and eastern Massachusetts in particular, was not in agricultural productivity. Had farming been as successful in Massachusetts as it would prove in Pennsylvania and Virginia colonies, the economic development of the Puritan commonwealth would have been remarkably different. Instead, by the 1640s, the North Shore coastline from the Mystic and Charles Rivers to the Merrimack River was dotted with coastal fishing settlements, fishing drying stages, and shipyards.

Indeed, Massachusetts shipbuilding began with the launching of *The Blessing of the Bay* on the Mystic River in 1631, while farming as the mainstay of the economy would decrease in importance after the first decade of settlement, giving way first to fishing and finally, the West Indies trade.

ECONOMICS, SPIRITUALITY, AND
THE HALFWAY COVENANT

As early as 1638, the Massachusetts-built vessel *Desire* was engaged in trade with the West Indies, returning home to Salem with the colony's first cargo of cotton, tobacco, and African slaves. During the next few decades, more vessels were constructed to engage in both the profitable businesses of fishing and maritime trade. By the mid-seventeenth century, this trade with the islands of the West Indies would create a wealthy upper class in Salem and Boston. Every year, hundreds of cargoes of New England lumber products and salt cod were profitably exchanged for return cargoes of molasses, sugar, rum, and African slaves.

This growing interest and success in maritime commercial activities, the making of profits and the increasing pursuit of secular activities in general, while perhaps encouraging to the colony's merchants and shipowners, was nevertheless worrisome to the Massachusetts clergy who soon began warning their congregations of the dangers of taking their eyes off the goal of creating a spiritually pure "city upon a hill." In his farewell sermon, Rev. Richard Mather, the father of Increase Mather, expressed his concern on this point: "Experience shows that it is an easy thing in the midst of worldly business to lose the life and power of religion, that nothing thereof should be left but the external form, as it were the carcass or shell, worldliness having eaten out the kernel, and having consumed the very soul and life of godliness."[25]

Indeed, as the commercial and economic success of Massachusetts Bay Colony rose through the 1640s and 1650s and settlers became increasingly prosperous and comfortable in their New World environment, there appeared to the New England clergy a perceptible decline in spirituality among the colonists themselves. This tendency toward secularization was most glaringly evidenced in the growing inability of newer generations to testify to an inward conversion experience needed to be received as a member of a Puritan congregation. Thus, as the population grew, and the colony thrived economically, fewer and fewer young people were willing or able to provide public testimony to having experienced the indwelling of God's Holy Spirit, or of living in a state of grace as a member of the elect. As a result, by mid-century, church membership was quickly declining as older members died with few replacements.

For this reason, a new idea was introduced to the churches of the Bay Colony, the so-called "Halfway Covenant," which although employed by several congregations during the 1650s, became officially sanctioned following a synod held in Massachusetts at the request of the Great and General Court in 1662. This official acceptance of the "Halfway Covenant" meant that being baptized into the church was now possible, as long as one's parents were also baptized—and even if they were not able themselves to testify to a conversion experience or to having been admitted to full membership within the congregation. What the "Halfway Covenant" did was bring hundreds of alienated and anxious parents and children back into fellowship with their local congregation as halfway members providing the parents were willing to publicly swear to uphold the conditions of that congregation's church covenant.

This was an important step in maintaining the momentum of the "errand into the wilderness" into and beyond the mid-century. Yet, it also became a source of deep internal controversy, dividing many congregations and alienating not a few pastors who felt that the "Halfway Covenant" represented a lowering of the spiritual standards for church membership, while encouraging backsliding among Massachusetts Puritans. In all, it took over a decade for independent congregational churches to uniformly accept this more liberal interpretation of what it meant to belong to a congregation. It also certainly had the permanent effect of weakening "the homogeneity of the New England Way by opening the possibility of still other forms of membership extensions and setting the clergy in fierce debate among themselves with a resulting loss of prestige for the ministerial class."[26]

The Massachusetts Body of Liberties and Colonial Coinage

Another important step in maintaining political momentum of the autonomous Puritan colony was the writing of the Massachusetts Body of Liberties by Rev. Nathaniel Ward in 1641. This document represents the first code of laws created by Europeans in New England. This earliest of Massachusetts law codes—drawn from both English and Mosaic law, essentially replaced English common law in Massachusetts Bay Colony.

The era of the English Civil War and Protectorate, that is from 1641 through 1660, was an especially trouble-free period for Massachusetts Bay Colony insofar that both the king and later, Parliament were essentially preoccupied with monumental domestic issues, and had little time or inclination to focus upon the activities of the Puritan colonies in New England.

Arguably the most startling new development was the introduction to New England society of the perceived threat of witchcraft resulting in the trial and execution of Alice Young of Hartford, Connecticut in 1647; Margaret Jones of Charlestown, Massachusetts in 1648; and Mary Johnson of Hartford, Connecticut in 1648. Prior to 1647, no episodes of alleged witchcraft had occurred in Puritan New England. After 1647, such incidents would become rather frequent occurrences only occasionally resulting in death by hanging. In the majority of such cases in both Massachusetts and Connecticut, accusations would be followed by an inquiry and in rare instances, a trial. Of the nearly 100 total accusations prior to 1692, 16 would result in death by execution. Interestingly, the appearance of "witchcraft" as a capital crime did not occur until the early 1640s in both Connecticut and Massachusetts Bay colonies.[27]

Another example of independent political action in Puritan New England took place in 1652 during the height of the power of Oliver Cromwell and his Protectorate. It is at this point that Massachusetts Bay Colony decided to mint its first coinage under the care of mint-masters John Hull (1624–1683) and Robert Sanderson (1587–1663), producing the now-famous silver pinetree shilling and six-pence. The reason for this initiative was allegedly the shortage of hard, standardized currency in the colony, but it could not escape English authorities that a colony that independently manufactures its own currency bearing no image of any leader, except the profile of a tree, clearly regards itself as distinctly outside the pale of any external authority.

Fortunately, until the end of Cromwell's life in 1658, Massachusetts was allowed nearly complete freedom to govern itself and conduct its own policies without direct interference from the government of the English Commonwealth. This would change with the restoration of King Charles II. In 1662, the king called the Massachusetts Bay Colony to account for its offense in minting coins, an act exclusively reserved by the royal mint. An audience between the new king and representative of the colony was arranged, and the Great and General Court of Massachusetts delegated Sir Thomas Temple to "placate offended Majesty." The tale of this incident is a tribute to seventeenth century spin-doctoring:

> He [Temple] began the interview apologetically. The colonists did not know they were doing wrong; they needed currency and had to make it themselves, since His Majesty, to their great grief, had been in no position to supply them. A [Massachusetts-made] shilling was produced and showed to the King. Charles inquired what tree that

was? Sir Thomas had the wit to declare it to be "the royal oak," which the good people of the Bay had placed on their coins as token of loyalty, daring not to incur the usurper's [Cromwell's] displeasure by using the royal name. The King was greatly pleased, called the New Englanders "a parcel of honest dogs," and allowed the Boston mint to continue its operations.[28]

AN OPPRESSED PEOPLE AND KING PHILIP'S WAR

In that same year (1662), King Charles II, while allowing the continued operation of the colony's mint, nonetheless wrote to the Great and General Court to reassert royal power over the autonomous and wayward Puritan commonwealth. In his letter, he required that all members of the Massachusetts government "... take the oath of allegiance, declare void laws contrary to those of England and ordered them to permit the Book of Common Prayer. Most important of all, he directed the [voting] franchise be granted to all freeholders of competent estates and not vicious in conversation, whether or not they were members of a Congregational church."[29]

This was the first time since 1631 that the ability to vote in Massachusetts provincial elections had been placed in the hands of any group other than the "visible saints," and represented a significant weakening of the political grip of the Puritan oligarchy upon the Bay Colony. Added to this threat was the report of the royal commission of 1664–1665, established by King Charles II, recommending that he fulfill his father's original plan to revoke the Massachusetts Bay Charter nullifying the present Puritan government, and placing the colony directly under royal control. Yet again Boston ministers warned that this first successful attempt on the part of royal authority to assert its power over the colony was nothing more than God's way of punishing the backsliding Massachusetts colonists for their refusal to repent their sinful ways. This warning would reverberate throughout New England in 1675 with the outbreak of King Philip's War, a conflict that would prove the most devastating and costly of all confrontations with the native people of New England.

The seeds of war were sown in 1671 when King Philip, or Metacom, the son of Wampanoag Chief Sachem, Massasoit, began arming his warriors with muskets at his primary settlement of Mount Hope near the colony of Rhode Island. Reports of this activity reached the ears of the authorities at Plymouth and King Philip was confronted by them at a conference near Taunton. Unable to satisfactorily explain his warlike preparations, he and his braves were required to surrender their firearms.

Resentment and hostility continued to escalate until 1675 when a new Wampanoag conspiracy against Plymouth was reported by a Christian Wampanoag, John Sassamon to Plymouth governor, Josiah Winslow. Within a short time Sassamon was found murdered. A Native American eyewitness to the killing identified and accused three Wampanoag warriors who were arrested by Plymouth authorities. Subsequently, these three suspects were tried, condemned, and executed for the murder of Sassamon by a court in Plymouth. King Philip was incensed at what he perceived to be a violation of Wampanoag sovereignty, and on June 20, 1675, a war party attacked the nearby English settlement of Swansea. In response, on June 28, militia from Plymouth and Boston attacked and destroyed the Wampanoag settlement of Mount Hope. These events mark the start of the war itself.[30]

From June 1675 to King Philip's death at the hands of a Christian Native American in August 1676, the conflict raged across the face of New England as other allied tribes, including the powerful Narragansetts, assisted the Wampanoags in their efforts to drive back the tide of Puritan settlement. In all, over 600 English settlers were killed in attacks which threatened Puritan settlements to within a 17-mile radius of Boston. By March 1676, war parties had attacked settlements as distant as Andover and Plymouth, penetrating deep into long-held regions thought safe by English colonists. By the war's end, nearly every male between 16 and 60 years of age was mobilized by a military draft, creating an armed force of more than 5,000 militia. Of these, nearly 500 would be killed wounded or captured. Thirteen Puritan towns would be totally destroyed and six others including Springfield, Massachusetts would suffer partial destruction.

By August 1676, the hostile Native Americans were suffering from an acute shortage of food and faced with the growing opposition of a significant number of warriors of the Mohegan tribe who had allied themselves with the English. These Native American allies and many "praying Indians" were recruited by the Puritans to wage war, and proved an effective force in tracking the dwindling bands of Narragansett and Wampanoag warriors. In New York and the western region of Massachusetts, the Mohawks and Iroquois refused to lend King Philip assistance, and grimly waited for the opportunity to extend their power into central Massachusetts when his alliance of tribes was defeated.

King Philip, Chief of the Wampanoag People. (From *The History and Antiquities of New England* by John Barber [1844]. Private collection.)

His demise finally came in the summer of 1676, as more Native American allies fled New England for Canada following a series of colonial victories. By July, over 400 warriors had surrendered to colonial forces. A raiding party of militia and native scouts penetrated the Assawomset Swamp, located King Philip's camp and attacked. He was shot by a "praying Indian" named John

Alderman, then hung, drawn, and quartered while his head was displayed publicly at Plymouth for the next 20 years. As a result, the power of the Wampanoags and Narragansetts was destroyed, their lands taken, and many prisoners sent to Bermuda and the West Indies as slaves. In all, nearly 3,000 Native Americans lost their lives due to warfare, disease, and starvation. Never again would the Native Americans of New England exercise so much military power and never again would the Massachusetts Bay Colony come so close to near complete destruction. But to the Puritan clergy, the measure of success experienced by the Native Americans during King Philip's War was merely a foretaste of what was to come unless the leadership of the colony placed the feet of "the elect" back onto the straight and narrow path.

EDWARD RANDOLPH, SIR EDMUND ANDROS, AND THE DOMINION OF NEW ENGLAND

While King Philip's War raged across New England, Boston was visited in June 1676 by another potential troublemaker, Edward Randolph, who had recently been appointed a special courier of the Lords of Trade. His mission was to demand that Massachusetts send agents to London to respond to serious charges that the colony essentially regarded itself as an independent commonwealth, was expanding its trade while ignoring the recently instituted Navigation Acts, persisted in making church membership a prerequisite for the voting franchise despite new legislation forbidding such distinctions, and still refused to compel its freemen to take the oath of loyalty to King Charles II. Added to this litany of suspected violations were two long-standing claims by Sir Fernando Gorges and Robert Mason that Massachusetts was in violation of *their* legal right to rule over the provinces of Maine and New Hampshire respectively, since the colony had acquired these territories without the sanction of the crown.

In a short time, Edward Randolph, in an effort to advance his own fortunes, succeeded in driving a wedge between the Lords of Trade and Massachusetts Bay Colony. First, by establishing a royal colonial government in nearby New Hampshire, he denied the Bay Colony their previously unchallenged authority to rule there. He next returned to Boston as the king's collector of customs and began to enforce, for the first time, the Navigation Acts against Boston's merchants and shipowners. More importantly, Massachusetts' inability to quell all suspicions of illegal activity and disloyal behavior prompted the commission to recommend to the king the revocation of the original Massachusetts Bay Charter by May 1678.

In spite of the impending danger, conservative elements in Massachusetts recommended taking a confrontational, almost rebellious posture, while a minority of the top leaders advocated conciliation with the Lords of Trade and King Charles II. The go-between diplomat in these delicate negotiations was again Edward Randolph who succeeded in alienating the Lords of Trade and the English government in general from the Colony of Massachusetts Bay, casting the Puritans leaders of New England in the most negative light possible in his reports. Adding to the growing suspicions of the king and Lords of Trade was the general attitude of most New Englanders that English law did not apply to them, and that the acts of a corrupt Stewart government needed to be resisted. This provided Randolph with exactly the evidence he needed in his campaign against the Puritan leadership.

On October 23, 1684, the High Court of Chancery, at the recommendation of the Lords of Trade, finally dissolved the Massachusetts Bay Charter. It would be another 18 months before a replacement government headed by Joseph Dudley would take over from the elected Massachusetts ruling elite. Dudley ruled the Council of New England with a personally appointed governor's council and no elected legislature from May 1686 until December of that year when he was replaced by Sir Edmund Andros. This delay in establishing an effective replacement government immediately after the revocation of the Massachusetts charter was probably attributable to the decline and death of King Charles II in February 1685.[31] Upon the coronation of Charles's brother, King James II, however, the situation would deteriorate quickly for Massachusetts with the creation and rapid expansion of the Dominion of New England and the hostile policies of the anti-Puritan, Sir Edmund Andros as its ruler.

One eminent historian described the Dominion of New England as "an experiment in imperial consolidation," for it was an attempt to place a group of diverse and often troublesome colonies under a single government, and at once bring them all in conformity with English law and colonial policies as expected by the new English monarch and the Lords of Trade. In addition, it was perceived as a means to raise revenue through Navigation Acts and uniformly provide for the unilateral defense of the frontier of the northern colonies from the threat of the French and their Native American allies.[32]

Had Joseph Dudley not been replaced, things might have been different. Had Sir Edmund Andros been possessed of a more sympathetic and diplomatic nature, things might also have been different. But Andros was wholly insensitive to the needs and insecurities of the colonists he governed, and quickly went about the business of alienating nearly everyone in the Dominion of New England, which by May 1688 included the people of the Province of New Hampshire, the Province of Maine, Massachusetts Bay Colony, Rhode Island Colony and Providence Plantations, Connecticut Colony, Plymouth Colony, the Narragansett Country or King's Province, the Province of New York, as well as the Provinces of East and West Jersey Colonies.

One of the more troublesome policies introduced by Andros during his brief tenure as governor included the elimination of all representative legislatures in all the colonies within his jurisdiction. This was a move hardly conducive to winning over a population of Puritan colonists largely accustomed to self-government and general elections. In Massachusetts and Connecticut especially, his policies only generated hostility among the elect who considered him a minion of Satan come among them to disrupt, and if allowed by God, to destroy the New Canaan.

Andros quickly went on to reform the judicial system in all the colonies of the Dominion, making it conform to the English system. Criticism in the press was severely censored restricting the ability of critics and editors to express their objections to the new government and Andros in particular. Particularly distressing for the Congregational churches in Massachusetts was his support of the Anglican Church which was forced upon the people of Boston when Andros demanded the use of the Third Church of Boston for the purpose of Anglican worship starting on Easter Sunday in 1687, giving the Church of England preferred status over the resident congregation of Rev. Samuel Willard.

Further resentment was generated by Andros's introduction of a governor's poll and land taxes without the approval of any elected representative body, or even the governor's council. This action so enraged Rev. John Wise of Chebacco Parish in Essex County that he began to write and preach against it, organizing resistance to the taxation policies of the Andros administration. The immediate response of Andros was to arrest and fine the dissidents and eliminate the long-standing custom of the quarterly town meeting in Massachusetts, allowing only one meeting per year to elect community officers. Moreover, towns in Massachusetts were prohibited by the governor to collect funds to support the community's Congregational Church.[33]

As a particularly bothersome step in reorganizing the former Puritan society of Massachusetts, and finding a new source of revenue, Governor Andros decided to apply a quitrent fee to all new land grants, and place all previous land grants under judicial review to establish their validity. If proven invalid, these land grants held by Puritan families for generations might be revoked, or if determined valid, they might be subjected to a quitrent fee. Thus, by 1688, Andros had succeeded in creating a social crisis among landowners in Massachusetts by threatening their legal claim to thousands of acres of essential real estate containing farms, homes, barns, warehouses, and businesses of many kinds. The situation had reached a crisis state and Puritan divines once again were warning their parishioners that such divine punishment was the result of God's wrath with the backslidden and sinful elements now living among the remnant of God's elect. In these sermons, Andros was regarded as an example of how God may raise a sinful ruler to power in order to discipline and chasten God's chosen people.

Only the Glorious Revolution of 1688, and the removal and exile of King James II in England succeeded in providing relief to the impending disaster by giving the Puritans of Boston the opportunity to arrest Andros and deprive him of his authority to rule. The action took place on April 18, 1689 when, following news of the successful invasion of William Prince of Orange, bands of armed Bostonians besieged Edmund Andros in a garrison house on Fort Hill, while Edward Randolph and other Andros supporters were arrested. A Council of Safety was formed under the leadership of former governor, Simon Bradstreet, accusing Andros of crimes against the people of the colony and demanding his surrender. Local militia companies responded to the revolt by coming to Boston in support of the Council of Safety. With no hope of escape, Governor Andros finally surrendered to the Council of Safety, and the Dominion of New England was no more.[34]

It would not be until May 1692 that a duly appointed royal governor, Sir William Phips, a native of the Province of Maine, would return to Boston from England accompanied by the esteemed father of Rev. Cotton Mather, Rev. Increase Mather, bearing the newly issued Massachusetts Colony Charter. The arrival of Governor Phips would mark the official beginning of Massachusetts's role as a royal crown colony and the unification of Massachusetts Bay

Colony and Plymouth Colony into a single political entity. Unfortunately, their long-awaited return in Boston was marred by the sudden realization that Massachusetts colony was, by May of 1692, embroiled in the first phase of the infamous Salem witch episode with a long list of suspects already in prison awaiting trial. For Governor Phips, and the Mathers, this crisis would prove to be the greatest challenge of their lives.[35]

NOTES

1. William Haller, *The Rise of Puritanism* (New York: Harper and Brothers, Publishers, Inc., 1957), 6–11.

2. Ibid., 49.

3. Ibid., 183–85.

4. The Massachusetts Bay Charter, AMDOCS: Documents for the Study of American History.

5. Samuel Eliot Morison, *Builders of the Bay Colony*, 33.

6. Morison, *Builders of the Bay Colony*, 34.

7. Cotton Mather quoted in Morison, *Builders of the Bay Colony*, 37.

8. Edmund Morgan, *The Founding of Massachusetts*, 36–37.

9. Morison, *Builders of the Bay Colony*, 80.

10. R. C. Winthrop, ed., *The Papers of John Winthrop*, vol. II, 430.

11. Morison, *Builders of the Bay Colony*, 84.

12. Francis J. Bremer, *The Puritan Experiment*, 58.

13. "Records of the Massachusetts Great and General Court," Massachusetts Bay Colony, Massachusetts State Archives, vol. 1, 163.

14. Morison, *Builders of the Bay Colony*, 85.

15. Morgan, *The Puritan Dilemma*, 175.

16. John Winthrop quoted in Edmund Morgan, *The Puritan Dilemma* (New York: Addison-Wesley Longman, 1998), 175–76.

17. Bradford quoted in James Ernst, *Roger Williams: New England Firebrand* (New York: MacMillan, 1932), 82.

18. Bradford, quoted in Edwin Gaustad, *Liberty of Conscience: Roger Williams in America* (Valley Forger, PA: Judson Press, 1999), 28.

19. Bremer, *The Puritan Experiment*, 62–63.

20. Ibid., 67.

21. Ibid., 68.

22. Morison, *Builders of the Bay Colony*, 123.

23. Bremer, *The Puritan Experiment*, 70.

24. Ibid., 66.

25. Richard Mather, "A Farewell Exhortation to the Church and People of Dorchester, in New England," quoted in Perry Miller, *The New England Mind: From Colony to Province* (Cambridge: Harvard University Press, 1939), 4.

26. Bremer, *The Puritan Experiment*, 165.

27. K. David Goss, *The Salem Witch Trials: A Reference Guide*, 4.
28. Morison, *Builders of the Bay Colony*, 152.
29. Thomas Jefferson Wertenbaker, *The Puritan Oligarchy*, 305.
30. Bremer, *The Puritan Experiment*, 169–70.
31. Wesley Frank Craven, *The Colonies in Transition: 1660–1713*, 173–74.
32. Francis J. Bremer, *The Puritan Experiment*, 175.
33. Ibid., 176.
34. Ibid., 178.
35. Ibid., 181.

2

THE IMPACT OF THE SALEM WITCH TRIALS ON THE MASSACHUSETTS BAY COLONY

It is wrong to assume that the outbreak of accusations, arrests, and the widespread fear of witchcraft in 1692 were in any respect new to Puritan New England. Witchcraft accusations, trials, and executions had been a part of the New England social landscape for many years, beginning with the execution of Alice Young in Hartford, Connecticut in 1647. But executions for witchcraft were relatively rare. In actuality, of the nearly 100 known accusations and nearly 60 trials, apart from those belonging to Salem, about 16 resulted in execution, with the majority of these cases being dismissed. This is somewhat at odds with the general public's stereotype of how New England Puritans handled cases of this kind.[1]

The case of witchcraft, which in all likelihood had the greatest impact upon the evolution of the Salem episode, was the well-publicized 1688 incident involving Rev. Cotton Mather, accused witch Mary "Goody" Glover, and the four children of Boston stonemason, John Goodwin. The so-called "Goodwin Case" began when 13-year-old Martha Goodwin accused the family laundress, a daughter of "Goody" Glover, of stealing linen. Immediately following this accusation, all four Goodwin children began to suffer severe pains, laboring "under the direful effects of a stupendous witchcraft."

Reverend Cotton Mather of Boston. (Library of Congress)

A detailed account of this episode was chronicled and published by Rev. Cotton Mather in his 1689 book, *Memorable Providences, Relating to Witchcrafts and Possessions,* a publication that sold hundreds of copies throughout the Boston area during the years immediately following the event. In Mather's interpretation of the Goodwin episode, all attempts to alleviate the torment of the afflicted children by prayer proved ineffectual. The evil effects of "Goody" Glovers's spell could only be alleviated by moving the children from the Goodwin home and into the homes of neighboring families. Unlike the Salem episode, accusations were limited to the Goodwin parents and children crying out against the Glovers, mother and daughter. In the end, only "Goody" Glover confessed to having committed acts of witchcraft, and was consequently the only person hanged. This was markedly unlike the Salem episode where nearly 50 persons confessed and none of those who confessed were executed. It also differed from the Salem event in that it was closely confined and did not spread quickly to a much wider audience. One of the primary reasons why the Salem witch trials were so devastating is that they directly and indirectly touched so many people, and no effort was made to limit public access to the proceedings.

The Salem episode itself began in 1689, when Rev. Samuel Parris accepted the invitation of the Salem Village congregation to become pastor of their church. Salem Village (present-day Danvers) was a small farming community located approximately three miles from the large seaport town of Salem, Massachusetts. Parris arrived later that year with his wife, Elizabeth, his daughter Elizabeth, a niece Abigail Williams, and two slaves he had purchased during his previous failed career as a West Indies merchant, John Indian and his wife Tituba.

Prior to his arrival in Salem Village, Samuel Parris had inherited a sugar plantation in Barbados from his London-born, merchant father, Thomas Parris in 1673. Withdrawing from his studies at Harvard, he tried his hand at making a living in the potentially profitable sugar trade. Unfavorable economic circumstances forced him to sell his West Indian property, return to Boston in 1680, and reestablish his business there. Failing in this, he finally attempted to reinvent himself as a pastor using his theological training from an incomplete college education. The call to the humble Salem Village pulpit in 1689 was, for a person like Parris who had once attained the status of a gentleman, a socially difficult step requiring an adjustment in both lifestyle and income. He managed to retain his domestic servants and his social standing as a gentleman, but at a reduced standard of living. The greatest adjustment for the Parris family was in all likelihood the transition from the fairly sophisticated, urban environment of Boston to living in a rural, agricultural community and depending upon a small congregation of largely uneducated farmers to sustain a gentleman's household.

The Parris household continued in a fairly normal pattern until the winter of 1691–1692 with Rev. Parris and his wife spending much of their time away from the parsonage calling upon the Salem Village parishioners. On these occasions, the care of the home and children was left in the hands of Tituba, the West Indian slave who would entertain the young girls with tales of magic and experiments fortune-telling. In time, the group would grow to include six other young girls in addition to Abigail Williams and Betty Parris. This gathering would come to be referred to as "the afflicted children," the primary source for spectral evidence presented during the Salem episode.

On one occasion during these afternoon meetings, Tituba, according to courtroom testimony, asked the girls if they would be interested in knowing the profession or "calling" of their future husbands. In response to their desire to tell the future, the slave woman prepared a simple "crystal ball" by suspending an egg white in a clear glass of water, holding it up to a glowing candle while instructing the children to gaze into the swirling liquid to discern images. This act of foretelling the future was, as all Puritan children were taught, an absolutely forbidden activity since God alone through His prophets reserved the right to predict future events. Such actions when undertaken by everyday people were regarded by Puritans as an attempt to contact satanic powers, and as such, regarded as a form of witchcraft.

Within a brief time, one of the girls claimed that she, to her horror, witnessed the ghostly image of a floating coffin. The result of this revelation was to cause the children to cry out in hysterical fits disrupting the otherwise quiet household of the Parris parsonage for an extended period of time. Upon returning home on this occasion, Rev. Parris after observing his daughter and niece, inquired as to the reason for their aberrant behavior. Receiving no satisfactory answer, he and his wife called upon the local physician, Dr. William Griggs, to examine the girls to determine the cause of their illness. Finding nothing physically wrong with them, Griggs declared his opinion that they were under "the evil hand" of witchcraft, and that their sickness was of a spiritual nature.

This was not considered a particularly bizarre diagnosis since, to the culture of the seventeenth-century Puritan there were two realms of reality—the physical world and the invisible spiritual world. Each was equally capable of impacting the other, and illness could as easily be brought on by evil spirits or by demonic beings as by exposure to an infected person or to the evil humors of the night air. In confirmation of this dualistic reality, Boston's noted cleric Rev. Cotton Mather, produced his classic work, *Wonders of the Invisible World* in 1692, describing the irrefutable, personally observed evidence of spiritual activity as it impacted daily life in the form of witchcraft.

Once Dr. Griggs's opinion concerning the spiritual nature of the girls' affliction became known, immediate and appropriate steps were taken to relieve their distress. Rev. Parris called for a convening of a group of local ministers who spent a day of fasting and prayer in an attempt to lift the curse from the children who, despite the ministers' efforts, continued in their crying out, hysterical fits, and general aberrant behavior. Finally, after days of questioning, the two girls mentioned the names of three individuals responsible for their torment: Tituba, Sarah Good, and Sarah Osborne. This new information was immediately passed on to the local magistrates, John Hathorne and Jonathan Corwin, who on February 22 issued warrants for the arrest of these three individuals. This marks the first step of the legal process in cases of suspected witchcraft requiring the suspects to be brought before a magistrate for a pretrial examination.

At their March 1 examination both Sarah Good and Sarah Osborne maintained their innocence while Tituba made a startling confession declaring that the Devil had come to her and bid her serve him. She went on to describe her association with a local coven of witches whose membership included Sarah Good and Sarah Osborne and two others she could not identify. As a result of this pretrial hearing, the three women, the first victims of the episode, were imprisoned under suspicion of witchcraft. The afflicted girls continued to provide testimony through March and April identifying additional suspected witches, many of whom were arrested and brought in for pretrial examinations. Those whose guilt appeared likely were placed in prison and held until a date for their trial could be set.

Trials for the growing number of suspected witches did not take place until the arrival of the newly appointed governor, Sir William Phips, who brought with him the newly issued Massachusetts Colony Charter from King William and Queen Mary. Only after Phips's return on May 14 could a "Special Court of Oyer and Terminer" be established for handling the trials themselves. That court was established between May 25 and 27, 1692, and from that point onward the cases could be tried. The first person to be tried and executed for witchcraft was Bridget Bishop who was hanged on Gallows Hill on June 10, 1692. The trials continued into the summer as more names were provided by the afflicted girls whose fits and convulsions also continued. By July 29, another group of eight convicted witches were hanged. This group included Sarah Good, Susannah Martin, Rebecca Nurse, Sarah Wildes, and Elizabeth Howe. A second group of victims were executed on August 18 including John Proctor, George Jacobs, Sr., Rev. George Burroughs, Martha Carrier, and John

Sir William Phips, Governor of Massachusetts Bay Colony.
(Library of Congress)

Willard. The last victims were hanged on September 22 including
Mary Eastey, Alice Parker, Martha Corey, Ann Pudeater, Margaret
Scott, Wilmet Redd, Samuel Wardwell, and Mary Parker. This was
the final incident of executions resulting from the trials. In all, 19
individuals died by hanging, while one victim, Giles Corey, was
pressed to death on September 19 (?) for refusing to cooperate with
the Court by entering a plea when charged with the crime of witchcraft. Altogether 20 deaths resulted from the proceedings of the
Special Court of Oyer and Terminer. Several other deaths resulted
from the unhealthy prison conditions suffered by the victims during
their period of confinement including that of Sarah Osborne.

The trials themselves continued unabated until October 29, 1692 when Governor Phips, bowing to public pressure and criticism, closed the proceedings in Salem. A new Superior Court of Judicature was convened in Boston in January 1693 to complete the process of trying the remaining group of suspects, but without the use of spectral evidence which had been allowed in Salem. Without any spectral evidence, the visions and testimony of the "afflicted children" was of little use to the Court. With no further convictions or executions, by May 1693, the governor, Sir William Phips, issued a general manumission freeing those still in custody. This action marks the official end of the Salem witchcraft episode, but the short- and long-term effects of this event would have a profound impact upon New England everyday life and society.

The most immediate and observable result of the trials was the undermining of the authority and reputation of Massachusetts governor Sir William Phips who was soon recalled to England to answer serious questions concerning incompetence and misuse of public funds.[2] He never returned to Boston, dying in London in 1694, before he could be brought to trial. His very promising political career was destroyed. Although not as dramatic, the authority and credibility of the Boston-area Puritan ministers was damaged to the extent that secular political authority and merchant leadership began to move ahead of the clergy in exerting influence in what had once been a theocratic commonwealth.

The people of Massachusetts colony, stunned by the enormity of the tragedy, were collectively repentant, and were asked by acting governor William Stoughton in December 1696 to participate in a day of fasting and prayer "so that all God's people may put away that which hath stirred God's holy jealousy against this land; that He would ... help us wherein we have done amiss to do so no more, and especially that whatever mistakes on either hand have been fallen into ... referring to the late tragedy, raised among us by Satan and his instruments, through the awful judgment of God, He would humble us therefore and pardon all the errors and people that desire to love His name." This followed close upon three years of bad harvests, outbreaks of smallpox, losses at sea to French privateers, and other misfortunes viewed as evidence of God's displeasure with the guilty commonwealth. Making tangible amends, the Massachusetts colonial government in October 1711, decided to compensate the victims' families with monetary awards which, after being distributed, came to a total amount of 578 pounds and 12 shillings ($394,600 in today's currency).

Governor William Stoughton of Massachusetts Bay Colony.
(Danvers Archival Center)

Significantly, several notable individuals as well as groups expressed their sincere regret for involvement in the 1692 episode. Foremost among these was the honorable captain Samuel Sewell, a former associate justice of the Court of Oyer and Terminer who attended Boston's South Church. Here, before his fellow congregants he stood while Rev. Samuel Willard read Sewell's confession declaring that he was "sensible of the reiterated strokes of God upon himself and his family . . . and that he desires to take the blame and shame of it, asking pardon of men, and especially desiring prayers that God forgive that sin and all others of his sins." In a similar scenario at Salem Village in 1706, Ann Putnam Jr. stood before the congregation as Rev. Green, Rev. Parris's successor, read her confession declaring that she "desired to be humbled before God" for having "been made an instrument for the accusing of several persons of a grievous crime, whereby their lives were taken away from them, whom now I have just grounds and good reason to believe they were innocent persons, and it was a great delusion of Satan that deceived me in that sad time, whereby I justly fear I have been instrumental with others, though ignorantly and unwittingly, to bring upon myself and this land the guilt of innocent blood."

Thus did the high tide of the Salem witch trial episode begin to ebb back into the flow of daily life for colonial Massachusetts. The general population was for many years thereafter imbued with a sense of guilt for wrongful accusations, unjust imprisonments, and unwarranted executions of innocent fellow-citizens. Never again would witchcraft as a crime rear its head in the colony of Massachusetts, although in nearby Connecticut Colony there were seven known cases in 1692 and a final incident in 1697, none of which resulted in a conviction.

From 1693 onward belief in witchcraft, while still publicly supported by the sermons and writings of many New England clergy and the majority of the devout populace, began to experience a perceptible decline. Fewer and fewer individuals saw witchcraft as a possible rationale for misfortune and natural disasters. This fact is borne out by the steady decline of perceived incidences, public accusations, and indictments for crimes of a supernatural nature as the eighteenth century began. Concurrent with this public decline in belief in things supernatural, was a growing tendency on the part of many colonists to drift away from the spiritual roots of their Puritan ancestors, a falling away in church attendance, and a general decline in piety which would finally prompt the counter-reaction of the Great Awakening by the 1730s and 1740s. Compounding this tendency toward spiritual complacency was the evergrowing influence of the contemporary writers of the Age of Reason whose ideas were beginning to gradually work their way into the minds of the educated elite of colonial society.

It is into this vibrant and transitional world of growing spiritual skepticism, whose roots still cling to the soil of Puritanism that we will now begin to explore in greater detail what daily life in the late seventeenth-century New England might have been like for most colonial settlers.

NOTES

1. David Hall, *Witch-Hunting in New England* and Richard Godbeer, *The Salem Witch Hunt*, 5.

2. Baker, *The New England Knight*.

3

DOMESTIC LIFE OF THE SALEM WITCH TRIAL ERA: HOMES AND FAMILIES

THE HOUSES OF LATE SEVENTEENTH-CENTURY NEW ENGLAND

With few exceptions, the domestic, built environment of New England in 1692 was made of wood, primarily consisting of houses with frames of white oak and exteriors of pine. Such structures were built in a style and method known as joined-frame construction, a regional adaptation of the medieval style of frame construction found in Elizabethan England. The major difference between the joined-frame structures of Old England and New England is that the American house exteriors were sheathed with solid pine weatherboards covered by overlapping layers of pine clapboards coated in dark pine tar to preserve the outside surface. This construction method reflected the ready availability of vast amounts of lumber in New England, a commodity long since depleted and in short supply in seventeenth-century England where half-timbered houses infilled with brick or wattle-and-daub walls which were more common. Such joined-frame houses were erected by craftsmen known as housewrights, who were skilled at creating a frame of oak timbers joined together by wooden pegs known as "trunnels" or tree-nails.

Whereas in Old England roofs might include thatch or slate in addition to shingles, in New England thatch roofs had long since

Old Balch House,
Built 1639, Beverly, Mass.

Colonial Framed House. (Private Collection)

given way to hand-split cedar shingles as the preferred covering
material. Both Old and New England house construction incorpo-
rated brick chimneys and fireplaces in every room used for human
occupation. Once again, while Old English houses used a variety of
materials for fuel—coal, peat, and wood—in New England, wood,
preferably hard wood was the exclusive heat source for domestic
structures. By the late seventeenth century, supplies of firewood
for Massachusetts homes were being shipped from the Province
of Maine. Indeed the greatest threat to New England houses of this
era was the "chimney fire" created from a spark or glowing ember
rising up a chimney flue coated in a layer of wood creosote, a
highly combustible residue of wood smoke. When such fires
occurred, the only practical response was to remove the residents,
save as many valuable household items as possible, and attempt
to prevent the spreading of fire to neighboring structures.

INTERIOR FURNISHINGS OF A LATE SEVENTEENTH-CENTURY HOUSEHOLD

The contents of a New England domestic environment of the 1690s
consisted primarily of joined-frame furniture which, like the house
itself, usually was constructed of oak and pine. These were, by the
late seventeenth century, produced by local craftsmen known as
joiners and cabinetmakers in a style generally reminiscent of

English Framed House. (Mary-Ellen Smiley)

English provincial furniture of a generation earlier. There was a definite stylistic lag in fashion and taste between the Old and New Worlds in the 1690s. Occasionally, members of the wealthy merchant class of Salem or Boston would import furniture from England for their more elegant urban houses, but such instances were exceedingly rare. The most fashionable furniture of this era was beginning to display surfaces of beautifully patterned walnut veneering with brass hardware. These case pieces were, once again, only commissioned and owned by the upper class of Salem and Boston, while most middle- and lower-class seventeenth-century colonists contented themselves with solid joined furnishings of oak and pine.

Contemporary household inventories of most middle-class homes of the late seventeenth century reflect a surprising diversity

Colonial Beams. (Courtesy of the Wenham Museum. Photograph by Mary-Ellen Smiley.)

in the domestic environment. Kitchens contained a various array of pottery to include American redware for everyday use, as well as European salt-glazed and tin-glazed ceramic vessels for more formal use. Fireplaces in kitchens usually boasted an elaborate display

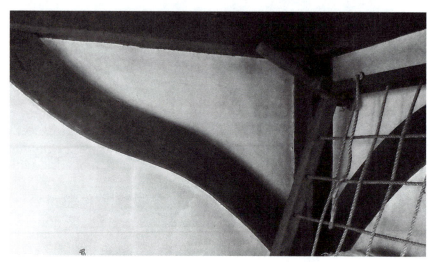

English Curved Braces. (Courtesy of the Wenham Museum. Photograph by Mary-Ellen Smiley.)

of iron cooking utensils which by the 1690s were manufactured locally by a blacksmith. Most valuable of all to the home of the 1690s was its collection of textiles which, for most families, consisted of domestically produced wool and linen items. Only the most affluent urban families possessed exotic textiles of silk and fine cotton since these were imported and therefore quite expensive. For the above reasons, in households boasting a bed with a canopy and curtains, such an item was regarded as the single most valuable of all household furnishings.

In the homes of the late seventeenth century all woven materials were carefully stored in chests, chests with drawers, chests of drawers, and linen cupboards. Clothes closets were virtually unknown in the design of New England joined-frame houses and the careful, enclosed storage of textiles was essential to ensure the longevity of clothing items. Most clothing was worn until it literally wore out, and was then repaired and reused for children or for

Seventeenth-century room. (Courtesy of the Wenham Museum. Photograph by Mary-Ellen Smiley.)

Joined-stool, late seventeenth century. (Courtesy of the
Wenham Museum. Photograph by Mary-Ellen Smiley.)

general household use as quilts, potholders, drying towels, and
cleaning rags. Rarely were textiles discarded for any reason, but
continued to serve some useful purpose for as long as possible.
This accounts for the fact that, with the possible exception of
relatively few items of upper-class clothing found in museum collections, nearly all examples of lower- and middle-class clothing
of the late seventeenth century have disappeared. What we do have
are household inventories from probate court records describing
clothing items as well as paintings of the merchant upper class to
help us envision the everyday appearance of New England's people of the 1690s.

EVERYDAY GENERAL APPEARANCE OF LATE
SEVENTEENTH-CENTURY NEW ENGLAND PURITANS

Contrary to the popular image, people of late seventeenth-
century Puritan New England did not present themselves in a uniform attire of black and white. Rather, daily attire was dictated by
one's occupation, financial resources, and social standing or status.
Social pressure in Puritan communities and the prevailing rules of
conduct generally discouraged persons of modest income or lower

Bible and Stand. (Courtesy of the Wenham
Museum. Photograph by Mary-Ellen Smiley.)

social standing from dressing in a manner above their station. This
emphasis was reinforced in New England by the use of "sumptuary laws" which outlined in specific terms what materials and
styles were acceptable on a daily basis. These laws were rarely
applied, but their presence in the law code underscores the
Puritan belief that all citizens should know their place and avoid
unnecessary extravagance in their manner of dress. It is therefore
possible to say that in the late seventeenth century, as in the
Middle Ages, it was possible to identify a Puritan gentleman from
a yeoman farmer by their general appearance as well as by the style
and material of their clothing.

During the Salem witch trial era, the average male of middle
income presented himself wearing a linen shirt with cuffs and

Side table, late seventeenth century. (Courtesy of the Wenham Museum. Photograph by Mary-Ellen Smiley.)

collar. The sleeves were always long and somewhat puffy in appearance. The shirt might be either tied or buttoned at both the neck and cuffs and long enough to serve as a nightshirt as well. Breeches went from the waist to below the knees and were usually of wool, although sometimes linen or a combination fabric known as linsey-woolsey was used. Colors of wool varied greatly, but dyes were usually natural and organic tending toward various shades of brown, green, blue, and gray. Black was worn but usually by persons of high social or economic status and on occasions demanding formality such as at church meeting, court, or on government business. Over the shirt and extending to the knees was the waistcoat of wool or linen, usually held together with a single row of pewter, bone, or wooden buttons leaving only the sleeves and collar exposed and covering all but the knees of the breeches. From under the breeches, a pair of linen, wool, or silk stockings would cover the calves and feet which were shod in leather shoes either buckled in brass or pewter or tied with laces by the late 1690s.

Panel-back chair. (Courtesy of the Wenham Museum. Photograph by Mary-Ellen Smiley.)

The average male of middle income wore a broad-brimmed, felt hat, preferably with a hat band and this was worn at almost all times. The wearing of a hat was not merely a fashion statement, but also was considered a means of protecting oneself from both the elements and evil humors which might adversely affect one's health. Finally, a wool or linen coat worn over the waistcoat by the late 1600s was replete with a collar, a long row of buttons, and side pockets with flaps and cuffs. Such coats could vary in color, cut, and condition, but were generally worn in public by all respectable men of the middle and upper class unless at home or

A full-length image of a late seventeenth-century
Puritan man. (Private collection)

engaged in an informal activity. Craftsmen and artisans when
engaged in their trade would work in their shirtsleeves, but usually
with a waistcoat to maintain the appearance of decency and decorum.

The average female of the late seventeenth century wore a linen
garment known as a chemise or undergown which covered from
the shoulders to the ankles, tying at the neck and elbows. Over this
were tied at the waist several petticoats which likewise covered
from waist to ankle. A pair of thigh-high woolen, linen, or silk long
stockings were held in place with garters while feet were shod in

A full-length image of a late seventeenth-century
Puritan woman. (Private collection)

leather shoes with slightly elevated heels. Over all of this was worn
an ankle-length, wool, or linen outer skirt, tied or fastened at the
waist. Over the chemise a bodice of wool or linen was worn, usually fitted to the waist and flaring out over the hips and the upper
portion of the skirt. The colors for such clothing were varied to an
even greater extent than for men. As with men, black wool garments for women were rare, but reserved for formal occasions.

   In a domestic setting, women often wore woolen aprons to help
prevent stains and extinguish the occasional spark from the fire.
The danger of catching fire was an omnipresent threat to housewives, and a frequent source of injury. Upon their heads, women
always wore a linen cap called a coif wherein was tucked their
exceedingly long hair. This house-cap was rarely removed in

public, and was often supplemented by a felt, broad-brimmed hat when traveling abroad. For women, the use of a coif was a means to keep the hair clean and out of sight, a mark of domestic modesty among Puritan housewives in the late seventeenth century. In cold weather, women wore hooded, ankle-length cloaks of heavy wool fastened at the neck with ties, clasps, or a hook-and eye.

Children of this era, except young boys who during the first few years wore skirts, dressed in much the same manner as their parents, with no stylistic distinctions made for the exigencies of child-life since Puritan culture, even as late as the 1690s encouraged parents to train their children to be devout, sober, obedient, mature, and responsible from the earliest age. They were essentially regarded and attired as little adults. Some baby clothing of the late seventeenth century has survived in some quantity, but these items tend to be linen and occasionally silk ceremonial christening robes, caps, and mittens and not everyday wear. Only the more elegant of these articles have been preserved in museum collections and reflect the infant attire of the children of the late seventeenth-century elite, while those of the more middle class have largely vanished.

FAMILY LIFE IN NEW ENGLAND OF THE 1690s

Of primary importance to the rank-and-file Puritans of the witch trial era was to create a domestic environment under the sober and firm guidance of a father strongly assisted by his wife and help-mate. Both were expected to follow biblical standards and set an example before their children as model Christian parents. Wives in the late seventeenth century assumed the role of "deputy hus-band" of the household, meaning that they were in command of all children, servants, domestic work, and all household activities and only subordinate to, but working closely with the husband. Indeed, in cases of the husband's absence from the home, or his inability to act in his legal capacity as the titular head of the family, the wife took his place and acted as the representative of the family.[1]

The ultimate goal and purpose of a family, in the eyes of these "saints," was to produce children who would glorify and honor God in every aspect of their daily lives, and secondarily support the family's household in every way possible through diligence and hard work. While every Puritan family varied slightly in its social dynamic, in general these domestic expectations and goals applied to the great majority of people of all classes and locations in New England during the 1690s and well before. Reinforcement of these ideals came regularly from the sermons of clergy, presented to all residents during mandatory church services offered in every meetinghouse in every community throughout the commonwealth. An insight into this perspective and its implications comes from Rev. Richard Baxter writing to Puritan parents, "it is no small mercy to be the parents of Godly seed, and *this is the end of the institution of marriage.*"[2]

In light of this, Puritan households had an easy time setting their priorities since the ultimate goal of every family member and the family as a whole was to glorify God through the efficient and judicious use of time and economic resources. The reason why a general acceptance of this belief was considered essential in the Puritan commonwealth was that families were seen as the foundation building blocks of a godly society, and therefore an essential key to the success of their colony. Baxter concluded by emphasizing this point, "The life of religion and the welfare and glory of both the church and the state, depend much on family government and duty. If we suffer neglect of this, we shall undo all."[3]

HUSBANDS AND WIVES OF THE 1690s

The individual upon whose shoulders responsibility for a godly family rested was the father and husband, often referred to by Puritan writers as the "high priest" of the family. It was generally understood that all actions taken by the wife or children directly reflected the will and leadership of the family's patriarch in a thoroughly male-dominated society such as Massachusetts of the 1690s.

It is important to recall that, even by the turn of the seventeenth century, the Puritan commonwealth was still strongly influenced by the teachings of reformer John Calvin whose doctrines did much to shape daily life in both thought and practice. Calvin's admonition to Puritan fathers was unmistakably precise: "Let the husband so rule as to be the head ... of his wife. Let the woman yield modestly to his demands." What is often misunderstood, however, is the manner in which Puritan husbands were to exercise their God-given authority. It was not to be done in a ruthless and demanding manner according to many late seventeenth-century contemporary writers, but in a spirit of love and leadership through compromise. Rev. Benjamin Wadsworth observed that a good husband will "make his government of her (his wife) as easy and gentle as possible, and strive to be more loved than feared."[4] The famous Rev. John Robinson in his exhortation to his Calvinist followers in Leyden noted that husbands must provide "love ... and wisdom" in the management of their families, and likewise love for their wives "like Christ's (love) to his Church: holy for quality, and great for quantity."[5]

Conversely, the wife was expected to acknowledge the "head-ship" of her husband in matters of family government, but with a mutually recognized responsibility to assist with advice in decision making and setting family policy, that is ruling the house, but not the husband. In this regard, the Puritan writer, William Ames noted that the roles of leadership in the Puritan family should be "mutual for husband and wife, and ... observed equally in all essential and principal matters, provided that that difference of degree between husband and wife—that the husband govern and the wife obey— be observed by all." There was never any question or doubt as to what the acceptable role and place of husbands and wives might be in New England homes of the late seventeenth century. Men were expected to lead, while women were placed in a responsible, but secondary role as helpmates to their husbands supporting him and assisting with the day-to-day management of all family affairs. Rev. William Gouge summed up the nature of the relation-ship between the two parents: "In general the government of the family ... belongeth to the husband and wife and both," while another cleric noted that while the husband was undoubtedly the "chief ruler" of the family, the wife was "the associate, not only in office and authority, but also in advice and counsel unto him."[6]

Finally, some basic generalizations about family life in Puritan New England may be made based upon a recent demographic study of Salem, Massachusetts between 1636 and 1683 by historian, C. Dallett Hemphill. First and most importantly, unlike the mid-Atlantic and Southern colonies, family life in Puritan New England was stable. This was not simply due to the high moral standards of the inhabitants, but was also a reflection of the remarkable longevity of the settlers themselves. Simply put, they lived longer in New England than elsewhere in the English North American colonies. Secondly, infant mortality was lower in New England during the latter 1600s when compared to other colonies, and children, to a greater extent than elsewhere, tended to live to maturity. This was due in large part to the healthier physical envi-ronment of New England when compared to the colonies further

Table 3.1

Age at Death of Persons Born between 1640 and 1669 and Surviving to the Age of Twenty

Age	Male		Female	
	No.	%	No.	%
20–29	13	14.1	2	4.5
30–39	4	4.3	5	11.4
40–49	2	2.2	5	11.4
50–59	10	10.9	9	20.5
60–69	16	17.4	6	13.6
70–79	25	27.2	9	20.5
80–89	19	20.6	4	9.1
90–99	3	3.3	4	9.1
100 and over	0	0.0	0	0.0

south. Historian Philip J. Greven, in his significant study of four generations of families living in Puritan Andover, discovered that men, women, and children in this rural community tended to live comparatively long and healthy lives. His statistical analysis of birth and death records of 92 males and 44 females provides an interesting glimpse into the average life expectancy of late-seventeenth century colonists (Table 3.1).

What Professor Greven has shown is that contrary to the traditional stereotype, in Andover at least, if not elsewhere in New England during the last years of the seventeenth century, "those who did survive to adulthood could anticipate long and healthy lives."[7] Such demographic analysis points to evidence that in everyday Massachusetts village life of the late seventeenth century, both men and women tended to live on average into their fifties or longer. This is about the same average life expectancy of Americans at the turn of the twentieth century.

Another stereotypical image of this era that is challenged by Greven's study is that men in the mid-to-late seventeenth century frequently outlived several wives. While some men certainly did marry more than once as a result of the death of a spouse, it might not have been as common an occurrence as had been previously thought. Greven notes that

[o]ut of thirty-four first generation men, twenty-three or 67.6% appear to have only had one wife during their lifetimes, with nine

or 26.5% marrying twice, and two marrying three times. The proportion of second-generation males marrying only once proved even higher with sixty-six out of a total of eighty-nine marrying only once—74.2%. Marriages broken by premature deaths clearly were the exceptions, not the general rule since both men and women lived far longer than many of us realized.[8]

And what was the typical sphere of these long-lived housewives of Andover in the late seventeenth century? Greven notes that "by the late seventeenth century, the great majority of women in the villages and towns of New England had been forced back into (their) traditional role. The home, not the farm, once again became her domain." It was within the domestic, household environment, managing interior chores and family activities, that the majority of late seventeenth-century women both urban and rural, would be found. But within these homes such women dominated and controlled all life, ordering and sustaining all domestic activities. Like a foreman or plant manager, the Puritan wife of the late seventeenth century wielded great authority and was expected to acknowledge only her husband as her superior. This was the theoretical ideal, but many court records and town proceedings testify to the fact that not all husbands were in actual control of their domestic environments or of their wives.

CHILDREN AND THEIR ROLES IN THE 1690s FAMILY

The subject of child-life at the time of the Salem witch trials has received a disproportionate amount of study due to the significant role played by the "afflicted girls" in leading the Salem Village community in their persecution of the trial victims. Some researchers, rather conspicuously and without justification, have attributed their behavior to a desire to break with the traditional pattern of boring household chores and the very subservient position usually occupied by children—especially female children—in the families of the late 1600s. Others, like Rev. Charles Upton in his two-volume history of the episode, assess the children's behavior as a desire for recreation or "sport" in a society which customarily discouraged fun and entertainment for young people. While it is certainly true that the families of the 1690s did not regard a child's "playtime" as a high priority, it should be observed that recreation was not as unknown and restricted as our stereotypical image would seem to indicate.

However, child-life begins with birth and babyhood and it is initially important to understand how infants were brought into the world of the 1690s and how they managed to survive. The birthing of children was most often attended by midwives as doctors were in short supply even by the late seventeenth century. Only in urban areas like Salem or Boston were professionally trained physicians available to attend births. Even with the assistance of midwives, infant mortality was considerably less than statistical figures in other North American colonies. Nonetheless, childbirth still held serious risks for both mother and child. In spite of the presence of an attending midwife or physician, the death of mother, infant, or both was not uncommon in the 1690s.

Like household fires, childbirth was yet another significant risk to the lives of women of this era. If the birth was successful, within a few days the newborn was expected to be baptized in the local meetinghouse during the Sabbath service by the resident pastor. On January 22, 1694, Judge Samuel Sewell, one of the magistrates of the Court of Oyer and Terminer that presided at the Salem trials, recorded in his diary, "A very extraordinary storm by reason of the falling and driving of snow. Few women could get to meeting. A child named Alexander was baptized in the afternoon."[9] Sewell continues to recall how his own child when only four days old was presented at Boston's Old South Meeting House for baptism in mid-winter, and although shocked by the splash of cold water in the unheated church, did not cry out.

This was the customary beginning of a child's life in New England of this period. A christening ceremony marked the first occasion of the Puritan family introducing their newborn to the community within the environment of the meetinghouse. It also marked the beginning of a family's commitment to raise their new child in the "nurture and admonition of the Lord" before their relatives, friends, and neighbors. It did in no way guarantee a child's salvation which, according to the teachings of John Calvin, could only be achieved by a transforming spiritual experience of God's free gift of indwelling grace after the child had reached the age of accountability.

Concerning parental responsibility to their child, most Puritan parents would acknowledge that their sons and daughters were gifts from God and that parents were merely God's stewards given the special responsibility of raising God-fearing offspring who might, if God so wills, obtain the gift of salvation. For this reason, child-rearing was a serious business to parents of the late 1600s.

A seventeenth-century baby's cradle. (Courtesy of the Wenham Museum. Photograph by Mary-Ellen Smiley.)

Rev. Cotton Mather, Boston's most famous minister of the era, observed that parents "must give an account of the souls that belong unto their families."[10]

A well-known American colonial historian once generalized the upbringing of colonial children such that "[t]he quality of a colonial childhood varied, as always, with the character of the parents as well as their religious and ethnic backgrounds. Congregationalists, Presbyterians and Quakers were stricter, Anglicans and Dutch Lutherans more easygoing with their children." Though broad, this statement underscores that Puritan parents, also known as Congregationalists, tended to place greater emphasis on the importance of their children's religious training at home than many other contemporary sects.[11] The reason for this is nothing less than the Puritans's awareness of the awesome responsibility a parent has for preparing one's children from infancy to receive the gift of salvation. Boston minister Richard Mather, in one of his most famous sermons, imagined for his congregation how children might confront their parents on "Judgment Day" for having overlooked their religious education: "All this that we here suffer is through you. You should have taught us the things of God, and did not; you should have restrained us from sin and corrected us, and you did not; you were the means of our original corruption and guiltiness, and yet you never showed any competent care that we might be delivered from it. Woe unto us that we had such carnal and careless parents."[12] This was the parents' greatest responsibility, but by no means their only one.

Nearly as important as one's religious training was one's occupational instruction. Massachusetts colonial law required that every father assume the responsibility to have his son trained "in some honest lawful calling, labor or employment, either in husbandry, or in some other trade profitable for themselves and the commonwealth."[13] This requirement sometimes resulted in the sons of a numerous family being apprenticed at an early age to learn a craft from a local artisan. The by-product of this condition was that the family was relieved of the responsibility to feed and house one of its members, "clearing space in a small house for another child coming along."

For an apprenticed boy to be torn away from his family and placed in a strange domestic and work environment where he would receive stricter discipline than under the care of his own parents was undoubtedly traumatic for many boys. The long-term result, however, was to create a class of self-supporting artisans who learned at an early age to be hardworking, productive, and responsible to both their master and themselves. Similarly, families not able to economically sustain a large number of female children might resort to sending them to live with more prosperous relatives to act in the role of household servants. As with a boy's apprenticeship, such girls would learn the skills of managing a household necessary to become successful wives and mothers. In both circumstances, the host family was responsible not only for the physical well-being of the child placed in their care, but also responsible for their discipline, education, and religious training in exchange for their labor.[14]

The majority of families living in New England during the Salem witch trial era owned farms and earned their living from agricultural activity. These families tended to be large by modern standards, an extreme example being that of Sir William Phips, governor of Massachusetts during the witch trials, who was one

of 26 children by the same mother. As another example of a large
family, Rev. Cotton Mather and his wife produced 15 children of
whom only two survived him.[15] The most obvious advantage to
large families on a colonial farm was the availability of free labor
for a wide variety of tasks; Puritan farming parents in general uti-
lized their children effectively to meet the demands of their agricultural way of life.

In cases where the economic well-being of a farming family was
more adequately met by the employment of the children performing daily essential tasks, everyone contributed their labor to meet
the needs of the family. On most farms no apprenticeships were
necessary, and by the late seventeenth century indentured servi-
tude was rare as every member of the household, from the young-
est to the oldest child, was busily engaged every day in some type
of agricultural or domestic household activity. By learning from a
young age the importance of work, such children quickly developed an increasing awareness of themselves and of their worth
as contributors to the family's common wealth. As one writer expressed this widespread phenomenon, on New England farms
"the boy's own father, or the girl's own mother, provided relatively
clear models for the formation of a meaningful identity. Here was
no awkward age, but the steady lengthening of a young person's
shadow."[16] This was a common facet to farm life in the late 1600s
and would influence the development of community life in rural
towns and villages across New England well into the nineteenth
century.

For late seventeenth-century farm children as well as their parents,
the work week included every day but Sunday. Every day was
begun with a simple breakfast often including leftovers such
as toasted bread and cheese with meat and turnips from the previous
night's supper, or an oatmeal or cornmeal mush, supplemented with
raisins or currants and molasses. Such cereal was washed down with
milk in the summer and apple cider or small beer in the winter which
Puritans of all ages consumed, but usually in limited amounts.
Contrary to our stereotype, Puritans had no problem with the consumption of a wide variety of alcoholic beverages, only with overcon-
sumption and drunkenness which was proscribed in both biblical law
and the civil statutes of the commonwealth.

As far as daily diet was concerned, the available foodstuffs
tended toward fresh and organic during the warmer months of
the year with a transition to more salted, smoked, dried and generally less fresh during the cold months of the calendar. This was in

large part due to the lack of food preservation techniques which greatly impacted both food availability and nutrition. Recent scholarship in seventeenth-century New England foodways has provided a fairly comprehensive overview of what the average middle-class family might have consumed. In her classic study, *Good Wives*, Laurel Thatcher Ulrich examined the household inventory of the 16-acre farm of Beatrice Plummer of Newbury, Massachusetts who died in 1672 with an estate valued at 343 pounds. Although a generation early, this document gives identifies in detail what types of food were available.[17]

On the day the inventory was written, the dairy house contained four-and-one-half flitches, or sides of bacon, "a quarter barrel of salt pork, twenty-eight pounds of cheese, and four pounds of butter." Stored in an upstairs bedchamber were 25 bushels of English grain including barley, oats, wheat, and rye. (English grain stood in opposition to Indian corn, which was an indigenous staple consumed by both colonists and farm animals.) Barley was often used by colonists to produce malt for home-brewed beer. The use of oats was varied from oatcakes and simple porridge to a "gelatinous dish flavored with spices and dried fruit" known as "flummery." The wheat and rye supply would have been primarily used in breads and pies baked in an interior brick oven introduced to most New England kitchens by the late seventeenth century. Beatrice Plummer also kept a bushel of dried peas and beans near the grain and a full barrel of cider in the cellar. Ulrich speculates, based upon her findings in other household inventories, that the Plummer family also consumed "pickles, preserves or dried herbs" as well as "cabbages, turnips, sugar, molasses and spices." Interestingly, neither chocolate nor tea was commonly found in kitchens of the late seventeenth century, nor were potatoes in common use.[18]

After the fall harvest, Ulrich speculates that Beatrice Plummer might have served roast pork or goose with apples, while in the spring, eel pie flavored with parsley or savory from her kitchen garden would have been well received. In the summer, a special treat might be a leek soup or gooseberry cream, but for most days the Plummers could have expected a steady diet of boiled meat with some kind of "sauce" of the season, supplemented by dried beans or peas, parsnips, turnips, onions, cabbage, and garden greens. Pudding was common in most households, prepared in a cloth bag placed on top of the boiling vegetables.[19]

Ulrich's study of seventeenth-century foodways concludes with what might be served for the evening meal: "Supper, like breakfast, was a simple meal." (The heavy meal was consumed at midday.) "Bread, cheese and beer were as welcome at the end of a winter day as at the beginning. In summer, egg dishes and fruit tarts provided more varied nutrition."[20] The danger of fireplace cooking for the housewife was constant since "the most basic of the housewife's skills was building and regulating fires. Summer and winter, day and night, she kept a few brands smoldering ready to stir into flame as needed. Seventeenth century housewives *did* stand in their fireplaces, which were conceived less as enclosed spaces for a single blaze than as accessible working surfaces upon which a number of small fires might be built." The fact that every woman wore a skirt that went, together with several petticoats, nearly to the ground only made the potential danger of fire worse for them, a situation ending sometimes with tragic results.[21]

When not occupied by more pressing domestic activities such as food preparation, time was also usually taken, either in the morning or early evening, for family "devotions" whereby the father and mother led the children in reading and discussing scripture

A Puritan Family being led by a father reading scripture. (Woodcut. Private collection.)

and also usually a time of corporate family prayer. While this activity may have been more commonly practiced in some households than in others, there is no doubt that the prevailing social and religious mores of Massachusetts in the late seventeenth century recognized the importance of such daily parental and domestic religious instruction in the maintenance of the family, the community, the church, and the commonwealth. Rev. Cotton Mather in his sermon, "Cares About the Nurseries"[22] had this to say about the necessity of religious instruction from Puritan parents: "Before all and above all, 'tis the knowledge of the Christian religion that parents are to teach their children." It was only after the family meal and the time of spiritual instruction that work on the day's chores was begun. In general, work was considered an essential, praiseworthy, and even a God-honoring activity to members of New England Puritan culture. However, in terms of day-to-day life, it customarily followed only after daily times of family fellowship and religious devotion. These were the priorities and values imparted by parents to their children in the family life of Puritan New England at the time of the Salem witch trials.

NOTES

1. Laurel Thatcher Ulrich, *Good Wives* (New York: Alfred A. Knopf, 1982), 36–37.

2. John Halkett, *Milton and the Idea of Matrimony* (New Haven: Yale University Press, 1970), 20.

3. Quoted in Edmund Morgan, *The Puritan Family: Religion and Domestic Relations in Seventeenth Century New England* (New York: Harper and Row, 1966), 143.

4. Ibid., 46.

5. Quoted in John Putnam Demos, *A Little Commonwealth: Family Life in Plymouth Colony* (New York: Oxford University Press, 1970), 91.

6. Quoted in Charles H. George and Katherine George, *The Protestant Mind of the English Reformation* (Princeton: Princeton University Press, 1961), 186, 286–87.

7. Ibid., 286–87.

8. Greven, *Four Generations*, 29.

9. Quoted in Alice Morse Earle, *Child Life in Colonial Days* (Stockbridge, MA: Berkshire House Publishers, 1993), 4.

10. From "Small Offers Towards the Service of the Tabernacle in this Wilderness" quoted in David E. Stannard, *The Puritan Way of Death: A Study in Religion, Culture and Social Change* (New York: Oxford University Press, 1977), 51.

11. David Freeman Hawke, *Everyday Life in Early America* (New York: Harper and Row, 1989), 67.

12. Richard Mather's "Farewell Exhortation" in Edmund Morgan, *The Puritan Family* (New York: Harper and Row, 1966), 92.

13. Massachusetts Law Code quoted in Edmund Morgan, *The Puritan Family*, 51.

14. David Freeman Hawke, *Everyday Life in Early America*, 68.

15. Alice Morse Earle, *Child Life in Colonial Days*, 11–12.

16. John Putnam Demos, from *A Little Commonwealth* quoted in David Freeman Hawke, *Every Day Life in Early America*, 67–68.

17. Ulrich, *Good Wives*, 19.

18. Ibid.

19. Ibid., 19–20.

20. Ibid., 20.

21. Ibid.

22. Edmund Morgan, *The Puritan Family*, 90.

4

BUSINESS, MARITIME COMMERCE, AND PIRACY IN THE 1690s

In terms of their approach to work and business, the Puritans, both in New and Old England, were highly successful. Their serious and tireless efforts to be productive created the modern business concept of the "Puritan work ethic" which is a term synonymous with the essential idea of hard-won economic success. By the 1690s, the settlers of New England and especially those of coastal Massachusetts had succeeded in creating a prosperous society which was already challenging England for the wealth of the transatlantic and especially, the West Indies trades. Their farms, created from the unpromising rocky soil of postglacial New England, already generated enough agricultural produce to meet the needs of the region's population with a surplus to send out as export.

Likewise, by the end of the seventeenth century, fishing had come to dominate the New England economy to the extent that exported salt cod would form the essential foundation of all the future fortunes of Massachusetts down to the industrial age. For this reason, it is no coincidence that hanging over the speaker's chair in the Massachusetts House of representatives is a four-foot-long gilt carving of a cod known as "The Sacred Cod" emblematic of the importance of the cod fisheries to the economic survival of colonial Massachusetts. In light of all this it is no wonder that these Puritan colonists viewed themselves as a people favored by God, having, with His care and blessing, overcome a hostile environment to create a North American promised land "flowing with milk and honey."

NEW ENGLAND'S FISHING INDUSTRY AT THE TIME OF THE WITCH TRIALS

By the last decade of the 1600s, several major ports along the coast of Massachusetts—Boston, Salem, Marblehead, and Cape Ann—had already established themselves as thriving and indeed famous, fishing centers focused clearly upon the catching, curing, and exportation of salt cod. This was the direct result of over 50 years of gradual development and exploitation of several so-called fishing banks where codfish swam in great abundance. These sources of cod were nearby Stellwagen Bank and the slightly more distant Georges Bank, both within easy sailing from the Massachusetts shoreline, and the more remote Grand Banks of Newfoundland.

Fishing at this time was still done from open or half-decked vessels with one or two masts, known as shallops or ketches. These popular vessels of the late seventeenth century were constructed largely of pine with an oak frame and keel, possessed a shallow draft making them ideal for coastal sailing, and had an overall length from bow to stern of between 35 and 50 feet. Although the earliest known vessels of this kind were brought from England during the 1620s and 1630s, by the 1690s, they were being commonly produced in shipyards along the New England coast.

Carrying a simple rig bearing one mainsail, and occasionally a foresail, these vessels could be easily maneuvered by a crew hauling upon several sets of oars with no sails required. They sailed close to the waterline when well ballasted and were generally very stable when floored with a catch of fish which made them ideal for the fishing business. The average shallop would require a crew of four to six men and might be sailed hundreds of miles either along the coast or into the open ocean. The care and maintenance of these vessels was easily handled by the fishermen themselves and required a patch of open beach where the vessel might be safely grounded, then careened to be scraped, recaulked with oakum, and covered once again with a thick coating of preservative pine tar.

As to the fishermen and their families, they frequently stood apart socially from the mainstream Puritan population of the late 1600s with communities of their own, often set apart geographically as

A New England Shallop of the 1690s (Private collection)

well from all other types of settlements. A fishing community was established at Winter Island in Salem in 1636, largely through the influence of Rev. Hugh Peter, and it retained its semi-independent status down to the end of the seventeenth century with no meeting-house but a well-known, infamous tavern called the Blue Anchor. A similar community of independent fishing folk was likewise established at Marblehead and another at Cape Ann; both had equally rancorous reputations for violating the basic social guidelines of New England Puritan life. Such settlements were often closely watched by officials who might arrest persons who flaunted authority by conducting themselves in an "unseemly" manner.

The business of fishing required individuals willing to risk everything, even their lives, for the sake of a good catch. It also demanded an array of specialized supplies and facilities in order to be conducted successfully. Among these were vast amounts of salt, usually imported from the Azores, Portugal, or Spain. Earlier in the century domestic saltmaking had been attempted with the construction of a saltworks in Salem, but with relatively little success since the demand for this substance was so great. To facilitate the processing of dried codfish, every fishing settlement required vast areas covered with *fish flakes,* or fish-drying frames where cod fillets would be laid out by the thousands in sunny weather. Each cleaned fish fillet would be heavily coated with coarse salt to draw the moisture from the fish flesh which would then be evaporated by the sun and dehydrating the fish to prevent spoilage. This process was an ancient means of food preservation and transformed the fish fillets from soft and moist to stiff and dry in a matter of 12 to 15 days in good weather. The pungent aroma of a seventeenth-century coastal fishing settlement—especially in the summer— might well have been another reason for their isolation from the main community of a seaport town.[1]

THE MARITIME MERCHANTS OF MASSACHUSETTS IN THE 1690s

As with New England's agricultural produce, the seventeenth-century fishing industry produced enough salt fish to meet the needs of the local population with a substantial surplus available annually for export. Interestingly, although the fishing community was possessed of seaworthy vessels, they did not engage in the actual transportation and sale of the vast quantities of salt fish which they produced. That task was the responsibility of the maritime merchants and sea captains who, each year purchased the surplus supplies of salt cod from the fishing stations of the Massachusetts coast, oversaw their placement into wooden barrels near the fish flakes, and transported them in the holds of merchant vessels to the various markets of the Atlantic—the British Isles, Catholic Europe, the colonies of Virginia and Maryland, and the sugar plantations of the West Indies.[2]

The underlying rationale for the need of salt fish on the sugar-producing islands of the West Indies was to serve as an inexpensive dietary source of protein for the thousands of slaves which, by the 1690s, labored on the English sugar plantations. Combined with cargoes of New England agricultural produce and lumber products like barrel staves, shingles, and sawn boards, salt cod formed the primary trading commodity from New England to the West Indies. Thus, wood and salt fish was exchanged at Barbados, St. Christopher (St. Kitts), Antigua, and Jamaica for vast quantities of molasses, sugar, rum, and African slaves. These cargoes in turn would be brought north to the ports of Salem and Boston where they would be sold. This so-called West Indies Trade, heavily based as it was on salt cod and molasses, formed the foundation of many pre-Revolutionary New England fortunes, and continued to be a profitable enterprise well into the nineteenth century.

Some of the best-known and wealthiest Massachusetts merchants who engaged in this profitable West Indies trade were John Turner, Philip English, William Browne, and Deliverance Parkman. These were among that elite group of late seventeenth-century entrepreneurs whom maritime historian Samuel Eliot Morison refers to as the "Codfish Aristocracy" since the base of their wealth rested upon the humble cod. A vivid representative image of the maritime commerce of Salem during the witch trial era is provided by historian James Duncan Phillips: "it is safe to say that as the century closed Salem was doing considerable foreign trade. Probably as often as once a month, one of the larger vessels owned in Salem left for Europe, stopping perhaps at Fuchal, Madeira, or Fayal in the Azores, and then going on to Bilbao or Oporto. Thence the vessel might proceed to London and then home."[3] Voyages such as this to Portugal, the Madeira Islands, or Spain were conducted by Massachusetts merchants in order to exchange salt fish, lumber products, and New England rum for citrus fruits, wine, and salt, the latter being so essential for the fishing industry. In trading with Catholic Europe during the 1690s, merchants needed to be careful to avoid invoking the penalties of the several Navigation Acts restricting trade and requiring American vessels to declare such transactions to English custom officers and pay the appropriate fees. At the center of this policy was the protection of the economic interests of English merchants and their business activities. In their view, American colonies should not be allowed to engage in economic competition with the mother country, rather their role was to support the economy of England by supplying raw materials and supplementary resources.

Although the government of England had, since the 1640s and through the 1670s, attempted to regulate New England maritime trade with various Navigation Acts, these laws were difficult to enforce, and were often entirely circumvented by the "codfish aristocrats" of Salem and Boston through bribery and smuggling. This gave them virtual autonomy in the handling of their maritime activities as well as huge profits. It is important to note that although any coastal community might engage in fishing and ship-construction, after 1683 only Boston and Salem in Massachusetts were authorized by the English government to engage in international maritime trade. For that reason, many smaller ports simply shipped all their outward bound cargoes of fish, produce, and lumber to one of these two mercantile centers to be shipped out to Europe or the West Indies.[4]

The sheer number and frequency of trading ventures also provides the observer with a sense that far from being a provincial backwater, Massachusetts of the 1690s was a bustling center of commercial activity: "As often as once a week a ketch came in from Barbados or some other West Indian port, having made a trading voyage first to Virginia and then on south. Wheat and corn made good merchandise to exchange for tobacco, horses, barrel staves, planks, hewed timber, butter, cheese and the ever-present codfish furnished the wherewithal to buy the sugar and molasses and to obtain the pieces of eight . . . highly desirable for foreign trade."[5]

THE MASSACHUSETTS SHIPBUILDING INDUSTRY OF THE 1690s

Related to all the region's maritime trade and fishing activities was yet another thriving colonial industry which, by the end of the seventeenth century, was on the rise—shipbuilding. During the 1690s, there were three prominent shipyards and several smaller ones in Salem alone, one in Marblehead, and several more in the area around Boston Harbor and the Mystic River. In 1690s Salem, the Becket family was the preeminent shipbuilding clan who operated a shipyard at the foot of the lane named in their honor. Next in order of prominence was the shipyard of Daniel Lambert, a prominent shipowning merchant and shipright. Likewise, several other merchants engaged in shipbuilding as well, owning and operating shipyards that supplied the needs of their own merchant fleets. Among these were Bartholomew Gedney, John Turner, and John Ruck, whose yard stood at the end of Ruck's Creek where it emptied into Salem Harbor.[6]

A report by Edward Randolph to the "Lords of Trade and Plantations" in England commenting on Massachusetts shipbuilding, pointed out that Massachusetts by the 1680s was already competing with the English shipbuilding industry by producing vessels more cheaply than they could be produced in the mother country. To make matters even worse, these American shipbuilders, not content with sailing their own homemade vessels, were beginning to transport them across the Atlantic Ocean, selling both the cargoes and ships which carried the cargoes to the merchants of continental Europe and even England at bargain prices.[7]

A stroll around the crowded waterfronts of Salem and Boston of the 1690s would clearly illustrate that the shipbuilding industry itself was responsible for fostering the establishment of several other supporting trades and businesses, such as ships-carpenters, anchorsmiths, ropemakers, sailmakers, caulkers, ships-chandlers, blockmakers, and riggers. Naturally, the success of these maritime support industries was largely predicated on the continued success and prosperity of the shipping and fishing activities of a seaport, but from this summit of the late seventeenth-century business economy, patronage also trickled down to a wide array of other businesses. This was the economic infrastructure supporting daily life in coastal New England in the 1690s.

Other Construction Activities in Boston and Salem of the 1690s

By the 1690s, the urban centers of Salem and Boston had built up a sizable community of artisans sustained by the patronage of others earning their living in some manner from the sea. Among these were housewrights who were kept steadily at work constructing new dwellings, many of which, despite the numerous town fires, are still in existence today. A related trend of the late 1600s among the seafaring merchant class was the construction of mansion-houses, large and complex domestic structures unlike any that had preceded them in the previous half-century. This was possible only because of the enormous influx of profits as a result of successful maritime trade which produced impressive works of architecture such as the Turner-Ingersoll House (1668) and the mansion of Philip English (1683).

Such large and impressive dwellings tended to change the essential character and physical appearance of the once humble waterfronts of Boston and Salem, dwarfing the earlier half-houses and vernacular structures of the previous two generations. In keeping with this tendency, some of the main streets in both seaports, which had previously been surfaced with compacted soil, began to be resurfaced with small, rounded cobblestones taken from the rocky beaches of nearby islands. This not only greatly improved the appearance of the main thoroughfares, but eliminated the tendency of pedestrians and vehicles to get bogged-down and muddied in inclement weather. Such improvements came directly as a result of the votes of male taxpayers at town meetings and the decisions of the town's elected selectmen who served as the municipal government. Each town conducted its business using a small group of elected or chosen volunteer and paid officers who provided

The Philip English House (1683), Salem, MA. (From *The Ships and Sailors of Old Salem* by Ralph Paine, 1908. Private collection.)

essential services to the residents of the community. These officers in the larger communities like Boston or Salem by the 1690s included a surveyor of fences, a surveyor of highways, a hog-reeve, a surveyor of weights and measures, a town constable, a night watchman, and a town crier as well as a committee for the care of the indigent residents of the town called "The Overseers of the Poor."

In addition to domestic house construction to accommodate a growing urban population, wharf and warehouse construction was an ongoing trend during the late 1600s to accommodate a growing trade. As vessels increased in size and number, merchant-shipowners acquired large segments of waterfront property to provide themselves with space for warehouses and vessel docking facilities. Very often such business-related amenities were placed conveniently near or adjacent to the residences of merchant shipowners giving the merchant easy access to his countinghouse and cargo storage as well as his vessels when they were in port. Wharf and warehouse construction not only helped increase the overall capacity of late seventeenth-century ports to accommodate more vessels, but provided additional employment to carpenters, joiners, and day laborers and additional sources of income to the already expanding middle and lower classes in Massachusetts seaport towns.[8] Historian James Duncan Phillips comments upon this tendency and notes that "[c]ommerce was evidently growing, for in March, 1684, no less than ten merchants were given the privilege of building wharves at Winter Island. It also suggests that the trade was being carried on in winter as well as in summer."[9] This expansion of the maritime infrastructure would continue until the American Revolution.

Another major and highly profitable industry of the 1690s, closely tied to both ship and house construction, was the lumber industry. Like fish, lumber in various forms—shingles, barrel staves, clapboards, framing timbers, masts, yardarms, and hewn logs—constituted a very important and economically significant export cargo from Massachusetts to England and the West Indies. Virtually all of Boston's and Salem's merchants shipped out cargoes of lumber at different times. These were purchased from suppliers from "down East" in either the Colony of New Hampshire or the Province of Maine. Such private ventures in lumber necessitated an exploitation of northern virgin forests which, by the 1690s, were already being severely cut back from the coast, creating a new landscape of denuded, rolling hills from the coastline to the foothills of the White Mountains in New Hampshire. Eventually, by the early nineteenth century, nearly all of the easily accessible forest of eastern and southern New England would be gone.

During the last decade of the seventeenth century, England itself sought a means to regularly acquire the best of what New England's forests had to offer, particularly for the use of the English shipbuilding industry. To this end, Sir William Phips, in June 1691 presented a proposal to the Lords of Trade and King William as to how he might accelerate the lumbering process on behalf of the crown. Emerson Baker elaborates on this innovative scheme: "In September, 1691, he (Phips) presented an explicit proposal concerning the timber resources of the Piscataqua ... and their value as a source of naval stores." This was only another attempt to commercially exploit the seemingly limitless timber resources of northern New England, while making money from England by supplying her shipbuilders and navy with an essential commodity. It was also an indirect way to curtail the efforts of the heirs of Sir Fernando Gorges and the Mason Family who were still attempting to press their claims to New Hampshire and parts of Maine.[10]

At the very heart of the lumbering industry was the safe access and availability of forests as well as who had the right to harvest them and sell the lumber. This question was a source of some concern to those colonists involved in the lumber industry of the 1690s and those that followed well into the eighteenth century. The Lords of Trade suggested that the Crown had a proprietary right to claim the best North American timber resources for the use of English shipwrights in the construction of naval vessels. Phips supported that perspective when he was summoned to appear in person before the Lords of Trade: "Sir William Phips attending, is call'd [sic] in and ordered to present to the Committee some proposals in writing concerning ship timber, masts and naval stores that maybe had in New England."[11] The end result was that from the 1690s onward, and largely because of the ongoing King William's War, British naval claims would challenge and compete with private suppliers of lumber as both factions sought to harvest vast amounts of New England timber for export and commercial sale to transatlantic markets.

FRENCH PRIVATEERS, PIRATES, AND KING WILLIAM'S WAR DURING THE 1690s

The negative side to all this increased exportation, maritime traffic, and growing prosperity is that it tended to attract French privateers as well as pirates of all nations, all of whom were frequently inclined to prey upon the shipping of Massachusetts merchants. James Duncan Phillips elaborates that "[t]he most serious threat against the Salem trade came with the outbreak of the Indian troubles in Governor Andros' time, which soon drifted into . . . King William's War which lasted from 1689 to 1697." During 1689, French privateers captured nine vessels and over thirty American seamen, taking them into the French colonial naval base on Cape Breton Island known as Port Royal. Such encounters and the resulting loss of property, finally resulted in the mounting of a military campaign under the leadership of Sir William Phips in 1690 prior to his appointment as governor of Massachusetts. As described by Emerson Baker, "with French vessels based in Port Royal putting increasing pressure on Massachusetts shipping—the House of Representatives resolved in favor of raising volunteers and appointing commanders for the reducing of the French on the coast of Acadia or elsewhere to the obedience of their Majesties of Great Britain."[12]

The primary purpose of this venture was to protect British-American mercantile interests on the high seas and secondly, to reduce the potential threat to New England of France's most dangerous naval base in the New World. It succeeded under Phips's leadership when he arrived at Cape Breton Island, Nova Scotia with a fleet of five ships: the 42-gun, 120-man *Six Friends*; the 16-gun, 117-man, *Porcupine*; the sloop-of-war *Mary*, the barque *Union*, and three small, armed ketches carrying Massachusetts militia. The total strength of this force in terms of manpower was 286 sailors and 446 soldiers and yet this modest force succeeded in causing the French fortress to surrender on May 12, 1690. This achievement, underwritten by the businessmen of Boston and Salem, helped to bring the French privateer threat under control—at least for a time.[13]

FRENCH AND ENGLISH COMPETITION
FOR THE FUR TRADE

The 1690 capture of Port Royal marks only a brief episode in an otherwise prolonged war with the French Empire that dominated most of the 1690s. This conflict was an ongoing struggle which added tension to the everyday life of New England's colonists, especially those engaged in any aspect of maritime trade and those living and working on the northern frontier. At its very heart was the issue of which European power would come to dominate the North American fur trade, which since the 1630s had become one of the most profitable businesses directly involving the Native American population. Virtually all the wars in North America between England and France, from the late seventeenth century to the signing of the Treaty of Paris in 1763, revolved around English and French attempts to control the fur trade conducted with several major tribes on the northern and western frontiers of New England. The French sided with the Algonquin, Abenaki, Mi'kmaq, Ottawa, and Ojibwa people while the English tended to ally themselves with the Iroquois Confederacy including the Onandaga, Oneida, Seneca, Tuscarora, Cayuga, and Mohawk nations. King William's War (1689–1697) was fought on both the sea and the land, and throughout the 1690s the entire northern frontier of New England was faced with the threat of attacks by Native American war parties or their French allies.

Since the early 1600s, European hatmakers had created a demand for beaver fur which was nearly limitless since beaver fur produced the finest quality felt for hats. By the mid-seventeenth century, the market for fur of all kinds gave rise to a transatlantic industry that would set England and France on a collision course as each tried to outdo the other in meeting the demand. The primary suppliers of fur to Europe were the above-mentioned Native American groups who not only sought to compete with each other for European goods in exchange for fur pelts, but often found themselves locked in conflict with either England or France as they struggled for control of international commerce. The fur trade was, for over 100 years, a constant source of colonial anxiety as well as monumental profits. But the French and Indians did not represent the only threat to Massachusetts settlers and their commerce. There were also pirates who cruised the New England coast and preyed upon New England shipping vessels.

The first trial and execution of pirates in Boston took place in 1672. This was a growing problem during the last quarter of the seventeenth century and figured prominently as a subject in Rev. Cotton Mather's book, *Pillars of Salt: An History of Some Criminals Executed in This Land*, published in Boston in 1699. In terms of the law, the Massachusetts Great and General Court enacted legislation on October 15, 1673, declaring that in all cases piracy was punishable by death in Massachusetts Bay Colony. But there were occasional exceptions. For example, in 1675, the Court of Assistants found John Rhoade and others of his crew guilty of piracy for robbing vessels off the coast of Maine. They were sentenced to be hanged after the lecture on the following market day (Thursday) in Boston. Immediately prior to their day of execution news reached Boston of the outbreak of King Philip's War, and in the state of emergency following this crisis, their execution date was postponed until finally they were released.[14]

On August 9, 1689, the ketch *Mary*, of Salem, was attacked and captured by pirates near Halfway Rock in Casco Bay, Maine. The Governor's Council of Massachusetts ordered the sloop *Resolution* under the command of Captain Joseph Thaxter with 40 men to pursue the outlaws, and by October they were captured after a brief battle in Martha's Vineyard Sound. The pirates flew a red flag and succeeded in killing and wounding several of their attackers before surrendering. They were later brought to Boston and condemned.[15]

In 1695, the ship *Essex* was attacked by pirates while en route back to Salem from Bilbao, Portugal, but her commander, Capt. Joseph Beal was successful in fighting off his pursuers and lost only one of his gunners, John Samson, in the running battle.[16] In the following year, the innovative Puritan businessmen of Salem decided to retaliate by outfitting the privateer *Salem Galley*, an American privateer, under the command of Capt. Richard Harris. Its purpose was to capture French merchantmen and bring them back as prizes of war to Massachusetts, a goal which was accomplished by August 1695 when two French vessels were sent to Salem, condemned, sold, and rechristened with new English names. It seems that even Puritan merchants were skilled at turning a profit from wartime activities.

The French responded to this initiative by increasing their efforts to cripple the fishing fleets of Massachusetts, and enjoyed some considerable success in nearly destroying the local economy. In 1697, John Higginson of Salem wrote to his brother, Nathaniel: "in the year 1689, when this war first broke out, I had attained a competent estate, being as much concerned in the fishing trade as most of my neighbors, but since that time I have met with considerable losses. Of sixty odd fishing ketches belonging to this town, there are now but about six are left."[17]

An interesting note to all the privateers and piracy of the 1690s is that one of the accusations leveled by critics against Massachusetts governor Sir William Phips prior to his removal is that "he had received cash generated by piracy." The possibility that the governor who was in charge of the court during the witch trial proceedings worked with pirates was revealed in September 1692. In a letter presented to the Lords of Trade, Nathaniel Byfield wrote that "a crew headed by a Captain Tew who have brott in vast quantities of gold and silver which they have got in all likelihood very wickedly" was allowed to land and stay in Boston. In Phips's absence, Lt. Gov. Stoughton issued a warrant for their arrest, only to see it reversed when Phips returned from his visit to Pemaquid, Maine. Finally, when Phips's alleged account papers were presented for examination, "the 'Accounts' attributed to him included both five hundred pounds in Arabian gold received from pirates in 1692-93 and one thousand pounds of Arabian gold in the year 1694 received of pirates he giving them liberty to come to Boston from Rhode Island."[18]

Reflections on Puritan Business Practice and Its Effect upon Their Religion

In light of all the above legitimate and questionable forms of profitable and profiteering activities being practiced by alleged Puritan businessmen and officials, it should come to no surprise that many ministers of Salem, Boston, and throughout the colony of Massachusetts were dismayed at how far community leaders had strayed from the original principles for which the colony had been originally established. Many contemporaries of the Salem witch trials warned their fellow citizens about the unbridled and immoral pursuit of wealth and its effects upon one's spiritual life. Rev. Cotton Mather, pastor of Governor Phips's congregation and advisor to Phips himself wrote in tragic irony, "(our) religion begat (our) prosperity, and the daughter devoured the mother."[19] And he later denounced his people's "[i]nsatiable desire after land and worldly accommodations . . . only so that they might have elbow room in the world."[20]

Mather's grandfather Richard, speaking to an earlier generation of Boston merchants expressed his concern in another way, "Experience shows that it is an easy thing in the midst of worldly business to lose the life and power of religion, that nothing therefore should be left but only the external form, as it were, the carcass or shell, worldliness having eaten out the kernel, and having consumed the very soul and life of godliness." Worldliness, in Mather's view, is the love of and pursuit of the "things of this world" with little attention paid to things of a spiritual nature, in short a love of materialism. In this way during the 1690s, the observer may detect, especially in Puritan urban life, an everwidening motivational breach between the religious leaders of the Puritan movement and the leaders of the Puritan business community. The Salem witch trials only further contributed to the breakdown of the Puritan movement as the disenchanted colonists began to place less confidence in the religious leadership and gradually turned to the leaders of the business community as their role models by the early eighteenth century.

NOTES

1. James Duncan Phillips, *Salem in the Seventeenth Century* (Boston: Houghton and Mifflin, 1933), 94–95.
2. Ibid., 251.
3. Ibid., 289.
4. Ibid., 282–83.
5. Ibid., 289.
6. Ibid., 327.
7. Ibid., 282.
8. Ibid., 282–83.
9. Ibid., 283.
10. Baker, *The New England Knight*, 124.
11. Ibid., 124.
12. Ibid., 82–83.

13. Ibid., 87–88.

14. George Francis Dow, *Everyday Life in the Massachusetts Bay Colony* (Mineola, NY: Dover Publications, 1988), 219.

15. Felt, *Annals of Salem*, 2nd ed., 242–43.

16. Ibid., 245.

17. Letter, *John Higginson to Nathaniel Higginson*, 1697, quoted in Phillips, *Salem in the 17th Century*, 214.

18. Nathaniel Byfield quoted in Baker, *The New England Knight*, 233–34.

19. Ibid.

20. Mather quoted in Ryken, *Worldly Saints*, 63.

5

POLITICS AND WAR IN THE 1690s

THE ARRIVAL OF GOVERNOR SIR WILLIAM PHIPS

The Glorious Revolution in 1688 brought with it many changes for both Old and New England. Not the least of these was the removal of King James II and the ascension of King William III and Queen Mary as England's first constitutional monarchs. It also ended the reign of Sir Edmund Andros as governor of the Dominion of New England since he was arrested and sent back to England by the Puritan elite of Boston. During this transitional period, Massachusetts temporarily reverted back to its old Massachusetts Bay Charter under the leadership of interim governor Simon Bradstreet, while the influential reverend Increase Mather traveled with three other colonial agents to London to appeal to Parliament and the king. Mather and his colleagues were vigorously lobbying with members of the House of Commons and several powerful political figures in an attempt to have restored to the colony all the rights and privileges taken away when the original Massachusetts Bay Charter was revoked under James II in 1684.

Since very little support for this idea was evident among those who would be responsible for the creation of a new colonial government, Rev. Mather decided instead to labor for the best political arrangement possible. Not all of his Massachusetts colleagues supported his decision to abandon the plan for a complete restoration of the old charter, but in practical terms there was little else to be done. It was Mather who, once told that all of the American colonies would soon become royal colonies, suggested that a native-born governor, such as military hero Sir William Phips, might serve both the best interests of the crown and the commonwealth. Since Phips had, in 1690, experienced a religious conversion as a member of Rev. Cotton Mather's congregation in Boston, he was regarded by both Increase and Cotton Mather not only as a fellow-member of the elect, but as someone they might be able to influence for the good of the people and the colony. Mather ultimately succeeded in his lobbying efforts on Phips's behalf.

In the final analysis, a compromise was struck and Massachusetts received its new charter in 1691 restoring many, but not all of the colonial rights removed during Andros's administration, and merging the adjacent colonies of Plymouth, New Hampshire, Maine, Nantucket, Martha's Vineyard, Nova Scotia and New Brunswick to the revised colonial entity known simply as the Province of Massachusetts Bay. However, the government of England was not willing to restore the right of the public election of a colonial governor as previously had been done in Massachusetts since the first election of John Winthrop. Instead, Massachusetts in 1691 became another royal colony meaning that, henceforth the monarch of England, not the freemen or freeholders of the colony, would appoint a governor to take over the reins of power in Massachusetts.

In May 1692, newly appointed governor, Sir William Phips, arrived in Boston with his patron, Rev. Increase Mather bearing the new colonial charter and replacing the interim governor Simon Bradstreet. Phips's arrival marked the start of an entirely new phase in the history of Massachusetts government, greatly affecting the colony down to the eve of the American Revolution. Governor William Phips would be, by far, the single most influential character in determining the activities of daily life, especially in the political sphere in Massachusetts from 1692 until his removal in 1694. In this respect, he is an important figure in understanding the handling of both the Salem witch trials as well as the often misunderstood frontier war which dominated the lives of the residents of Massachusetts during this brief period.

BIOGRAPHY OF GOVERNOR SIR WILLIAM PHIPS

Unlike his royally-appointed predecessor, Sir Edmund Andros, Phips was a product of the lower edge of New England agrarian society. He was born of a non-Puritan farming family in 1651 in a frontier town located in the Kennebec region near present-day Woolwich, Maine. Without any social advantages or formal education, he began his remarkable rise in fortune as a ship's carpenter. Traveling to the provincial capital of Boston, he soon met and in 1673 married Mary Spencer Hull, the wealthy widow of a successful Boston shipowning merchant, John Hull. Using her inherited resources, Phips built a ship of 117 tons and became a sea captain. By the early 1680s, he began a series of treasure-hunting expeditions in the Caribbean, resulting in the successful plundering of a wrecked Spanish galleon, the *Concepción*. The resulting wealth— 68,511 pounds of silver and 25 pounds of gold worth between 205 and 210 thousand pounds sterling (between $143,500,000 and $147,000,000 in today's currency)—was shared with King James II who knighted Phips on June 26, 1687 "in consideration of his loyalty, and good services in a late expedition."[1]

By 1688, the year of the Glorious Revolution and the overthrow of King James II, Phips found himself serving the Dominion of New England as the newly appointed provost marshal-general during the administration of Sir Edmund Andros in Boston. The position was a royal appointment with the responsibility of supervising the colony's county sheriffs under the new, unpopular dominion government. Phips was not equal to the task as he lacked any legal or previous government experience. He further proved an ill-chosen candidate for an office requiring good diplomatic and administrative skills. Thus, Phips came to be viewed by many officers already in the Dominion of New England as "at best, an unwelcome intruder and at worst, a contemptible upstart."

In actuality, Phips was a native New Englander of humble origins seeking to somehow "establish himself as a member of the ruling elite."[2] By quickly siding with the political faction in Massachusetts opposing Andros, he made every effort to curry favor with the powerful colonial oligarchy, and was selected by their leadership to command a force of Massachusetts militia against the French base at Port Royal in Acadia, present-day Nova Scotia. The expedition resulted in the surrender of the French garrison in May 1689. The capture of Port Royal was negotiated by Phips and the French governor of Acadia, Louis-Alexander de Meneval. Encouraged by this initial success, Massachusetts led an intercolonial conference of northern colonies the following year in "directing a two-pronged attack on French Canada"; Phips lead an amphibious assault on Quebec with 2,200 Massachusetts troops under his command, while Fitz-John Winthrop attacked Montreal commanding a force consisting of New York and Connecticut militia supported by Native American allies. Unfortunately, both of these efforts resulted in failure. In the case of Phips's attack on Quebec, the city was held by renowned French governor Louis de Buade, comte de Frontenac, who refused Phips's demand for surrender. Within a week, he forced Phips and his forces to withdraw after two failed skirmishes. The disastrous affair, according to Rev. Cotton Mather, who considered himself a supporter of his parishioner, Phips, estimated that it cost the Massachusetts Bay Colony "[f]orty Thousand Pounds, more or less, now to be paid, and not a penny in the Treasury to pay it withal."[3]

But despite this reversal, Phips emerged with his reputation as the victor of Port Royal intact and immediately returned to England to seek the nomination for the replacement of Sir Edmund Andros as the next royally appointed governor of Massachusetts. With the support of Rev. Increase Mather and several prominent English political figures, his candidacy was ultimately approved and in May 1692, he returned to his native country of New England bearing the new Massachusetts colonial charter and a new vision for the New England colonies.

CHANGES IN MASSACHUSETTS WITH THE NEW CHARTER OF 1691

In terms of new political policies, the arrival of "The Second Massachusetts Charter" would create a colony markedly different in purpose and function than that which had existed previously. The "errand in the wilderness" was now no longer the God-ordained objective for the colony, nor indeed was the colony ever again to be a Puritan commonwealth. Henceforth, not only would the colonial governor be royally appointed, but also the governor's secretary and deputy governor would now require royal approval as well. Other changes included the creation of a revised House of Representatives whose members are elected annually, not by free-holders whose membership in the Puritan church qualified them to vote, but by freeholders whose taxes reflected an "estate to the value of forty shillings per annum at the least," or were possessed of property "to the value of forty pounds Sterling." Every town in Massachusetts was expected to elect, from among its prosperous residents, two such legislative representatives, and from these delegates new colonial laws would be created—provided they be reviewed and approved by the King's Privy Council—a process that was essentially new. Most disturbing to many Puritan clergy was the charter's reinforcement of the Act of Toleration whereby "forever hereafter there shall be a liberty of Conscience allowed in worship of God to all Christians (except Papists)."[4] Henceforth all Christians, be they dissenters or radical sectarians, as long as they were not Roman Catholics, must be tolerated by the Puritan majority without fear of exclusion or persecution.

In addition, the new royal governor, Sir William Phips, would now hold absolute power to veto any legislation generated by the Great and General Court, or as the charter states, "in all elections and acts of government whatsoever to be passed or done by the said Great and General Court ... the Governor of our said province of the Massachusetts Bay in New England for the time being shall have the Negative voice and that without his consent or Approbation signified and declared in writing, no such orders, laws, statutes, ordinances, elections or other acts of government ... shall be of any force, effect or validity." This made Phips a very powerful political figure in Massachusetts.[5]

As previously suggested, there is little doubt that, despite his obvious failures, one of the primary reasons why Phips was chosen to serve as the first royal governor of Massachusetts was his previous military experience leading the successful campaign in 1689 against Port Royal, the great French fortress in Acadia, present-day Nova Scotia. As a direct consequence of this, the additional support of Rev. Increase Mather and because many English political figures were uneasy about the current war with France, Phips also received a royal commission granting him supreme command of all the colonial militias in New England.[6]

This was precisely what Phips had desired since his chief aim was to redeem his failure in 1690 by launching a new direct military assault on Canada, defeating the French forces as well as attacking their Native American allies, the Wabanaki of Maine. His goal was to annex the unsettled part of Maine and the "maritime provinces" including present-day Nova Scotia, New Brunswick, and Prince Edward Island to the newly expanded Colony of Massachusetts. The result of this maneuver, if successful, would be to make Phips's reputation and fortune while denying the French access to the fishing grounds of Newfoundland. Most importantly, it would secure for England dominance of the lucrative fur trade in Northeastern Canada, while controlling seaborne traffic through the mouth of the St. Lawrence River, the only waterway access to the French trading centers of Montreal and the City of Quebec.[7] It was indeed fortunate for Phips that his military success at Port Royal in 1689 consistently

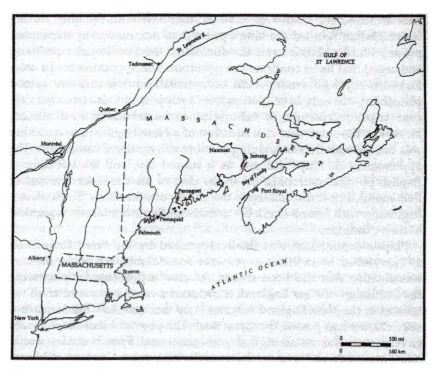

Map showing Phips's expanded vision of Massachusetts Bay Colony.
(Dr. Emerson Baker)

overshadowed his failure at Quebec in 1690, and his appointment as
governor was approved despite some serious misgivings by some of
England's leading political figures concerning his military ability and
leadership skills.[8] That military preparations were already being
planned by the English government to take the offensive against the
French in Canada is reflected in a letter sent by Privy Council committee member, William Blathwayt, "Sir W. Phips is made the king's
Governor of the Massachusetts and Commander-in-Chief of all the
other colonies of New England by which means his Majesty's authority is to be resettled in those parts."[9]

As his first step to securing a well-defended boundary for
Massachusetts, Phips requested that the northeastern coast immediately south of Canada be fortified. In response, in the original instructions to Phips and to the Massachusetts agents in London "was the
provision for 'Ten Great Guns' to be sent to New England and for
Phips 'to take care that our Fort of Pemaquid be forthwith restored,
and the said Guns placed within the same.' "[10] This fortress would

serve as the primary guardian of the Massachusetts coastline in the event of a northern invasion by French forces headed toward Boston.

To help Governor Phips further protect New England's coast from a French seaborne assault, and to enable him to support a future invasion of French Canada, the Royal Navy assigned to him a single, 24-year-old frigate, a fourth-rate warship called, somewhat ironically, the HMS *Nonsuch* commanded by Captain Richard Short. A future political enemy, it was this captain of the *Nonsuch* who would "exert significant and unexpected influence on the course of Phips' career as Governor, notably after Phips had accused Short of insubordination," then publicly caning him on a Boston wharf in January 1693. Clearly, in addition to military leadership shortcomings, Governor Phips also lacked diplomatic skill and the demeanor of a gentleman as well.[11] Captain Short's hostility was, in part, the result of what was perceived by him as an act of high-handed robbery by Phips in refusing to share the proceeds of a captured and condemned French prize vessel.

It was on board the HMS *Nonsuch* that Phips made his crossing from London, England to Boston in May 1692. England was locked in a state of war with France. During this seven-week crossing, the British frigate bearing Phips captured a French merchantman, the *Catharine*, en route to La Rochelle from Martinique in the West Indies bearing a valuable cargo of sugar. Upon arriving in Boston with his French prize, Phips "took her (the *Catherine*) from the said Captain Short promising the ships' company satisfaction, yet never made them any recompense." Normally, a naval vessel responsible for a prize capture would expect to receive prize money from the sale of the captured vessel and her cargo. Such prize money was customarily divided among the captain, officers, and crew of the naval vessel. Apparently, this did not happen and Short and his naval contingent resented the governor's self-aggrandizing intervention and Phips appears to have kept a significant portion of the proceeds of the prize auction for himself. Politically, this was a bad first step since Phips needed the full cooperation and support of those royal naval officers and vessels assigned to protect Massachusetts and support his future military assault on Canada.

Phips's personal secretary, Benjamin Jackson, countered implications of wrongdoing with the explanation that Captain Short "had failed to appear before the vice-admiralty court to make any claim to the prize."[12] In actuality, Phips used his newfound political power to control the appointments to the admiralty court positions, and on this case and several other valuable prizes he either sat in judgment himself, or placed political friends on the bench. By investing in privateers himself, then controlling the verdict as well as the disposition of prize money, Phips began his political career as a war profiteer in grand style. It would become one of several controversial political issues to call him back to London to face charges of corruption in 1694.

Thus, from his first days of official authority as governor of Massachusetts Bay Colony, Sir William Phips was already sowing the seeds of political controversy and animosity between himself and the commander of his largest royal naval vessel. In addition, it appears that Governor Phips also succeeded in offending his only other naval commander, Captain Robert Fairfax of the Boston-based, fifth-rate warship HMS *Conception*. In later testimony, Fairfax remarked that he too objected to the rude treatment that he received from the Puritan leadership: "None that ever commands his majesty's ships in this place (Boston) was ever used with common civility." Thus it was from 1692 onward that relations between the Royal Navy and the Phips administration were strained and would not improve.[13]

Governor Phips was faced with two additional problems of a critical nature upon his arrival in May. The first involved the ongoing King William's War which had evolved into northern frontier conflict with the Wabanaki of Maine. This war had become for the Wabanaki a war of containment and survival fighting against the encroachment of English settlements into Wabanaki territory, a conflict which could be traced back to the 1670s. Although the Wabanaki were compelled to sign a treaty with Massachusetts Bay Colony in 1678, periodically renewed hostilities would result in terrifying raids upon the frontier settlements of Maine producing large numbers of colonial casualties and displacing many more settlers from their farms and villages. In January 1692, a Wabanaki attack had struck the town of York, Maine, resulting in the death or capture of over 100 people. Phips was personally very much affected by this event since he was originally a native of the province of Maine. Attempting to resolve this looming frontier crisis would occupy much of Phips's time and energy during his brief tenure as governor.[14]

The second and better-known major crisis faced by Phips upon his arrival, was an outbreak of suspected witchcraft activity in the area near Salem Village, a small farming community outside Salem, Massachusetts. Phips addressed this emergency with the creation of a "Special Court of Oyer and Terminer" to handle the growing backlog of witchcraft court cases. This was necessitated by dozens of pretrial examinations of suspected witches by local justices John Hathorne and Jonathan Corwin. Of these, 42 were, by the time of Phips's arrival, already imprisoned by them awaiting trial. An attempt to try them all in the existing colonial court system would, in all likelihood, tie up the courts for months and prevent the regular dispensation of justice. Instead, Phips decided to create a special court of "oyer and terminer" specifically for the purpose of trying the suspected witches, leaving the trying and execution of witches to those he deemed better qualified for the task. In accomplishing this, Phips claimed later that he selected as judges "people of the best prudence and figure that could then be pitched upon."[15]

Phips's actual court selections are unquestionably representative of those individuals who, in 1692, were considered among the "most prominent lay leaders of New England" beginning with the notable chief justice, Deputy Governor William Stoughton who brought with him the prestige of his rank as deputy governor and a former minister, but also more than two decades of continuous public service. It is Stoughton who, as chief justice of the Court of Oyer and Terminer, is most often regarded as the individual ultimately responsible for its course of action. Stoughton's fellow justices were absolutely representative of the best men the colony had to offer: Samuel Sewell, Wait Winthrop, Bartholomew Gedney, Nathaniel Saltonstall, William Sargent, and John Richards.[16] It would be their task to call juries and try those already awaiting trial in the privately owned jails of Salem, Ipswich, and Boston.

The Phips-appointed court went immediately to work trying the case of accused witch, Bridget Bishop in June. Much of the evidence presented against her was circumstantial and of a spectral nature. Despite its controversial nature, Chief Justice Stoughton decided to allow it. On or about June 8, Col. Nathaniel Saltonstall had had enough, and became the only court justice to resign from the Special Court of Oyer and Terminer, avoiding responsibility for the death of Bridget Bishop and all the others that would follow. Governor Phips replaced Saltonstall with Salem's Jonathan Corwin who earlier had worked with Hathorne conducting pretrial examinations. Corwin would remain on the bench until October of that year.

After Bishop's execution on June 10, the court went into a recess, and in an attempt to affect the outcome of future trials, Governor Phips and his council requested that a group of clergy meet in

Cambridge to discuss the role of spectral evidence being allowed as admissible proof of guilt. Phips was so concerned about their findings on this subject that he attended every meeting. In actuality, the "spectral evidence issue" was an important point of procedure since most of the evidence against the remaining accused was of a spectral nature. Without the use of spectral evidence presented in the testimony of the "afflicted children," the trials would have been nearly impossible.

The committee of 12 Boston ministers, after due deliberation, produced a proposal on June 15, 1692 entitled, "The Return of Several Ministers" to guide the Special Court of Oyer and Terminer in all future cases. Unfortunately, although it specifically recommended "a very critical and exquisite caution" in the use of spectral evidence by the court, and called into question "several of the tactics the magistrates were employing in their dealings with the suspects," it, nonetheless, concluded with a final statement endorsing the good work undertaken by the court: "We cannot but humbly recommend unto the government, the speedy and vigorous prosecutions of such as have rendered themselves obnoxious, according to the directions given in the laws of God, and the wholesome statutes of the English nation, for the detection of witchcrafts."

The equivocation of this document on the acceptability of spectral evidence proved critically important in the future direction of the court proceedings from June 1692 onward. Far from being seen as a cautionary warning to the court, the "Return of Several Ministers" was interpreted carelessly by Chief Justice Stoughton, and consequently had little deterrent effect on the handling of future cases. To quote historian Mary Beth Norton, "They [the ministers] did not contest the validity of the sufferings of the afflicted young people, nor did they challenge the belief that those torments originated in the invisible world. They did not dispute the reality of the girls' spectral visions, but instead asked whether those visions could be trusted unhesitatingly."[17]

In short, "the justices in fact might well have interpreted much of the ministers' statement, not simply its final paragraph, as an endorsement of their efforts."[18] Had the "Return of Several Ministers" been understood by Chief Justice Stoughton as an unequivocal warning to stop using spectral evidence, the trials would have almost certainly ended more quickly and Governor Phips's political career might have been saved. As it turned out, the trials, which dragged on from June through September 1692, would depend heavily upon the visions and specters of the afflicted children. Tragically, spectral evidence would not be declared inadmissible until 19 people were hanged by the end of September. By that time, public sentiment had begun to turn against the trials and was also turning against Phips himself. Things might have been very different for Phips and Massachusetts had the he chosen to remain more directly involved instead of placing the problem into the hands of Chief Justice Stoughton and his special court.

Rather than personally oversee the court proceedings in Salem, Governor Phips chose to focus his energies on the ongoing frontier war with the French and the Wabanaki nation which had resurfaced so recently in Maine. This was, in his view, a regional upheaval of a more tangible nature, and one which he, as an experienced military leader, could effectively manage. Phips's most recent wartime experience in this area was acquired from the aforementioned failed expedition against Quebec between August and October 1690, when both his fleet on the St. Lawrence and Fitz-John Winthrop's army of New York and Connecticut militia on Lake Champlain were soundly defeated. The only positive aspect of the 1690 campaign came in October when Plymouth Colony's captain Benjamin Church, leading his force of colonial rangers, had successfully attacked the Wabanaki headquarters taking as prisoners the wives and families of sachems, Kankamagus and Worombe. Following this, a treaty was negotiated, prisoners exchanged, and an uneasy peace was established that would only last until May 1, 1691.

Not surprisingly, in contemplating the military reverses at Quebec and on Lake Chaplain, the elderly, acting governor Simon Bradstreet saw God's hand—remarking that the bad weather and adverse winds experienced by the invasion fleet "plainly revealed the finger of God therein." In his view, the citizens of Massachusetts needed to seek God's face, humbly beseeching His forgiveness for those sins "that have provoked so great an anger to smoke against the prayers of his people."[19] Despite these prayers of repentance seeking God's favor, the war was renewed on June 13, 1691 when Kennebec sachem Moxis and 200 Wabanaki warriors attacked the town of Wells, Maine while on January 24, 1692, the Wabanaki struck the town of York, Maine, killing or capturing over 100 colonists. By the spring of 1692, the problem of retaliation, and the prevention of further bloodshed was firmly placed in the hands of Governor Phips—a challenge he readily accepted.

GOVERNOR PHIPS' MILITARY CAMPAIGN OF 1692

On July 5, Governor Phips commissioned frontier fighter, Col. Benjamin Church as commander of all New England's forces of militia. Then, going before the governor's council on July 8, he demanded that Massachusetts initiate a new war effort, and begin generating revenue to fund the creation of defensive fortifications against attacks in the "Eastern Parts" of the province. The result was the creation of an official "committee of war" and the raising of a small army of nearly 500 Massachusetts militiamen. The committee of war immediately began requisitioning military supplies for a campaign to take place in Maine. By August 1692, at the very height of the infamous witch trials, Gov. Phips and Maj.-Comm. Benjamin Church set sail from Boston with about 450 men to re-establish a fortified position near Pemaquid, Maine, arriving on August 11. The result of this expedition was the rebuilding and remanning of Fort William Henry, a fortification that had been destroyed by the Wabanaki with French assistance in 1689, but would now serve as "the northeastern-most station of Massachusetts Colony."[20]

On this occasion, two companies of militia were tasked with rebuilding the Pemaquid fort in field stone. While Fort William Henry was under construction, Benjamin Church and his troops raided the several local villages of the Wabanaki as a warning that Massachusetts power had been re-established in the region. Throughout this period, Sir William Phips was absent from Boston overseeing the reconstruction of Fort William Henry, and arrived back in Boston on September 29, 1692, after the last witch trial executions had taken place at Salem. Upon returning he discovered that the "afflicted children" had cried out against his wife, Lady Mary Spencer Phips, and remarked in his formal report to the officials in England, that "on enquiry into the matter, I found that the devil had taken upon him the name and shape of several persons who were doubtless innocent."[21] As a result of this, after Phips's return from Maine, the Salem trial proceedings began to wind down and because of his direct intervention, they were relocated to Boston.

By late October, Phips's response to the general public dissatisfaction was to ask the Great and General Court to dissolve the special Court of Oyer and Terminer, a bill that was passed by a margin of only four votes. In November, Phips appointed William Stoughton to serve as chief justice of a newly created Superior

Court of Judicature to try the remaining cases of witchcraft in Boston without the use of spectral evidence, a process that continued through the winter and into spring of 1693. Phips concluded the episode by ordering a general pardon and release of all persons held in custody in May 1693. But his challenge to rule the province was far from over.

The one major positive achievement by Phips during this period was the re-establishment of an Anglo-American presence on the Maine frontier. More than any other action, the rebuilding of Fort William Henry served notice to the Wabanaki that any future alliance with the French would be closely observed and resisted. Moreover, with Fort William Henry well-manned by militia at all times, the Maine coast would be under the constant protection of Massachusetts troops in the event of any further raids in the areas of Wells or York, Maine.

GOVERNOR PHIPS AND KEEPING PEACE WITH THE FRENCH

Other efforts to secure the areas of Maine and Acadia were not as successful during 1692. The previously captured French base of Port Royal in Canada was visited in June 1692 by the Boston-based naval vessel, HMS *Nonsuch* under the command of Captain Short. Short was given orders to persuade the French inhabitants to take the oath of loyalty to King William and Queen Mary, but the most he could manage was a promise of neutrality in any future conflict between the French and the English over control of the fur-trading base. In a later report to England, Phips claimed that the oath of loyalty was finally taken by the French residents at Port Royal, but as with so many of Phips's claims, there was always some doubt as to its truth.

In the fall of 1692, Phips received a smuggled report brought by French deserters from Quebec, claiming the French were about to launch a surprise maritime attack on Wells, Maine, the Isles of Shoals, and the area near present-day Portsmouth, New Hampshire. The result was an unorthodox and ill-conceived plan by Phips who sent the French deserters to kidnap or assassinate the French leaders of the attack. Unfortunately for Phips, the deserters were betrayed, caught, and executed, casting him in a negative light as a bungling incompetent, unable to devise an effective retaliatory strategy. Fortunately, the alleged French attack amounted to several ineffective coastal raids that were easily driven off by colonial forces.[22]

The overall strategy of Sir William Phips as governor of Massachusetts throughout 1692 was to keep the Acadian base of Port Royal in English hands by providing occasional shipments of supplies to the French fur-trading population of that region. At the same time, he sought to avoid a major military confrontation with the French land or sea forces, while keeping their native allies in Maine in constant fear of possible raids from Fort William Henry at Pemaquid. Essentially, Phips and the Massachusetts Bay Colony, in spite of their mutual desire to expand into French-held Canada, lacked the monetary and military resources to make such a move practical. At the end of Phips's tenure as governor, the French military commander in Canada wrote to his superiors in France, "I do not believe they (the New England militia) will come and see us very soon."[23] His overall assessment was absolutely correct.

It might be mentioned that during this period, while the witch trials raged in Salem, minor confrontations of another sort occasionally took place. Most notable was the problem of keeping peace between the French inhabitants of occupied Acadia and their English overlords. One such incident took place at the Acadian town of Beaubassin in the spring of 1693 when the crews of "two New England supply vessels had gratuitously attacked the inhabitants; or according to the New Englanders, they themselves had been ambushed by a 'party of French and Indians.' "[24] Either way, the incident underscores the fragile nature of the peace that existed between the two factions, and the problem would continue well beyond Phips's tenure as governor.

For Phips's government, the most important political and military accomplishment of his administration was the reconstruction of Fort William Henry, an achievement which helped enforce control over the Wabanaki and give a presence to English authority in the Province of Maine. Sir William himself personally took a direct interest in the fort's construction while actually leaving the daily operations of the colony in the hands of Dep. Gov. Stoughton while Phips traveled to Pemaquid seven times between August of 1692 and July 1694. The physical appearance of this fortification was impressive, providing a far more formidable defense than the wooden palisade structures preceding it. The new coastal bastion measured "more than one hundred feet on each side" with walls that "ranged from ten to twenty-two feet in height." Rev. Cotton Mather wrote that behind these walls, the fort boasted a battery of "fourteen guns mounted, whereof six were eighteen pounders" while a French military report recorded that it possessed a battery of 16 twelve- and sixteen-pound guns as well as several four- and six-pound guns. With walls constructed from "more than two-thousand cartloads of fieldstones," it was defended by a full-time garrison of approximately 60 soldiers.

Phips showed justifiable pride in his military accomplishment in a letter to his patron, the Earl of Nottingham in 1693: "I have caused a large stone fort to be built at Pemaquid . . . and have kept an army in readiness wherewith I have attacked the Indians whenever they appeared upon our frontiers, and often drove them from their quarters. The Fort is sufficient to resist all the Indians in America."[25] Ironically, despite his extravagant claims, the fort was taken by a combined force of French troops and Wabanaki warriors in August 1696 just two years after Phips's departure for England. The best that can be said for Fort William Henry is that Rev. Cotton Mather credits its presence as being the reason for bringing the Wabanaki to the treaty table to sign a temporary peace accord on August 11, 1693. This treaty provided the Massachusetts frontier with a much needed, though brief respite from Native American attacks.

The essential substance of this early treaty with the Wabanaki provides an overview of the key issues that affected the everyday life of settlers along the frontier, the very profitable fur trade, and the concerns of the colonial government. In Emerson Baker's text, *The New England Knight*, these diplomatic concerns are reviewed: "The terms set down were unprecedented in Wabanaki-English relations. Attributing years of bloody war to Wabanaki adherence to the 'ill counsells' of the French, the paper signed by the Wabanaki promised 'hearty subjection and obedience to the Crown of England' on behalf of 'all the Indians belonging unto the several rivers aforesaid, and of all other Indians . . . from Merrimack River unto the most Easterly bounds of Massachusetts.'" The treaty went on to address the future of relations concerning the fur trade and frontier war: "Peace was to be established and captives returned; the Wabanaki were to abandon the French alliance; the English fur trade was to be regulated by the Massachusetts government and future disputes were to be settled in English courts."[26]

The absolute bottom line with the new Wabanaki treaty was that it reinstated and regulated the all-important English fur trade. This was important to the economy of Massachusetts and also would help pave the way for Governor Phips to achieve his personal economic goal of dominating the redrawn boundaries of Massachusetts Bay Colony and possibly gaining a profitable share of the fur trade. As to the personal importance of the fur trade, he wrote in a conspiratorial letter to English Privy Council member Blathwayt: "This peace hath put into *our hands* an opportunity of doing something that may be of considerable advantage *to both of us* if you are pleased to accept it ... It is concerning the beaver and peltry trade with those Indians which I know will be worth two thousand pounds per annum if not much more."[27] The plan called for both gentlemen to invest 500 pounds each in New England fur trading, while Blathwayt was asked by Phips to: "procure for me their Majesty's Letters (of) Patents for that trade." In actuality, in a second letter to Blathwayt, Phips enclosed an ambitious petition for presentation to the crown requesting "a monopoly of the fur trade 'from Saco eastward to the utmost bounds of Massachusetts.' " Blathwayt did not respond to either request, and as with so many of his plans, this venture did not materialize for the Massachusetts governor, or as one historian summarizes, "Phips' efforts to use his governorship to advance his aspirations as a projector on the frontier of New England thus ended in failure."[28]

For the people of Massachusetts Bay Colony, the political and military activities of the Phips governorship between 1692 and 1694 secured for them a brief period of safety followed by a renewal of warfare on the Massachusetts frontier of Maine and New Hampshire within two years following his departure. The period of the Salem witch trials was an extremely tumultuous one, and it is worth noting that several of the so-called afflicted children had been victims of attacks and were recently relocated from the northern frontier to Salem Village. Several historians in recent studies have suggested that psychological tensions felt by the people of Essex County as a result of periodic native raids were a contributing factor to the outbreak of witchcraft fears in Salem Village and the surrounding area.

NOTES

1. Baker, *The New England Knight*, 54–55.
2. Ibid., 66.
3. Rev. Cotton Mather from "Humble Address," April, 9, 1691, quoted in Emerson Baker, *The New England Knight*, 104.
4. "The Second Massachusetts Charter" (October 7, 1691), in Jack P. Greene, ed., *Settlements to Society 1607–1763* (New York: W. W. Norton, 1975), 206.
5. Jack P. Greene, *Settlements to Society 1607–1763*, 209.

6. Baker and Reid, *The New England Knight* (Toronto, Canada: University of Toronto Press, 1998), 127.

7. Ibid.

8. Michael G. Hall, *The Last American Puritan* (Middletown, CT: Wesleyan University Press, 1988), 256.

9. Letter, William Blathwayt to Francis Nicholson, December 5, 1691, Colonial Williamsburg, *Blathwayt Papers*, vol. 15, folder 2.

10. Baker and Reid, *The New England Knight*, 129.

11. Ibid., 130.

12. *Record of the Admiralty Court*, July 27, 1692, Public Record Office, CO5/ no. 10.

13. Letter, Capt. Robert Fairfax to James Sotherne, Public Record Office, CO5/ 857, no. 22.

14. Emerson and Reid, *The New England Knight*, 136–39.

15. Letter, Sir William Phips to William Blathwayt, October 12, 1692, Public Records Office, CO5/857, no. 7.

16. Baker and Reid, *The New England Knight*, 145.

17. Mary Beth Norton, *In the Devil's Snare* (New York: Vintage Books, 2002), 214.

18. Ibid.

19. Letter, Governor Simon Bradstreet to Massachusetts agents in London, November 29, 1690, *Documentary History of the State of Maine*, vol. 5, 171.

20. Baker, *The New England Knight*, 152.

21. Ibid., 153.

22. Ibid., 160.

23. Robineau du Villebon to Pontchartrain, 1694, in Webster, ed., *Acadia at the End of the Seventeenth Century*, 71.

24. Baker, *The New England Knight*, 160.

25. Ibid., 162.

26. Ibid.

27. Ibid., 170.

28. Ibid., 176.

6

RELIGION, LAW, AND EDUCATION IN DAILY LIFE IN THE 1690s

Few areas have received more attention concerning the Puritans than that of their religion, and yet interestingly, few people have a realistic understanding of the fundamental nature of their religious beliefs and how those beliefs impacted daily life. The essential issue here revolves around the theology that underlay the preaching every Puritan colonist heard at every Sabbath service. This weekly preaching session was an essential aspect of daily life and therefore shaped public attitudes concerning marriage, education, childrearing, job performance, gender roles, personal and public morality, prejudices, and social interaction. It is also important to bear in mind that by 1692, Puritan ministers had been exclusively impacting Puritan society in Massachusetts for three generations, that is, since the late 1620s. Theirs was a society without religious diversity, which offered a narrow focus with few options, and greatly limited the perspectives of what an individual might believe. To the average Puritan of the 1690s, one's religious faith was as much a part of life as breathing and considered nearly as essential.

What is difficult to fully appreciate is the central and all-encompassing nature of the Puritan's religious faith. As mentioned in previous chapters, every household was expected to provide religious instruction to their children and to participate in daily

Portrait of John Calvin, Reformer of Geneva.
(Library of Congress)

family worship. Every Sunday each week, on the only day free of work, the entire family was required by law to attend the only meetinghouse in their community. Indeed, the present-day Congregational denomination is the lineal descendant of the original Puritan churches of New England. This accounts for the widespread phenomenon that throughout New England, every village and town usually features a Congregational church or meetinghouse on its common or green. These centrally located centers of religious activity were regarded as the focal point of Puritan community life where all religious services took place as well as town meetings. The only exception to this single meetinghouse concept applied to communities with large, urban populations such as Boston or Salem. By the 1690s in the larger Puritan cities, the sheer size of the population required more than one meetinghouse, each with its own senior pastor and usually an assistant pastor. Such was the case in Boston where Rev. Increase Mather was the senior pastor of the North Church congregation while his equally famous son, Rev. Cotton Mather served as the assistant pastor. In addition, there were two additional major congregations located at two separate meetinghouses.

How was religion taught in the Puritan community and what were the essential Puritan religious teachings? Foundationally, the essential source of all religious teaching for the Puritans was the Bible, both the Old and New Testaments. This was because Puritans believed that the Bible alone was the only absolutely inerrant source of spiritual truth, coming directly from the mind of God and written down by prophets and apostles inspired by God Himself. And while it needed to be read and memorized regularly by all men and women, the exposition and interpretation of scripture, as well as its translation, was left in the hands of university-trained theologians and clerics.

But not all translations or editions of the Bible were acceptable to the Puritan ministers of Massachusetts Bay Colony and their congregations. The well-known Vulgate, or Latin, translation by St. Jerome, used throughout the Roman Catholic Church, was absolutely not suitable since it reflected the theological perspective of the Roman Catholic Church, and Puritans were profoundly anti-Catholic. In all likelihood, the New England Puritan owned and read the Geneva Edition of the Bible translated and interpreted by John Calvin. This was much preferred over the so-called King James version of the Bible sponsored by King James I in 1611, and used extensively throughout seventeenth-century England in the Anglican worship service. The reason for a preference for Calvin's translation is simply that most New England Puritans were Calvinists, that is, followers of John Calvin, and believed that his version of the Bible most accurately reflected what God was saying to His church through the scriptures. It was from the Geneva Edition translation of the Bible that Puritan theologians developed their ideas concerning the Christian faith, and from that translation all scriptural references used in sermons were taken.

The essential religious doctrine expressed in the writings of John Calvin of Geneva were the foundations of the Puritan faith, and this was no less true in Massachusetts of 1692 than it had been when the colony was first established in the 1620s. At the very heart of their faith was the *doctrine of grace*—sometimes referred to as the "covenant of grace" which was understood to mean that God's grace (or mercy) cannot be earned by "human merit," good works, or by following a prescribed formula of ceremony or behavior. In this doctrine, Puritans stood directly opposite the Roman Catholic position which promised that eternal salvation was obtainable by closely following the teachings and practices of the Roman Catholic Church. To the Puritan, salvation was the unmerited free gift of God to those persons whom He had chosen as "the elect of God."

SALVATION OF THE ELECT IN PURITAN THEOLOGY

Closely tied to this principle is the *doctrine of predestination* which is another Calvinist teaching that suggests to the prospective believer that God, since He knows all things past, present, and future, also knows in advance specifically who will be saved. In other words, in the grand scheme of the human race, a very specific and limited number of people will be saved, and these are referred to as "the elect." Their salvation is guaranteed by God, and they, by God's free gift of grace, will experience *personal regeneration* or *justification*, through no merit or deed of their own. Conversely, many devout followers of the Christian faith who pray and read the scripture regularly following all the teachings of Jesus Christ, *will not be saved or experience the free gift of grace*, because God, for reasons known only to Himself, has decided that these individuals should not obtain salvation. In other words, no act of man and no number of good deeds will influence God's decision to save or damn an individual's soul; it is entirely up to God to make the decision as to who is saved and who is lost.

John Winthrop in his sermon, "A Model of Christian Charity" used predestination to explain the inequities in human society when he said: "God Almighty, in his most holy and wise providence, hath so disposed of the condition of mankind, as in all times some must be rich and some poor, some high and eminent in power and dignities, others mean and in subjection."[1] In this way, predestination takes into account the all encompassing authority of God to influence all things; "it is a description of life as the saints lived it, a natural explanation of happenings in the real world. God, they knew, was sovereign in all things, not only in broad natural cycles like the movement of the stars or the change of seasons, but in the most ordinary details of everyday life as well."[2] This was the all encompassing impact of predestination as a universal element in the lives of late seventeenth-century Puritans.

Another equally important aspect of Puritan thought concerning their relationship to God was the concept of "covenant" which is a binding, spiritual contract or promise between God and His elect or those who are saved. To the Puritans of Massachusetts, nothing was more important than honoring the mutual agreement existing between themselves and God. Each individual who accepted God's free gift of grace (salvation) entered into a *Covenant of Salvation* or "justification," and did so with the understanding that in return for the free gift of salvation, God expected human faithfulness in worship and obedience to His commandments. The true believer was now expected to give evidence of his or her faith through a change in outward behavior resulting in a natural tendency toward "good works" reflective of his or her new status as a follower of Christ. This transformation of one's character and behavior from the sinful "old person" to the righteous "new person" was called "sanctification." Such a dramatic change in personal behavior was not easily achieved as spiritual help was needed; this necessitated the supportive presence of God's Holy Spirit in the daily life of every believer.

THE ROLE OF THE HOLY SPIRIT IN SALVATION OF THE BELIEVER

The Puritans believed that the presence of God's Holy Spirit helped the new believer to achieve this expectation of a transformation of both character and behavior. Immediately after the conversion or personal regeneration of an individual, that person was considered "sanctified," that is in-dwelt by God's Holy Spirit. "Sanctification" was the natural result of justification, since it gave clear evidence of one's salvation through holy behavior in all aspects of life. In other words, once a person received God's irresistible gift of grace, the Holy Spirit now living within him or her prompted the person to conduct him- or herself with new "holy behavior" reflective of a changed spiritual state. Doing good works was therefore not considered a means to achieve salvation, but outward evidence of salvation.

The Idea of Covenant in Puritan Church Structure

On a more corporate level, any gathering of believers who decided to establish a church congregation prayerfully asked God to bear witness that they would, as a community of believing Christians, pledge themselves to keep their fellow churchmembers in a close spiritual relationship one to the other and toward God. For this reason, the Puritan "church covenant" was absolutely central to the creation of Puritan congregations and served as a document which clearly outlined for everyone what was expected of each individual churchmember to maintain their relationship as a member of the "body of Christ." Such church covenants would literally be written down and recited periodically in a church service by the assembled congregation and then bear the signatures of those members of the congregation who were either forming or later joining the church. It was a means of establishing an accepted code of community behavior since everyone in the community was required to attend the church meeting every Sunday and quickly became familiar with the document. This was also an essential step in becoming a member of a Puritan church congregation. And for most of the seventeenth century, no male (or female) citizen over eighteen years of age could vote in church decisions or provincial government elections unless they were members of a church, and had signed a church covenant.

Church Membership

What exactly was the process of becoming a church member in the 1690s? More than merely signing their name on a covenant, prospective members were required to present themselves to the church officers known as the Board of Elders, that is, a voluntary group of laymen elected by the congregation who shared the management of the church with the minister. The Board of Elders served as the interview panel for prospective members. The elders and the minister would examine a prospective candidate for membership in a private interview. If they were satisfied that the petitioner was a likely candidate, an appointment was set for the candidate to go before the congregation and give testimony to his conversion experience. Questions were asked of the candidate by the church membership. If no evidence to the contrary was presented, the congregation voted on accepting the candidate into church membership. Following this vote, the candidate was allowed to sign the church covenant and was then welcomed into the congregation.[3] It should be also mentioned that while female church members had the right to vote and participate in church-related decisions, they were not given the voting franchise in colonial political elections in Massachusetts Bay Colony.

The aforementioned Board of Elders was an important part of church and community life in seventeenth-century New England and had additional church management responsibilities such as

Hingham Meeting House, 1680. (From *The History and Antiquities of New England* by John Barber [1844]. Private collection.)

visiting and praying for the sick members of the community. They also called and dismissed the congregation when church business meetings were held and prepared the agenda for such meetings. Most importantly, they served as watchdogs over the behavior of the church membership to determine if there were those who violated the church covenant or in some other way led un-Christian lives. Anyone discovered living or acting in a manner contrary to the church covenant would be censured and brought before the Board of Elders for disciplinary action. All church members were expected to report any violations of conduct when discovered since "the covenant one swore to in joining a congregation made each member his brother's keeper."[4]

ORIGINAL SIN IN THE PURITAN THEOLOGY

Theologically, perhaps the most essential and important religious belief drawn from the teachings of John Calvin and consequently followed by the congregations of New England is that all human beings are born into a state of original sin, and that human nature is therefore inherently corrupt and sinful. The reason for this sinful state, they believed, was that Adam and Eve, the first man and woman created by God, were given by Him the ability to choose right from wrong, and as a result of this free will, disobeyed God in the Garden of Eden. In so doing they established "original sin."

This disobedience, described in the Book of Genesis in the Old Testament of the Bible, brought about the fall of humankind and forever separated humankind from God the Creator. Puritans therefore believed that from the time of Adam and Eve, "original sin" passed from generation to generation setting the human race in spiritual opposition to God who cannot live in fellowship with sinful humankind. Thus, the physical results of "original sin" were spiritual separation from God, as well as pain, suffering, illness, and death. In addition, spiritual effects of "original sin" resulted in humans who were self-centered, headstrong, and selfish with their souls corrupted, alienating them spiritually from a holy and pure God. For this reason, the Puritan theology taught that humans are spiritually lost and therefore incapable of recognizing the need for a proper spiritual relationship with God. Rather, they are enslaved by Satan, and inclined to follow the temptations and promptings of Satan leading them away from God and into sin. A simple and essential verse found in most Puritan reading primers reads: "By Adams Fall, we sinned all."

THE COVENANT OF WORKS AND COVENANT OF GRACE

Thus, according to Puritan teaching, since all humankind is alienated from God and lost in human corruption and sin, all humankind deserved God's judgment and damnation to an eternity of Hell and total separation from God. Puritan theologians saw this as a fair and just sentence. But because God is a merciful as well as a righteous judge, and in order to provide humankind with a means of escaping judgment for sin, God in His goodness chose to save some people in spite of their unworthiness. In the Old Testament in the *Book of Genesis*, God introduced a "Covenant of Works" to Abraham, and promised Abraham to protect and save his descendants, the nation of Israel, as long as in return, they faithfully kept all of his laws and commandments and they only worshiped the one true God—Himself. This exceedingly difficult covenant between God and Israel, according to Puritan teaching, lasted only until the birth of Jesus Christ, considered by Christians to be God's only son, when God replaced it with a more practical "Covenant of Grace." Under the Covenant of Grace, rather than depend entirely upon following every aspect of Levitical Law and the Ten Commandments as the only means of salvation, a believer may be forgiven his or her sin by confessing his or her sin to God in true repentance, and then receive the free gift of salvation from God "paid for" by the sacrifice of God's son, Jesus Christ, on the cross.

This new covenant between humans and God extended salvation beyond the old nation of Israel, and offered salvation to all other people of the world—Europeans and English included. This is why Puritan writers often referred to the Puritan "elect" as God's "new Israel" since they truly believed they were the latter-day replacements of the descendants of Abraham, the old "Children of Israel." They, therefore, also believed that like the ancient Children of Israel, they enjoyed the special favor and protection of God, provided they keep faith with Him, following His commandments and worshiping only the one true God. For this reason, all Massachusetts legislation produced by the Great and General Court from the 1630s through 1692 not only had to conform to English common law, but also had to conform to the teachings of Jesus Christ in the New Testament, the Ten Commandments, and many of the laws of moral conduct laid down for the Children of Israel in the Old Testament.

THE RELIGIOUS BASIS FOR BLUE LAWS SUCH AS THE BANNING OF THE CELEBRATION OF CHRISTMAS

The influence of Puritanism changed somewhat with the arrival of the 1691 Massachusetts Bay Colony Charter in May 1692. Since the renewed Massachusetts Bay Colony was, by the time of the witch trials, under the direct authority of a royally appointed governor and his administration, the input of the Puritan religion and control of religious leaders gradually lessened, although many religiously oriented laws, previously enacted by earlier administrations, remained on the books for hundreds of years. The most notorious of these laws were generally identified as "blue laws" which enforced public behavior so as to conform to the teachings of a specific religious faith. In the case of Massachusetts Bay Colony, such laws were reflective of the moral standards of Puritan theology. An excellent example of one such law on the books until the nineteenth century in Massachusetts was the banning of the celebration of Christmas. It read as follows:

> For preventing disorders arising in several places within this jurisdiction by reason of some still observing such festivals as were superstitiously kept in other communities, to the great dishonor of God and offense of others, it is therefore ordered by this Court and the authority thereof that whosoever shall be found observing any such day as Christmas . . . shall pay for every such offense five shillings as a fine.[5]

The underlying rationale for this law is that Christmas was considered a pagan holiday adopted by the Roman Catholic Church, and therefore a reproach to God. While that in itself would alienate most Puritans, in addition, they objected to the waste of much needed financial and domestic resources, and most especially, rejected what they regarded as the outrageous revels that frequently accompanied the celebration of Christmas in Old England involving dancing, drunkenness, pagan customs, and sexual promiscuity. The fact that non-Puritan, English Christians justified such activity as being intended to honor the birth of Christ was seen by the Puritans as blasphemous. One described a procession in London led by the "Lord of Misrule" at Christmastide: "Then march this heathen company towards the church and churchyard, their pipers piping, drummers thundering, . . . and in this sort (of behavior) they go into the church, though the minister be at prayer or preaching, dancing and swinging their handkerchiefs over their heads . . . with such a confused noise that no man can hear his own voice. Then the foolish people, they look, they stare, they laugh, . . . they mount upon forms and pews to see these goodly pageants."[6]

LAWS AND PUNISHMENTS IN PURITAN MASSACHUSETTS

Such strict laws were put into place to guarantee public adherence to not only English common law, but a new code of public morality far more rigorous than any found in England itself. Those who settled and lived in Massachusetts understood that their behavior was subject to many new and revised laws based in large part upon biblical guidelines. Not surprisingly, the punishments for violating those guidelines were imitative of harsh Old Testament "eye for an eye, tooth for a tooth" justice, and not always in keeping with the spirit of English law itself.

The religious foundation for this Massachusetts Bay hybrid of common law and biblical statutes was found in the Preface to the Code of 1648: "So soon as God had set up political government among his people Israel, He gave them a body of laws for judgment in both civil and criminal causes. These were brief and fundamental principles, yet withal so full and comprehensive as out of them clear deductions were to be drawn in all particular cases in future time."[7]

For this reason, the people of late seventeenth-century Massachusetts were subject to a system of laws created over a relatively brief span of time which drew heavily from not only biblical principles, but from the Calvinist interpretation of those principles. In order to handle the resulting number of violations, the colony of Massachusetts created three distinct levels of legal jurisdiction to handle offenses: (1) the Massachusetts Court of Assistants which primarily limited its interest to cases of a major kind, such as capital offenses involving death, banishment, or dismemberment; (2) the County Courts (i.e., Essex County Court) which were four lower or inferior courts designed to "absorb the overflow" of hundreds of lesser cases involving petty crimes and deviant behavior; (3) the church court, which could be created on an "as needed" basis in every church in the colony, and exercising dual jurisdiction with the county courts trying and punishing offenses committed by members of its own congregation.

Between 1673 and 1692, the Court of Assistants dealt with 97 criminal actions including murder, arson, and piracy, all of which were punishable by death by hanging—the only allowable form of public execution. Of the four county courts, the one which provides the most complete picture of crime and punishment is the Essex County Court between the years 1641 and 1689. This court convicted 1,369 persons of 2,382 offenses during that period, most penalties being limited to fines or corporal punishments such as whipping, branding, earcropping, noseslitting, or placing the person in the stocks or pillory for public humiliation on market day. Kai T. Erikson's study *Wayward Puritans*, provides insight into the pervasive nature of crime and punishment in Puritan society: "In a given day, for instance, the court might take notice of persons who drank too much, who 'were without the use of their reason,' who lived a scandalous life, who dressed in inappropriate clothes or let their hair grow too long, who swore, bragged, or talked too much, who disobeyed their parents or engaged in frivolous games."[8] All of these offenses, while completely permissible in Old England, were punishable offenses in the Puritan colonies of New England. The remarkable aspect of this is the general acceptance of such a more strenuous code of behavior by the general population which underscores the faith-based foundation of the Massachusetts legal system, or as Erikson concludes: "The saints did not appreciate the distinction invented by later generations between persons who infringe the customs of the group and persons who flatly violate the law, for the Word of God governed everything and had to be protected with all the machinery at the state's disposal. The court's responsibility, then, extended to every mode of behavior which might offend in the eyes of God."[9]

What sort of behavior might offend God? In a recent study on deviance and crime in seventeenth-century Massachusetts, the types of crimes are divided into seven basic categories including: (1) crimes against the church such as disturbing the congregation, absence from church, or showing contempt of the ministry; (2) contempt for authority such as criticism of the government, contempt for the court, or abusing public officials; (3) sexual crimes such as adultery and fornication, including charges against married parents whose child was born too soon after the wedding; (4) disturbing the peace such as public drunkenness and disorderly conduct; (5) crimes against property such as vandalism or theft; (6) crimes against persons such as assault, slander, and defamation of character; and (7) crimes which are so unusual and infrequent that they cannot be categorized easily. An example of the latter might be a violation of sumptuary laws, such as the case of the wife of Joseph Swett who was fined ten shillings for wearing a silk hood.[10]

If, for example, a Puritan court were presented with evidence that someone had attempted to harm another by placing a curse upon them or their property, such a deed was a punishable crime. For example, Francis Usselton was presented before the Essex County Court for the charge that he had attempted to place a curse upon the sow of Henry Haggert by saying "a pox o' God upon her and the Devil take her."[11] Such threats invoking divine wrath and retribution were taken seriously by Puritan justice and were regarded as inherently offensive "in the eyes of God" since to call down upon anyone a curse of any kind was contrary to biblical law.

The problem with the enforcement of such an overtly faith-based civil code is that it necessitated the involvement of every citizen to discover and prosecute violations of the commonly accepted pattern of behavior. Consider the moral concern Puritans had for using their time wisely and productively. A law to this effect was put into place to protect society from developing such bad habits: "It is further ordered, that no person, householder or other, shall spend his time idly or unprofitably, under pain of such punishment as the Court shall think meet to inflict; and this end it is ordered, that the constable of every place shall use special care and diligence to take knowledge of offenders of this kind, especially of common coasters (drifters), unprofitable fowlers, and tobacco takers."[12]

In order to make such laws viable, Puritan society of the late 1600s demanded that every citizen become a watchdog upon the activities of his or her neighbor, prepared to report any violations to the proper authorities when witnessed. This important point greatly affected attitudes between neighbors, friends, congregations, and even families on a day-to-day basis, or as Erikson observes: "Puritan discipline was largely a matter of community vigilance, and each citizen, no matter what his official function in the control apparatus, was expected to guard the public peace as carefully as he would the peace of his own household." This aspect of enforcement of the moral code necessitated the involvement of everyone in every community, giving each citizen a "license to watch over his neighbors or even to spy on them, to inquire about their business or disrupt their privacy, so long as his main purpose was to protect the morality of the community."[13] Thus, the role of the minister as the guardian of public behavior was extended to virtually everyone in a congregation who was expected to observe and report any immorality and violations of scriptural principles.

THE ROLE OF THE PURITAN MINISTER

The interpretation of scripture and the teaching of the lessons of the Puritan faith, however, was strictly the responsibility of the Puritan clergy. All public religious instruction came through the minister of each congregation to the assembled citizens of the meetinghouse each Sunday. Such church attendance was required by law, and unexcused absence from religious services was punishable by fine or public humiliation when discovered. At these services, which continued from morning until afternoon with a break for lunch, the minister would present sermons or lectures drawn from the Bible in an attempt to provide instruction as to how his parishioners might live better lives in accordance with the teachings of Jesus Christ and the apostles of the New Testament, as well as the prophets of the Old Testament. The idea behind such sermons was to come as close to the scripture and its plain and true meaning as possible since it reflected the inspired word of God, and was therefore essential to the understanding of every true Christian.

Puritan ministers took the role of spiritual instructor of a congregation very seriously since the eternal salvation of his hearers might well depend upon the way in which his words were received and understood. One well-known Puritan clergyman observed insightfully: "it is no small matter to stand up in the face of a congregation, and deliver a message of salvation or damnation, as from the living God, in the name of our Redeemer. It is not an easy matter to speak so plain, that the ignorant may understand us; and so seriously that the deadest hearts may feel us; and so convincingly, that contradicting cavaliers may be silenced."[14]

New England's Puritan pastors were, almost without exception a well-educated group. Virtually all were college graduates, and prepared sermons that were intellectually demanding for their hearers as well as strongly rooted in the scriptures. Indeed, every sermon was drawn directly from a specific biblical text. Despite their bent toward theology and doctrine, Puritan ministers greatly favored writing and preaching sermons clarifying a specific passage of scripture for the benefit of their congregation. In term of priority, they took seriously the idea that a sermon be grounded in God's truth. This approach of focusing squarely upon scripture, they believed, lessened the input of people and their often faulty ideas and interpretation, and ensured that what was taught from the pulpit was trustworthy in helping God's people in living their lives in a godly manner. In short, helping people live godly lives was the entire point of sermon preaching in a Puritan community.

The Organization of a Sermon

In practical terms, Puritan ministers followed a formula or method in developing sermons for the consumption of the listeners of a congregation. Usually, a typical Puritan sermon consisted of three and occasionally four parts. Leland Ryken, an expert in Puritan preaching technique refers to a contemporary source:

> The outline that appears at the end of William Perkins's *The Art of Prophesying* can be taken as the prototype of the organization of a

Puritan sermon: 1. To read the text distinctly out of the canonical scriptures. 2. To give the sense and understanding of it being read, by the scripture itself. 3. To collect a few and profitable points of doctrine out of the natural sense. 4. To apply, if he have the gift, the doctrines rightly collected to the life and manners of men in a simple and plain speech.[15]

Ryken goes on to clarify what were the essential elements of every sermon, breaking its construction down into three simple components: "If we regard reading the biblical text as preliminary to the sermon proper, we end up with the following three parts of the sermon: (1) interaction with the surface meaning of the (scriptural) text, (2) deducing doctrinal or moral principles from the text, and (3) showing how those principles can be applied in daily Christian living."[16] Once again the emphasis for preaching in the Puritan faith is on making God's truth applicable to everyday life, and this reflects how sermons directly impacted daily life on a weekly basis in Puritan New England of the late 1600s.

It was the ultimate goal of every Puritan sermon to make people better Christians by awaking their conscience to sin, and prompting them to repent and change their daily behavior and thus reform their character in a way honoring to God. As one Puritan preacher recommended to his listeners, "remember always at the hearing of God's word to be applying the things delivered always to thyself."[17] In this way, Puritan pastors differed from the non-Puritan priests of the Anglican Church of England, who offered their hearers homilies, or mini-sermons containing generalized truths and platitudes about how people should behave under very broad circumstances. Conversely, the Puritan ministers sought to be as narrow and specific as possible, convicting and teaching their congregations precisely within the context of their day-to-day existence in New England.

In speaking to their congregations, ministers attempted to get them thinking about their inner spiritual state and how it might be improved. Moreover, they sought to prompt their hearers to respond to intellectual arguments while at the same time calling upon the Holy Spirit to make each sermon understandable and applicable to each individual. The fact that such focused and hard-hitting congregation-specific sermons were presented at every Sunday church service, morning and afternoon, had a dramatic impact upon the way the people of that community lived throughout the rest of the week.[18]

For this kind of preaching Puritan clergy thought simplicity of expression was the best approach, and was preferred over the more intellectually challenging "high" or academic style of preaching. In this way, the maximum number of listeners could understand and apply the lessons to be learned. Concerning this approach, Puritan author Perkins stressed the need for clarity in that every sermon "must be plain, perspicuous, and evident . . . It is a by-word among us: *It was a very plain sermon:* And I say again, *the plainer, the better.*"[19]

Learning from Sermons

Finally, how exactly did the Puritans of the late seventeenth century internalize the moral lessons drawn from such sermons and convey them into their domestic environments, touching the lives of every member of the family? First, careful listening was a highly developed skill on the part of congregational members, or as Ryken says: "For the Puritans, listening to a sermon was an active exercise that required the full attention of the listener."[20] Often to supplement active listening by the most serious hearers, ink, paper, and quill would be used during the sermon to take notes—often using a form of shorthand to keep up with ideas as they were introduced. Finally, postsermon meditation and discussion among friends and family was the most frequent manner of dispensing the truths expounded by a minister's preaching. One writer of the time observed that sermons must be consumed and digested like a meal: "you must eat it, and not only eat it, but concoct it, and digest it. . . . One sermon well digested, well meditated upon, is better than twenty sermons without meditation."[21]

Upon returning home after spending the day participating in a worship service at the community's meetinghouse, Puritan families were expected to not only discuss the main points of the minister's sermon, but attempt to reconstruct it from memory. The case of Theophilus Eaton was not untypical of how families internalized the Sunday sermon. As head of his household, he gathered his family in the evening of the Sabbath "and in an obliging manner conferred with them about the things with which they had been entertained in the house of God, shutting up all with a prayer for the blessing of God upon them all."[22] Puritan fathers were always considered the leaders of the family, no less so in their spiritual lives. To one observer, a good father should always pay attention to the religious instruction he heard in public so that it might be "repeated in private, to whet it upon himself and his family."[23]

The typical Puritan family therefore paid a great deal of attention to what took place in the meetinghouse every Sabbath. But what exactly took place in a Puritan religious service? First and foremost, the religious service of New England Puritans was orderly and organized. It tended to be systematic and goal-oriented, avoiding ceremony and distracting rituals. Concerning the inappropriateness of such flamboyant demonstrations in worship, Rev. Richard Greenham noted that "The more ceremonies, the less truth." As with their sermons, the emphasis on their worship service was on clarity and simplicity. In his assessment of a typical Puritan worship service, Ryken says:

A typical order of worship in such service books looked like this: 1. Confession of sins; 2. A prayer of pardon; 3. A metrical psalm; 4. A prayer of illumination; 5. A scripture reading; 6. The Sermon; 7. Baptisms and publication of Banns (engagements); 8. Long Prayer and Lord's Prayer; 9. Reciting of Apostle's Creed; 10. A metrical Psalm; 11. The Blessing.[24]

Thomas Lechford described a fairly typical service in Boston which began when the pastor delivered "a solemn prayer continuing about a quarter of an hour. The teacher then readeth and expoundeth a chapter, then a psalm is sung. ... After that the pastor preacheth a sermon, and sometimes extempore exhorts. Then the teacher concludes with a prayer and blessing."[25]

The business-like manner of Puritan worship and the complete absence of chants, repetitive prayers, incense, candles, Latin liturgy harmonic music, vestments, prayer books, statues of saints, crosses as images, and stained glass windows underscored the anti-Catholic nature of a truly reformed and purified Protestant faith. This radical rejection of all things ceremonial is exemplified in a satirical passage by the famous Puritan writer John Foxe describing a liturgical service in a Roman Catholic or High Anglican Church. He was amazed at the extent of the "turning, returning, half-turning and whole turning, such kissing, blessing, crouching, becking, crossing, knocking, ducking, washing, rinsing, lifting, touching, fingering, whispering, stopping, dripping, bowing, licking, wiping, ... shifting, with a hundred things more."[26]

Needless to say Sunday, or the Sabbath as the Puritans called it, was a very special day of the week, and the only day set aside exclusively for the honor and worship of the Lord. All other days were work days, Sunday was not. Every Puritan family was expected and required to attend Sabbath meeting and would be fined or censured by the community if they did not.

Upon entering a Puritan meetinghouse a visitor would be struck by the basic simplicity of the large, rectangular meeting room. The walls were usually whitewashed, that is covered with a thick coating of lime and water over plaster. The windows, if glazed, consisted of clear glass to emit pure sunlight with no stained glass of any kind. At the front of the meetinghouse would be placed a simple, rectangular wooden communion table, replacing what in a Roman Catholic Church would have been an altar. Most meetinghouses followed the tradition of having a pulpit located in the front of the room, elevated above the congregation often with a sounding board suspended above it to help amplify the voice of the minister. The pulpit would be reached by means of a set of stairs. Perched upon the edge of the pulpit would be a lectern or sloping shelf bearing a large Bible from which all scripture readings would be read. Next to the lectern, an hourglass would be placed to serve as a visual reminder of the passage of time to both the preacher and his congregation. In some cases, especially in rural parishes, a large bowl might be placed upon a stand to serve as a baptismal font for the practice of infant baptism.

The hearers sat on either long benches or, in more urban meetinghouses of the late seventeenth century, in walled wooden cubicles. Each cubicle was reserved by and for a single family for an annual fee paid to the church. Occasionally, the rear of the meetinghouse would feature an elevated gallery area high above the floor where single individuals, poor, servants, and nonmembers might be allowed to sit as "hearers" of the service.[27] Usually a "tithingman" or church officer was assigned the task of patrolling the meeting room during the service bearing a rod to awake those that might fall asleep during a lengthy sermon. Psalms were sung in contemporary English without the benefit of musical accompaniment led by the minister who would sing the first phrase alone, followed by the congregation in the same meter and key. As with all other aspects of their worship, music was simple and its purpose direct—to honor God with voices raised in praise of Him.

Funerals were held in churches and could be elaborate affairs depending upon the status or level of wealth of the deceased. It was the custom by the 1690s to give gifts to those who attended the funerals of the well-to-do. Such gifts included gold rings, scarves, and gloves. In 1691, the cost for "ringing the bell of the church for a man or woman was three shillings," as was the cost of digging a grave.

The only two sacraments playing a role in a Puritan worship service were communion, also known as The Lord's Supper, and if needed, infant baptism. This also reflected a further simplification of worship in contrast to the Roman Catholic faith which identified seven sacraments as essential for imparting of God's grace to the believer. In fact, the Puritan believed that sacraments were merely outward signs of God's salvation, but did not impart salvation in any way. Everything about Puritan worship turned the hearer away from complexity and ceremony and toward simplicity and those basic elements essential for worship and the understanding of scripture.

THE ROLE OF EDUCATION IN THE TRAINING OF MASSACHUSETTS YOUTH

Every person capable of doing so brought with them to the service an English translation of the Bible, usually the Geneva edition, in order to follow along as passages of scripture were cited by the minister during the sermon. This was because another important aspect of worship was the collective reading of the Bible by the congregation, including women and children. For this reason, literacy was deemed essential by the colony leadership in order that every person might be able to read and study the scriptures on a regular basis without assistance. As a direct result of this requirement, a high degree of emphasis was placed upon public education and the establishment of schools to foster the per capita literacy rate, and to prepare a well-educated population.

As previously noted, in 1636, only six years after John Winthrop's arrival at Salem with his fleet of ships and nearly 1,000 colonists, Harvard College was created with an allocation of 400 pounds from the Massachusetts Great and General Court. But the educational system of Massachusetts Bay Colony began at a much more fundamental level—at home with the family. It was the responsibility of both father and mother to instruct their offspring, beginning at an early age, in basic reading, religion, and if possible, arithmetic. As one historian observes, "Reading and writing were taught in the home, usually by a parent, occasionally by an elder brother or sister."

Overall, the Puritan understanding of God's creation viewed education as an important element to an understanding of God Himself. As Francis J. Bremer notes: "Knowledge, they believed was important for reasons of religion—God revealed himself in nature, history and the Scriptures, and it was man's responsibility to study and learn the lessons thus provided him."[28] Beyond this, the Puritans were a people on the defense against possible attacks from the Roman Catholic Church, foreign powers, and even from English royal authority. Education was important to prepare the next generation intellectually in understanding their religion as well as their rights under the law and how to protect those rights against potential tyrants.

As early as 1642, Massachusetts citizens were required by law to take the matter of their children's education into their own hands. The Great and General Court demanded every town's Board of Selectmen should "take account from time-to-time of all parents and masters, and of their children, especially of their ability to read and understand the principles of religion and the capital laws of this country."[29] Reading was, to the colonial leadership, a prerequisite to Bible study, and to the understanding of Calvinist principles as well as the basic laws by which the colony operated. Under the education law of 1642, reading and writing were required to be taught at home, "usually by a parent, occasionally by an elder brother or sister. Family reading sessions around the hearth in the evening offered children of some households excellent opportunities to improve their skills."[30]

Not to be overlooked, by the late seventeenth century some women had begun to operate "dame schools" to help families without sufficient training to educate their children in reading and writing for a small monthly fee.[31] The simple fact is that from the first arrival of Puritans to the end of the seventeenth century, education was always a high priority. Consider the recollections of the anonymous author of *New England's First Fruits* published in 1643: "After God had carried us safe to New England and we had builded our houses provided necessaries for our livelihood, reared convenient places for God's worship, and settled the civil government, one of the next things we longed for and looked after was to advance learning and perpetuate it to posterity."[32]

The big push by Massachusetts for public education came in 1647 with the passage of the so-called "Old deluder Satan" bill:

> It being one chief project of that old deluder, Satan, to keep men from the knowledge of the scriptures, ... it is ordered that in every township in this jurisdiction, after the Lord hath increased them to the number of fifty householders, shall then forthwith appoint one ... to teach all such children as shall resort to him to read and write and

require also that where any town shall set up a grammar school, the master thereof being able to instruct youth so far as they may be fitted for the university.[33]

This follows a decade after the precedent set by the residents of Boston who hired Philemon Pormont to serve the community as a schoolmaster in 1635. Pormont's task was to prepare Boston's young men, who might enroll as young as seven, to develop the knowledge and skills necessary to apply to and manage the curriculum of Harvard College by the age of 15 or 16.

By the late seventeenth century, some towns with public schools began to admit girls, but this was unusual since it was not thought seemly for females to be educated above a basic elementary education. For public-school scholars, however, the subjects covered in the curriculum of a public school were similar to what one might receive at college, or as Bremer notes that "its curriculum emphasized Latin and included at least an introduction to Greek, and in some schools, Hebrew as well."

The intellectual position of the Puritan in New England was strongly in favor of the liberal arts education in spite of the fact that they were facing an unsettled wilderness and survival was considered of great importance. For them the study of all aspects of academic study was not viewed as antithetical to their Christian faith, but rather an extension of it. Students at late seventeenth-century Harvard "not only learned to read the Bible in its original languages and to expound theology, but also studied mathematics, astronomy, physics, botany, chemistry, philosophy, poetry, history and medicine."[34] Another authority describes the Puritan education at Harvard in the 1690s as one where there was "no distinction between a liberal and a theological education, and its two sources were first, Calvinism and second, Aristotle."[35]

The physical appearance of the seventeenth-century schoolhouse in New England was distinctive. Usually constructed with an oak frame and pine weatherboards and clapboards (unless in an urban area when the structure might be of brick) public schools were "sparse and small, perhaps twenty-nine feet long, slightly less in width, with a six-foot ceiling. Windows were few. Desks were attached to the walls and light and heat were both provided by a large fireplace, excessive for those near it and insufficient for those far away."[36] Sadly, scholars in Puritan public schools enjoyed no summer vacation as classes were held year-round. Classes were also held on a Monday through Saturday schedule, and all learning was done by memorization. As part of the Monday academic curriculum at one such Puritan school, the headmaster examined his students on the previous day's sermon, teaching them religious lessons every Saturday in preparation for church service on Sunday.

Here in Massachusetts in the late seventeenth century, religion and education were inextricably linked together and were part of a prevailing life philosophy that a well-educated individual is also well-versed in scripture and its meaning. This idea is no where better expressed than in the prayer of famous Puritan Indian missionary, John Eliot: "Lord, for schools everywhere around us! Oh! That our schools may flourish! That every member of this assembly may go home and procure a good school to be encouraged in the town where he lives."[37]

NOTES

1. John Winthrop, "A Model of Christian Charity" quoted in Kai T. Erikson, *Wayward Puritans* (New York: John Wiley and Sons, 1966), 191.

2. Kai T. Erikson, *Wayward Puritans*, 190.

3. Francis Bremer, *The Puritan Experiment*, 110.

4. Ibid.

5. From: *The Records of the Great and General Court, Massachusetts Bay Colony,* May 11, 1659.

6. Philip Stubbes, "Anatomy of Abuses," quoted in Mary Caroline Crawford, *Social Life in Old New England* (New York: Grosset and Dunlap, 1914), 499–500.

7. George L. Haskins, *Law and Authority in Early Massachusetts* (New York: Macmillan, 1960), 56.

8. Kai T. Erikson, *Wayward Puritans* (New York: John Wiley and Sons, 1966), 168.

9. Erikson, 168–69.

10. *Essex County Records*, vol. 1, p. 103; found in Erikson, *Wayward Puritans*, 169 and 171.

11. *Essex County Records*, vol. 2, 50.

12. Essex County Records, vol. 1, 109.

13. Erikson, *Wayward Puritans*, 170.

14. Richard Baxter, "The Reformed Pastor," in Horton Davis, *Worship and Theology in England: From Andrewes to Baxter and Fox, 1603–1690* (Princeton: Princeton University Press, 1975), 162.

15. William Perkins quoted in *The Art of Prophesying*, in Leland Ryken, *Worldly Saints: The Puritans as They Really Were* (Grand Rapids, MI: Academie Books, 1990), 99–100.

16. Ryken, *Worldly Saints: The Puritans as They Really Were*, 100.

17. M. M. Knappen, ed. *Two Elizabethan Puritan Diaries* (Gloucester, MA: Peter Smith Press, 1966), 108.

18. Ryker, *Worldly Saints*, 103.

19. William Perkins in Charles H. George and Katherine George, *The Protestant Mind of the English Reformation, 1570–1640* (Princeton: Princeton University Press, 1961), 338.

20. Ryken, *Worldly Saints*, 103.

21. Edmund Calumny in "The Art of Divine Meditation" quoted in U. Milo Kaufmann, *The Pilgrim's Progress and Traditions in Puritan Meditation* (New Haven, CT: Yale University Press, 1966), 119; Ryker, *Worldly Saints*, 103.

22. Cotton Mather from *Magnalia Christi Americana* quoted in Edmund Morgan, *The Puritan Family*, 102.

23. Patrick Collinson, *The Elizabethan Puritan Movement* (Berkeley: University of California Press, 1967), 377.

24. Ryken, *Worldly Saints*, 120–21 from Horton Davies, *Worship of the English Puritans* (Westminster: Dacre, 1948), 209.

25. Bremer, *The Puritan Experiment*, 110.

26. John Foxe quoted in Horton Davies, *Worship and Theology*, 74.

27. Ryken, *Worldly Saints*, 121.

28. Ibid., 118.

29. Ibid.

30. Bremer, *The Puritan Experiment*, 118.

31. Ibid.

32. Quoted in "Modern Education and the Classics" in *Essays Ancient and Modern*, vol. 2 (New York: Harcourt, Brace and World, 1936), 701.

33. "Laws of Massachusetts Bay Colony" quoted in Francis J. Bremer, *The Puritan Experiment*, 119.

34. Ryken, 164–65.

35. J. W. Ashley Smith, *The Birth of Modern Education: The Contribution of the Dissenting Academies, 1660–1800* (London: Independent Press, 1954), 71.

36. Bremer, *The Puritan Experiment*, 119.

37. John Eliot, in Mary Caroline Crawford, *Social Life in Old New England* (New York: Grosset and Dunlap, 1914), 12–13.

7

THE ROLES OF WOMEN
AND MEN IN THE 1690s

In recent years, much research has been done exploring gender roles in colonial New England. The result of this research has been to determine that whereas in the past historians assumed that there was a sharp dividing line between the domain of the housewife and the working world of her husband, "in reality no such barrier existed. Male and female space intersected and overlapped. Nor was there the sharp division between home and work that later generations experienced."[1] In other words, there were occasions when tasks needed to be done and whoever in the family was available to perform the task did so regardless of gender.

On a very broad level, researchers have discovered information on colonial women performing work and even crafts formerly thought to be the exclusive purview of men. Colonial newspapers "yield evidence of female blacksmiths, silversmiths, tin-workers, shoemakers, shipwrights, tanners, gunsmiths, barbers, printers and butchers as well as a great many teachers and shopkeepers."[2] It is important to recognize that, as surprising as these findings may be, they represent the extreme minority of the colonial female population. At the time of the Salem witch trials, most women sought the role of wife and mother, serving their family as the "deputy-husband" and helpmate to their husband who was head of the household. But exactly what sorts of tasks did husband and deputy-husband perform? It will be the purpose of this chapter to explore the daily tasks and responsibilities of men and women in late seventeenth-century New England.

By far, the majority of late seventeenth-century Massachusetts families were living in rural areas, outlying towns, and villages like Salem Village, maintaining farms which provided the essential staples and support for their communities. On a daily basis, farmer's wives were given an enormous burden to handle such tasks as "cooking, washing, hoeing vegetables, bargaining with neighbors and, in season, herding and milking a cow."[3] Naturally, a good wife's domestic chores varied with the size of the farm, the size of her family, and the complexity and wealth of the household. But even by the standards of the more settled late seventeenth century, a farmer's wife labored from dawn to dusk and beyond in order to meet the heavy responsibilities to her family.

The "ideal" woman to a Puritan community of the witch trial era was one who attempted to conform to the biblical description of the "virtuous woman" found in the Old Testament, in the Book of Proverbs 31: 10–31. This series of verses, often referred to as "The Bathsheba model," was often presented by Puritan ministers to their congregations as descriptive of the proper female attitudes and skills expected by God and by a godly husband:

> Who can find a virtuous woman? For her price is far above rubies. The heart of her husband doth safely trust in her, so that he shall have no need of spoil. She will do him good and not evil all the days of her life. She seeketh wool and flax, and worketh willingly with her hands. She considereth a field and buyeth it: with the fruit of her hands she planteth a vineyard. She layeth her hands to the spindle, and her hands hold the distaff (a tool used in spinning to keep the flax fiber untangles before being spun into thread). She stretcheth out her hand to the poor; yea, she reacheth her hands to the needy. She maketh fine linen, selleth it; and delivereth girdles unto the merchant. Strength and honor are her clothing and she shall rejoice in time to come. She openeth her mouth with wisdom; and in her tongue is the law of kindness. Favor is deceitful, and beauty is vain; but a woman that feareth the Lord, she shall be praised.[4]

It is worth noting are the numerous references to textile production by the "Bathsheba model." This domestic role for Puritan farmer wives as textile producers is borne out in the numerous household inventories of Essex County farms after about 1670 where large numbers of spinning wheels and looms and other textilemaking devices appear. Flax was "carded," that is combed, spun, and woven into linen by countless farmers' wives and their daughters, while the large number of sheep grazing on Essex County fields clearly indicates that wool production was also a major domestic industry.

Recent scholarship has determined that not all weaving was done by women, but that a significant number of men were skilled in that aspect of the clothmaking process. However, there is no question that "women were an integral part of the economy in general and a highly visible component of the textile trades specifically" throughout the colonial era.[5] Far from being limited to home-textile production, many rural women supplemented their incomes by producing products which ultimately found their way to shop shelves in villages and towns across the region. Such products included far more than "homespun" textiles since the late seventeenth-century world was a place where, "female hands spun thread and where quilts, curtains, sheets, towels, tablecloths and napkins were either handmade or finished by women."[6]

Besides spinning thread and making cloth, and other textile products at home, Puritan wives were involved in the process of making dairy products such as churning butter and pressing cheese. These specialized crafts were possible as a result of the cows kept by most rural families to serve as a source of fresh milk. Not surprisingly, the early morning task of milking the cows was also a chore left to the wife or children of the farmer. Cheesemaking was a true skill passed down from generation to generation of women, and was responsible for the abundant supply of cheese— or "white meat"—in the diets of the colonists of late seventeenth-century Essex County. The supply of butter and cheese manufactured by women on New England farms was so plentiful that by the late 1600s, they became standard export cargoes on vessels to the West Indies.

A description of the colonial technique to produce New England cheese is found in *Good Wives* by colonial historian Laurel Thatcher Ulrich:

[S]he heated several gallons (of milk) with rennet dried and saved from the autumn's slaughtering. Within an hour or two the curd had formed. She broke it, drained off the whey, then worked in a little of her own fresh butter. Packing this rich mixture into a mold, she turned it in her wooden press for an hour or more, changing and washing the cheese cloth frequently as the whey dripped out.

Repacking it in dry cloth, she left it in the press for another thirty or forty hours before washing it once more with whey, drying it and placing it in the cellar or dairy house to age.[7]

Among the most important domestic manufacturing techniques employed by New England housewives of this period was the brewing of beer and the fermentation of hard cider, the two most important commonly produced beverages of rural Massachusetts. Traditionally, a Puritan housewife produced beer in three stages. Beginning with cracked malt made from sprouted and dried barley, she placed the malted liquid into an iron pot over an open fireplace steeping it at just below boiling temperature. This was known as the "mashing" process. It was important not to let the brew get too hot, otherwise acetic acid developed which soured the beer. The next stage was the "brewing" process when herbs and hops were added to the malted liquid. The final phase was when the yeast was added to the brew and cooled. The process was completed after 24 hours following the addition of the yeast. The result was a sufficient supply of beer to provide for the needs of New England's farming population, but with little left for export.

Cider, on the other hand, was produced in much larger quantities, and because it was the product of the simple fermentation of apple juice, it was very easy to make. Virtually every Puritan farmhouse had barrels of apple cider, with an alcohol content of about 5 to 7 percent, sitting in the root cellar. Like dairy products, cider met the demand of the local population with a sufficient overabundance in quantity to become another New England export cargo.

Besides all the above specialty skills, a productive and hardworking farmer's wife of the late 1600s was expected to prepare the winter's supply of meat, turning a slaughtered pig's flesh into safely preserved salt pork, sausage, bacon, and smoked ham. Occasionally, even the slaughtering of farm animals such as chickens, ducks, geese, and small pigs was also a task left to the farmer's wife.

Beyond such unpleasant chores, the farmer's wife was expected to produce an abundant supply of baked goods each week on "baking day." This was accomplished in the recently developed interior bake ovens which, by the late seventeenth century, had begun to appear as built-in brick ovens in the newly renovated chimney fireplaces of New England kitchens. The possession of all these skills made a rural young woman a valuable commodity and guaranteed her a desirable marriage since "a wife who knew how to manage the ticklish chemical processes which changed milk into cheese, meal into bread, malt into beer and flesh into bacon was a valuable asset to a man."[8]

ROLES OF URBAN WOMEN IN THE LATE SEVENTEENTH CENTURY

City wives differed from their country counterparts in many respects, but one of the greatest differences had to do with the manner of food production and its acquisition. In a town like Salem, housewives did not require the kind of specialized skills to be expected in Salem Village or some other rural location. The reasons for this have to do with the urban economy and the presence of a ready market available to women willing to act as bargainers and negotiators. Surviving inventories from Salem households of the late seventeenth century provide a glimpse of how the urban and rural lives of women differed. Whereas a country wife was required to brew her own family's supply of beer, in Salem, beer might be purchased from a tavern or local brewery. While a rural farm kept a small herd of cows for an ample supply of milk, cheese, and butter, urban women kept only one or two cows, hardly sufficient to produce a family's annual supply of cheese or butter. Such products were readily available, however, from a variety of sources, all of which found their way to Salem where in the 1690s, "there was no center of retail trade, [so] assembling the ingredients of a dinner involved many transactions. Sugar, wine, and spices came by sea; fresh lamb, veal, eggs, butter, gooseberries, and parsnips came by land. Merchants retailed their goods in shops or warehouses near their wharves and houses. Farmers or their wives often hawked their produce door-to-door."[9] In other words, although the cooking process followed in urban Salem over an open fireplace might have been virtually identical to that of the rural farmer's kitchen, the acquisition of the various ingredients required a different skill set on the part of the urban housewife.

In contrast, what other actions and work activities set urban wives apart from their rural counterparts? In some instances, urban wives kept retail shops in their homes. Such stores, or "cent shops" were a means for seamen's wives, whose husbands were absent from the family for extended periods of time, to supplement the family income with the sale of a variety of goods. In the inventory of one such shop owned by Salem goodwife, Hannah Grafton, one is impressed with the variety and selection "offering door locks, nails, hammers, gimlets, and other hardware as well as English cloth, pins, needles, and thread."[10] In other words, the urban environment, while stifling to the development of specialized domestic manufacturing skills such a brewing and cheesemaking for women, was perfectly suited for housewives to become entrepreneurs taking advantage of the surrounding concentrated population as a prospective market.

In an urban environment, women had a greater degree of latitude concerning their choice of occupation. For example, the first woman in the Salem witch trials to be hanged in June 1692 was Bridget Bishop who kept a tavern, and although "women were less likely than men to run a distillery or tavern," many nonetheless did so. The problem with the role of women in the economy of the late seventeenth century is not that they did not have occupational diversity, but that their occupations were generally low-paying. They, therefore, did not occupy positions of high economic status, and largely for that reason their significant contribution to American colonial history has, until recently, been largely overlooked. This point is emphasized by historian Elaine Forman Crane who notes that historians generally "have overlooked the many women whose pervasiveness throughout the economy ensured the successful functioning of the mercantile community. Thus, any construction that continues to assume the marginality of women must recognize that those margins encroached on the entire text of urban life. Moreover, women were not merely a support system to a hierarchal order: their skills and participation were central to the very existence of that order."[11]

By the late seventeenth century, women began to outnumber men in the seaport towns of New England. This was in part due to natural population growth and the high mortality rate among men engaged in dangerous occupations such as maritime trade and fishing. As a direct result of this population shift in gender parity, many women, thrust upon their own resources, found themselves in circumstances that prompted them to pursue livelihoods outside the home. For them, "not only did the demographic imbalance cloud marriage prospects for many, but women whose husbands were off on voyages were left to fend for themselves. In practical terms this created a paradox: although women were brought up to be dependent, they had independence thrust upon them, and both married and single women had a strong incentive to earn an income."[12] For these reasons, in places like Boston and Salem, both married and unmarried women earned their living by the skill and labor of their hands. Current research has uncovered a surprising variety of female occupations in urban Massachusetts during the witch trial era. "If most white women acquired money or goods through the needle trades or from the production and exchange of food staples, many more supported themselves or added to the family economy by charging for what would have been unpaid labor if done for the immediate family."[13]

As a result, while the type of domestic work for some women remained the same as it ever was, they nevertheless were able to gain income by doing the work for nonfamily members. This type of labor included renting rooms and preparing meals for boarders or mariners, and washing clothes and ironing for "other transients." "Some mended, cooked and cleaned for teachers and ministers whose live-in students were too occupied to tend to such chores." Other women "boarded the poor and infirm for the town and received compensation" while some "found employment as midwives, wet nurses, and servants." Moving beyond traditional female occupations, other women of the late 1600s taught school, ran inns, and taverns, leased land, rented houses, warehouses, horses, slaves, and lent out money at interest.[14]

Moving even further in the direction of occupational areas traditionally associated with men, in seaport towns of the late seventeenth century researchers have found that lower- and middle-class women "whitewashed houses, drove milk carts, ran lotteries, ground chocolate, sowed the ground, wintered the town bull, taught dance and sold dung." They also worked as "shipwrights, apothecaries, and brasiers or brass founders." On rare occasions, women were called upon to cart wood or hay, repair the town highways, and keep the post office. They even made "buttons and mourning rings in partnership with jewelers and prepared the dead for burial." Such diversity and high degree of occupational skill often demanded specialized training and, in cases like the apothecary and shipwright positions, the completion of an extensive apprenticeship.

From the specialized to the mundane, historians are now aware that female labor was an essential part of the economic life of every major community and seaport town, playing a part in the actual development of maritime commerce. "Women made candles for export, nets for fishing voyages, and ships' bread for slaving ventures. They embroidered chair seats for upholsterers and painted Windsor chairs for cabinetmakers. They retailed the goods imported by merchant grandees and made wigs to cover up their scalps."[15] What is interesting is that women in New England seaport towns, regardless of their social status, took their roles as housewives, or "goodwives," seriously and rarely neglected their traditional responsibilities and domestic activities.

Even the most prestigious ladies, such as Salem's Mary Vial Holyoke, wife of Dr. Edward Augustus Holyoke, took pride in keeping a daily journal noting her domestic activities, many of which were not especially ladylike. She notes with some pride her recent accomplishments such as "scoured furniture brasses & put up the Chintz bed & hung pictures," "[b]ought a pig to keep, weighed 12 ½ pounds" and later, "killed the pig, weighed 164 pounds, age 11 months." As distinct from the actions of a typical farmer's wife, the wife of a Salem doctor was also required to perform tasks reflecting a sophisticated household. For example, "She was also a 'pretty Gentlewoman' [who] did not spin, and frequently sat at tea with friends." She was also a gentlewoman "not just because she had wine and silver on her table, but because she was interested enough in the fine points of cooking to 'dress' a calf's head 'turtle fashion' rather than simply dropping it into the pot." This refinement for the late seventeenth and early eighteenth century reflects the upper-class urban society's culinary fascination with "sea turtle soup" which was considered a rare delicacy. Calf's-head broth prepared in this manner was colloquially known as "mock turtle soup," and hardly a meal one might expect on a 1690s rural farm, but perfectly serviceable at a sophisticated Salem "turtle frolick."[16]

Besides examining personal journals such as that of Mary Vial Holyoke, household inventories also provide a glimpse at the role of women of prestige in the late seventeenth century. The probate inventory of the widow Ursula Cutt, "taken in August, 1694, allows us to rummage among her belongings" and illustrates clearly what physical items one might expect to find among the possessions of a gentlewoman of the late 1600s.

In a chest of drawers is found an interesting assemblage of items and materials such as a "mounted pin cushion" with its "own little drawer beneath containing silver thimbles and an English half-crown. Twelve dozen silver and gold breast buttons, a spoon, a pair of 'agget pendents' and remnants of stitching and sewing silk." In another drawer is "jewelry (a necklace of small seed pearle and four gold rings) plus some of her best wearing linen, cambric aprons fine sleeves, caps, and neckerchiefs." Beyond these refinements, the inventory lists "remnants of old silk," and "several small swatches of silver lace," and "[o]ne tufted Holland cloak with silver clasps."[17] In the world of the late seventeenth century, such a woman was distinguished from the common woman by wealth (silver, gold, and pearls), specialized skills (silk embroidery), and especially by a prevailing attitude reflecting "an enlarged sense" of her own importance as evidenced by fine sleeves, lace petticoats, and a tufted cloak.

MALE OCCUPATIONS IN THE 1690s

Men in late seventeenth-century Massachusetts dominated the world of work as the primary wage earners and in keeping with both Puritan and Western European tradition, the head of the household. It is no exaggeration to say that from throughout all levels of Puritan society, the principal figures of authority were males. At the very top of the Puritan social hierarchy were the political leaders, royal governor, assistants, deputies, and town representatives down to the local town officers and of course, the voting electorate. All of these individuals were, according to law, male. Similarly, in the religious hierarchy no females were allowed to attend seminary, take a degree in divinity, become pastor of a church, or occupy a leading position in a congregation. Those roles were, as in the political sphere, exclusively the realm of men.

By the 1690s, Massachusetts seaport towns such as Salem and Boston had evolved another class of elite citizens—merchants and shipowners who dominated the maritime commercial activity of the community. This group, though never large in proportion to the rest of the population, controlled the shipping and trade that was carried in and out of port, and employed, directly or indirectly, hundreds of others who worked in maritime-based industries. In Salem of the 1690s, the shipowning merchants paid for new shipping to be built, lived in the largest and most comfortable dwellings, spent extravagant amounts on entertainment, and dressed in the most fashionable clothes allowed. These men were the "codfish aristocracy" who began their fortunes by peddling the collective catches of area fishermen, and gradually built up a sophisticated international trade where codfish was only one of many profitable cargoes.

The importance of this group of gentlemen cannot be overemphasized when reviewing the overall economic impact they had upon New England seaports. Their ships and trade literally sustained blacksmiths, coopers, blockmakers, shipchandlers, ropemakers, woodcarvers, carpenters, shopkeepers, dockworkers, sailmakers, boatmakers, and dozens of other craftspeople. From these "codfish aristocrats," the patronage and wealth trickled down to the remainder of the population to such an extent that one of the most common drinking toasts of the era was simply, "Success to our trade!" Thus to residents of seaport towns of the 1690s, it was understood that if maritime trade prospered, all other members of the community stood to benefit economically. In this way, the 1690s may be viewed as a period of economic transition as the maritime trade of Massachusetts began to expand from mere coastal and occasional West Indies activity to become a truly international marketplace.

In rural regions of New England in the 1690s, the world of manual labor was still male-dominated, but it also included a larger proportion of females. Nevertheless, as stated above, those women who entered areas of occupations traditionally reserved for men were in the extreme minority. Virtually no known women served in the militia, or voluntary military force raised from every village and town. And while the heavy agricultural manual labor—clearing land, building stone walls, plowing—was still heavily reserved for males, and no evidence has been presented otherwise, it would be presumptuous to say that in all cases no women ever became involved.

Beyond any doubt, however, it is safe to assert that men also dominated New England's fishing, lumbering, and fur trading businesses. The need for endurance and physical strength, not to mention the sheer weight of tradition, necessitated that these trades be conducted entirely by males. And while other occupations such as herding livestock might be dominated by men, there is little doubt that out of necessity, occasionally women assisted in these tasks as with gardening, feeding livestock, and the making of beer and cider. Thoroughly male-dominated fields of endeavor tended to be those requiring apprenticeships—something customarily denied women. Among these areas of expertise are included that of blacksmith, carpenter, joiner, cabinetmaker, boatbuilder, cooper, tin and pewtersmith, brickmaker, glassblower, housewright, ship-wright, sailmaker, and potter.

But the occupational field in the 1690s which held the attention of the greater majority of males in Massachusetts was farming. As historian Virginia DeJohn Anderson notes concerning the new arrivals during the Great Migration, "most became farmers, producing crops and raising herds that supplied their families' subsistence needs and generated a modest surplus that could be exchanged in the marketplace."[18] However, New England farms were different from those in the southern colonies. The large plantations of the southern colonies annually produced lucrative crops of staples such as tobacco and later, rice, both of which were in great demand as export cargoes. The stony and unfertile soil of Massachusetts initially barely provided enough produce for the families who lived upon it, and only through determination, thrift, and a commercially enterprising spirit did New England's agricultural produce, such as cheese, butter, and cider, reach the markets of the world.

Secondly, the farmers of Puritan Massachusetts did not require large numbers of slaves to meet their labor demands, although slaves were indeed present, and constituted a small minority of the population supplementing the dwindling population of indentured servants. These workers labored as farmhands where the family was of insufficient size, and only occasionally served as domestic servants. But New England farmers very often worked their own land with the able assistance of family members—sons, daughters, sons-in-law, and occasionally a helpful neighbor when a task was especially difficult.

The actual work of a Massachusetts farmer of this time period was also somewhat different than elsewhere in the colonies. For example, in Massachusetts unlike in the southern colonies, farmers were required by law to enclose their fields. This was because in the Bay Colony, cattle and sheep were allowed to graze freely, often on common land, and were not always were supervised. According to a law voted into effect by the Great Court of Massachusetts in 1642, "every man must secure his corn and meadow against great cattle" and "if any damage be done by such cattle, it shall be borne by him through whose insufficient fence the cattle did enter."[19] And for this reason, Massachusetts farmers became adept at the construction of several fence types.

What is somewhat surprising is that recent research of inventories has revealed that many, if not most Massachusetts farmers, supplemented their agricultural incomes by pursuing an additional trade. For example, as previously mentioned, many farmers also followed the trade of weaver. This popular choice of secondary occupation was made desirable because of a longstanding shortage of labor and textiles in the New England colonies. It also put to good use the skills of the thousands of Puritan immigrants who originally came from textile-producing regions of England, or as Virginia DeJohn Anderson remarks: "Most immigrant cloth workers tried to work part-time at their former trades while devoting most of their efforts to managing farms. Many of the weavers who had brought their looms with them apparently continued to use them, mainly producing fabrics for themselves and their neighbors."[20] This was a long-standing condition in Massachusetts since as early as 1656 the Great and General Court had ordered that "all hands not necessarily employed on other occasions, . . . shall and hereby are enjoined to spin according to their skill and ability."[21]

Other farmers went beyond weaving to include additional, much needed trades, such as Thomas Payne of Salem who farmed, wove textiles, and ran a local mill, or Anthony Thatcher of Yarmouth, Maine who farmed and worked as a cooper or barrelmaker. While weaving, milling, and barrelmaking were trades easy for farmers to follow in New England, other specialized, secondary skills demanded creativity in order to survive in a somewhat less sophisticated economy than that of England. For example, one farmer who possessed the skills of a locksmith, found it necessary to transition into the role of a blacksmith in order to make ends meet.[22] A significant number of Essex County farmers also engaged in shoemaking. In this pre-industrial economy, farmers would employ themselves and their families working in the kitchen of their home or in a small shoeshop, or "ten-footer" located near the dwelling where lower-quality shoes might be produced in limited quantities by hand during the fallow days of winter when farming was less demanding. These would be brought to the nearest commercial center or town to be sold.

Other men, not devoted to farming, were able to practice their trades in New England on a full-time basis. The post popular and common of these trades were those dealing with wood and leather. Every community in New England of the 1690s placed a high demand on those who produced sawn boards, house frames, joined furniture, and "treenware," that is, wooden bowls, cups, plates, and household utensils. In towns and more densely settled areas, full-time leather dressers, tanners, harnessmakers, and shoemakers also produced a wide variety of leather goods including high-quality leather boots, shoes, buckets, aprons, harnesses, saddle bags, and other such material culture.

NOTES

1. Laurel Thatcher Ulrich, *Good Wives*, 38–39.
2. Ibid., 35.
3. Ibid., 31.

4. Proverbs 31: 10–31, *The Bible*, King James Version (Grand Rapids, MI: Zondervan Publishers, 1995).

5. Elaine Forman Crane, *Ebb Tide in New England: Women, Seaports, and Social Change, 1630–1800* (Boston: Northeastern University Press, 1998), 101.

6. Ibid., 101–2.

7. Laurel Thatcher Ulrich, *Good Wives*, 22.

8. Elaine Forman Crane, *Ebb Tide in New England: Women, Seaports, and Social Change, 1630–1800* (Boston: Northeastern University Press, 1998), 23.

9. Ibid., 27.

10. Ibid.

11. Ibid., 102.

12. Ibid., 103.

13. Ibid.

14. Ibid.

15. Ibid.

16. Laurel Thatcher Ulrich, *Good Wives: Image and Reality in the Lives of Women, 1650–1750*, 70–71.

17. Ibid., 72.

18. Virginia DeJohn Anderson, *New England's Generation*, 132.

19. David Freeman Hawke, *Everyday life in Early America*, 34.

20. V. D. Anderson, *New England's Generation*, 139.

21. Nathaniel B. Shurtleff, ed., *Mass. Bay Records*, vol. 1, 294, 322.

22. V. D. Anderson, *New England's Generation*, 141.

8

MARRIAGE, COURTSHIP, AND SEX IN THE 1690s

PURITANS AND THEIR ATTITUDE CONCERNING MARITAL SEX

Courtship and marriage were extremely important facets of the Puritan way of life, in fact they were essential elements to their view of what constituted a holy and happy society. Contrary to the common stereotype, New England Puritans of the late seventeenth century were not repressed or sexually inhibited, but rather stood in direct contrast to the prevailing view of the Roman Catholic Church which, since the Middle Ages, had extolled virginity and the virtues of a celibate life. In this regard, the more liberal attitude toward sex and marriage of the Puritans challenged the teachings of some preeminent "church fathers" who had dominated religious thought on the subject for centuries. For example, St. Augustine of Hippo (354–430 CE), while acknowledging the necessity of marriage warned against the sin of engaging in marital sex for pleasure, and encouraged couples to abstain whenever possible. For Puritans, personal and shared pleasure was an important part of the sexual union between and man and wife, and essential to their continued happiness as a couple.

This is not to say that Puritans advocated promiscuity or sex outside marriage, but rather encouraged men and women to find life partners, love and marry them and as part of their normal behavior, enjoy each other sexually throughout their married life together.

On this point, Leland Ryken observes that: "The Puritan doctrine of sex was a watershed in the cultural history of the West. The Puritans devalued celibacy, glorified companionate marriage, affirmed married sex as both necessary and pure, established the ideal of wedded romantic love, and exalted the role of the wife."[1] Indeed, it could be argued that women in Puritan society exercised a greater degree of authority in many spheres than in any other society of Western Europe. Beyond this, in seventeenth-century Massachusetts there are several cases where wives took their husbands to court, successfully charging them with neglect of duty for their unwillingness to have conjugal relations.

In general, the greatest concern of Puritans in dealing with issues involving the interrelationship of husbands and wives is domestic harmony and what is necessary to foster peace and happiness between marriage partners. For this reason, they expected that important decisions involving family activities would be reached equitably by both the wife and husband in close consultation. David Hackett Fischer, in his work *Albion's Seed*, underscores the surprisingly evenhanded balance which usually rested between married couples in Puritan New England: "Agreements for the sending out of children referred to both the husband's and wife's consent. Business ventures were often undertaken jointly. Men and women were not equals in these relationships, but they were partners in the conduct of their affairs." And this partnership included their attitude concerning the marriage relationship and sexual activity between husband and wife.

One of New England's first published poets, Anne Bradstreet, in her poem "To My Dear and Loving Husband" provides insight into the special and somewhat idealized relationship that might well have served as a model for Puritan couples:

If ever two were one, then surely we.
If ever man were loved by wife, then thee;
If ever wife were happy in a man,
Compare with me ye women if you can....
Thy love is such I can no way repay,
The heavens reward thee manifold, I pray.
Then while we live, in love let's persevere,
That when we live no more, we may live ever.[2]

This idea of romantic reciprocity between spouses was often the subject of Puritan sermons and letters between spouses. Rev. William Secker, a late seventeenth-century Puritan minister, countered the Roman Catholic view of Eve as temptress and subordinate of Adam in his sermon, "A Wedding Ring Fit for the Finger" by stating that God made Eve "a parallel line drawn equal" to Adam, taken not from the head "to claim superiority, but out of the side to be content with equality."[3] This view was even endorsed by John Calvin who made it clear in his writings that while a wife should be subject to her husband, she was nevertheless his equal before God, having also been created in God's image.

As an equal creature, Puritans tended to treat wives with an admiration, tenderness, and respect not common in seventeenth-century European society. Even the controversial Rev. Cotton Mather referred to his wife as "a most lovely creature, and such a gift of Heaven to me and mine that the sense thereof . . . dissolves me into tears of joy."[4] Most insightful is Boston minister, Rev. Thomas Hooker, who a generation earlier laid down in a published sermon, what he and his parishioners should view as the ideal marital relationship: "The man whose heart is endeared to the woman he loves dreams of her in the night, hath her in his eye and apprehension when he awakes, museth on her as he sits at the table, walks with her when he travels. . . . She lies in his bosom, and his heart trusts in her, which forceth all to confess that the stream of his affection, like a mighty current, runs with full tide and strength."[5] In this way, the contemporary stereotypical image of Puritans and their attitudes concerning marriage and marital relationships is at odds with the realities of the views expressed in their formal writings.

Even in their informal writings, the surviving personal correspondence between Puritan spouses speaks to their sense of mutual love and respect in a manner not often found in the writings of their non-Puritan contemporaries. The letters of Gov. John Winthrop to his wife, Margaret, frequently reflect this attitude. He begins one such letter with "My dearly beloved wife, . . . my heart is at home, and specially with thee my best beloved . . . with sweetest kisses and pure embracings of my kindest affection I rest thine." He regarded her as "the chiefest of all comforts under the hope of salvation" and concluded with "I kiss my sweet wife and remain always thy faithful husband."[6] Such was the marriage ideal under the Puritan view of the partnership relation between men and women committed to only each other for life. It went without saying that, in Puritan society, it was expected that prior to the marriage itself, neither partner had sported or "dallied" with others of the opposite sex, so that the marriage commitment was unsullied by promiscuous behavior by either party.

How then and under what circumstances did marriages occur in Puritan Massachusetts? Interestingly, once again the stereotypical view is not close to the reality. Far from being anxious to marry at a young age, Puritan young people actually displayed remarkable patience and discipline before "tying the knot." According to several recent demographic studies, the average age of males at the time of marriage was 26, while the average age of females was about 23. Even more surprising is that these marriage ages persisted in New England until well into the eighteenth century. Another marriage fact has surfaced that by the late 1600s, although most people waited until well into their twenties to marry, nearly everyone married. David Hackett Fischer estimates that over 94 percent of women and nearly 98 percent of men managed to find marriage partners in Puritan Massachusetts. This contrasts sharply with the situation in England in the late seventeenth century where as many as 27 percent of the nation's adult population "reached maturity without ever marrying." Those few women who did not marry were colloquially referred to as "thornbacks," a seventeenth-century slang term akin to "old maid" meaning an elderly, unmarried woman. To the Puritan culture, the inability to find a marriage partner was an indication of God's disfavor, for there was nothing worse than not achieving one's highest calling as a woman to become a wife and mother.[7]

Thus, in Massachusetts at least, while nearly everyone found a marriage partner, social pressure worked to encourage marriage if at all possible since "the marriage imperative was very strong" among Puritans. They, therefore, encouraged their unmarried young men and women to always be attuned to God's leading for a prospective life-partner. For this reason, no single men or women were expected to live alone for fear that they might fall into temptation or sin. As Fischer says, "relationships between men and women were highly charged with sexual tension in this culture. It was assumed by the courts that if healthy adult men and women were alone together, they would probably be engaged in a sexual relationship." For this reason, in Puritan communities of the seventeenth century, single women were not allowed to live alone, but usually assigned to live with a family if they did not have local relations of their own. Similarly in most communities, single young men also were expected to reside with a family, or a master of apprentices, unless able to live with relations of their own. A possible exception to this rule was those male students living in dormitories at

Harvard College who were under the constant scrutiny of fellow students and their schoolmasters.[8]

Young unmarried persons were also expected to see each other only in public places, or were entertained in each other's homes while chaperoned to avoid any hint of scandal or inappropriate physical contact. Even older "married men and women were generally forbidden to meet privately with others of the opposite sex," unless they were related by blood. For this reason, residents of Puritan communities served as the watchdogs of social behavior for all persons, married and unmarried, to ensure that biblical mandates concerning personal behavior were consistently met. Puritan society did not trust young people to be able to conduct themselves in an appropriate manner alone in private, and therefore greatly limited the opportunities that might lead to sexually risky situations. But the system was not foolproof. The occasional offenders of the moral standard were always publicly denounced in church whenever discovered and often made to wear a sign about their neck identifying their particular sin. The prospect of public humiliation in this manner proved to be yet another form of deterrent, since many young single people were reluctant to embarrass themselves before their disapproving family and friends. For these reasons, illegitimate births in Puritan New England were the lowest of all the other North American colonies.

In order to find, court, and marry an appropriate marriage partner, it was necessary to follow some equally stringent social guidelines common to the understanding of the Puritan community. First and foremost, it is important to understand that "marriage was never just a private contract between a husband and wife, it was an alliance of families and a lynchpin in the social structure" of Puritan society.[9] This was especially the case where the two families involved owned a significant amount of personal property or real estate which may be passed to the prospective marriage couple. Usually no prospective match could be even considered without the young couple consulting both sets of parents for their permission and blessing for the match. In some rare cases, sons and daughters were brought together as the result of negotiations between their parents in a type of arranged marriage, but more often male suitors initiated the courtship proceedings by presenting small gifts to the parents to prepare them for his request to be allowed to court their daughter.[10]

Not surprisingly, the laws of Massachusetts Bay Colony closely controlled the actions of prospective marriage partners and their families. For example, they absolutely prohibited "an offense called 'self-marriage' which meant marrying without the consent of parents or magistrates." Likewise parents were warned by law that they "were forbidden to withhold their permission arbitrarily." There are several cases where children seeking marriage, but being denied permission by their parents, successfully brought suit against their parents "for refusing permission to marry."[11]

Once permission to court a daughter had been given, it remained for the prospective couple to establish a relationship and determine if they would be happy to be wedded to each other. Exactly how this fact was discovered depended upon the amount of time they were able to spend together and their ability to determine their mutual compatibility. During this early courting period, usually a daughter conferred her parents to ascertain their opinion of her prospective suitor. Occasionally, differences of opinion did arise at this point.

One account found in Laurel Thatcher Ulrich's classic work, *Good Wives*, involves the case of Sarah Woodward, a young woman who in trying to choose a suitor consulted her parents, while trying to ignore her personal feelings on the issue. While she clearly preferred a neighbor, Joseph Lee, her parents preferred an ambitious and hardworking fisherman, William Row. She bowed to the pressure of her family, yet her mother cautioned her, "Sarah, have a care what you do. If you can love him (Row) take him: and do not say that I persuaded you, it's you that must live with him and not I." Similarly she sought the advice of her aunt who urged her to consider the matter carefully since it was better to "break (it) off now than afterwards." Sarah responded by saying she could love Row "well enough."[12]

After the "banns were published," that is, after the engagement to Row was publicly announced, Sarah finally expressed her opposition to the marriage, but it was too late. Her father demanded that she fulfill her promise to marry Row, and she settled in as a fisherman's wife. During the protracted absences of her husband at sea, however, she began to be visited at her home by Joseph Lee, who derided her for having married Row. These unsupervised visits came to be known in the community of Ipswich, and within a few months "Sarah was in Essex County Court on trial for her dalliance with Lee." Sarah's minister, Rev. William Hubbard, sympathized with Sarah since she had been a servant in his household when a young girl. He claimed that neither he nor his wife had approved of the match with Row, "fore-seeing what has come to pass."

The problem was Sarah's unwillingness to assert her own wishes in the face of parental authority, or as Ulrich expresses it: "Sarah's mother and her aunt had urged her to consult her feelings. Yet the ability of a daughter to express and perhaps even to recognize her own feelings depended upon the amount of autonomy she had been allowed in growing up. In a deferential society a young woman who had been used to following her parents' direction, might have great difficulty in trusting her own judgment, even when invited to think for herself."[13] Late seventeenth-century Puritan Massachusetts was such a deferential society, and undoubtedly not all decisions reached concerning the choice of spouse proved satisfactory to all parties involved.

From the male perspective, problems also frequently arose in the general manner of how best to approach and woo the prospective bride, or as Fischer states: "Puritan males made awkward suitors." One notorious example of such awkwardness involves the well-known witch trial magistrate, Samuel Sewell, while courting Katherine Brattle Winthrop: "She asked him to help her 'draw off' her glove. He bluntly refused, and made a clumsy joke that 'twas great odds between handling a dead goat (apparently a kid-skin glove) and a living lady."[14] This lack of sophistication on the part of a well-educated Puritan male, speaks to the tendency of Massachusetts Puritans to discourage training in courtly behavior and the general niceties of manners so common in the higher social circles of late seventeenth-century England.

But awkward manners aside, the courting process was generally done under the watchful eye of the prospective bride's family, and the indication of love between the couple was always an important consideration. Indeed, it was always taken into account in weighing the desirability of a prospective marriage partner. If there was no love at all, the match was generally not deemed a good one. For example, after spending a good deal of time with her suitor, Puritan maid Mary Josselin refused him for several reasons including a lack of love. Her father wrote later in his diary: "Mary quitted Mr. Rhea. Her exceptions were his age, being fourteen years older, she might be left a widow with children. She checked at his estate being not suitable to her portion . . . and he seemed to her not loving."

Courting frequently involved house visits by the prospective groom to the home of his intended bride. These courting visits could go on from several months to up to a year or more. On these occasions every attempt was made to allow the couple the opportunity to engage in private conversation and enjoy as much intimacy as was allowed in Christian society. One such method, employed commonly in rural Puritan communities was the custom of "bundling," whereby "the courting couple were put to bed together, 'tarrying' all night with a bundling board between them. Sometimes the young woman's legs were bound together in a 'bundling stocking' which fitted her body like a glove." Another similar device was the "bundling apron" which tightly bound the female's legs together, but left rest of the torso unfettered.[15] The use of the bundling apron device is memorialized in an old New England ballad as follows:

But she is modest also chaste,
While only bare from neck to waist,
And he of boasted freedom sings,
Of all above her apron strings.[16]

Daniel Scott Smith and Michael S. Hindus in their study, "Premarital Pregnancy in America, 1640–1971," assess the bundling practice of New England Puritans as a common ground between the Puritan establishment's code of moral conduct and Puritan young people who wish to assert their wishes in the face of that code. It is "a compromise between persistent parental control and the pressures of the young to subvert traditional familial authority." Laurel Thatcher Ulrich conversely argues that bundling is nothing more than a "ritualized form of courtship," where prospective marriage partners may explore their future roles symbolically in a "marriage bed" under tightly controlled circumstances. Ulrich points out that "marriage not sociability is the issue" under consideration in a bundling bed. Concluding "a daughter who wanted to subvert her parents' authority, forcing a marriage against their wishes, could not be stopped by bundling."[17]

In his analysis of the Puritan courting ritual, Fischer discusses the "courting stick," a hollow tube between six and eight feet in length which was used by couples sitting in a room surrounded by family members in order to conduct intimate conversations between themselves without the eavesdropping of others. In his view, "Bundling boards and courting sticks were not merely pieces of amusing social trivia. These two ingenious folk-inventions were instruments of an important cultural purpose. They were designed to reconcile two requirements of New England courtship—the free consent of the young, and strict supervision by their elders. Both of these elements were thought necessary to a covenanted marriage."[18]

After it was decided by both parents and children that a marriage between the couple was desirable, the next step toward a wedding in Massachusetts Puritan society was the betrothal ceremony which was sometimes referred to as the "walking out" or "coming out." By the late seventeenth century, the ceremony had come to be commonly referred to as "The Contraction," or as Rev. Cotton Mather describes it: "There was maintained a solemnity called a contraction a little before the consummation of a marriage was allowed of. A pastor was usually employed and a sermon was preached on this occasion." For this "Contraction Sermon," the bride was customarily allowed to choose the biblical text for the pastor.[19]

Nearly simultaneous with the contraction service, was the publishing of the intended wedding couple's "banns" or formal intention to marry. This announcement would be made verbally by the town clerk in the meetinghouse, then posted at the meetinghouse of both prospective spouses according to colony law "three Sabbaths before the ceremony was performed, so that anyone who knew of any reason why such a marriage should not take place might appear and make an objection."[20] Failure to fulfill this requirement would result in the charge of "disorderly marriage" with the risk of a fine and a court appearance. If no evidence of a previous engagement, knowledge of a sexual impropriety, or other serious objection to the marriage were presented, a wedding date was set.

Puritan weddings were not generally held in the meetinghouse since marriage was not considered a holy sacrament, but rather a legal contract between a man and woman involving "no holy vows or wedding rings." This was in sharp contrast to the Roman Catholic view of marriage as a holy institution ordained and blessed by God. Instead, the wedding usually took place in a private home, most often that of the bride's family, in a simple civil ceremony performed by a court magistrate. In Massachusetts after 1686, weddings were legally allowed to be performed by a minister, but the practice remained rare for many years. The ceremony itself consisted of the couple being asked if they agreed to become husband and wife for life, and if they freely agreed to this, the happy couple were pronounced married by the magistrate. The service was immediately followed by the signing of the town clerk's register.[21]

According to Fischer's research, the civil ceremony was customarily followed by a "small celebration" but "not a great feast." The reason for such moderation being that Massachusetts Puritans "did not approve of wild wedding parties" while their clergy "condemned extravagant display as 'vain marriage.' " The most important part of the dinner was the singing of a psalm. Dancing was strictly forbidden; so also were "excessive dining and drinking."[22] After the night's modest repast, the bride was dressed in a gown especially for the first-night occasion, and the couple were accompanied to their bedchamber by their friends. This last part of the marriage ritual was a custom known as "chambering" and was one of the few marriage traditions from Europe maintained by the Puritans without a scriptural justification.

As to how marriages might be broken or nullified, Massachusetts law specified only a few justifiable grounds for divorce: adultery, desertion, physical violence, cruelty, or failure to provide support. Interestingly, in Puritan Massachusetts neither spouse was allowed to physically harm the other. Husbands had no right under the law to discipline or "correct" their wives, thus wifebeating was illegal under the law codes of this period. For Puritan society, this was a reaffirmation of the partnership that existed between man and wife and in their dignity as co-equal creations before God their creator and sustainer. Fischer concludes his analysis of the Puritan marriage with the observation that to these people "it was to be a close and companionate relationship, a union of love and harmony, an act of sexual fulfillment, and an institution with a firm economic base. All of these requirements were part of the Puritan idea of the marriage covenant, which could be dissolved if any of its major terms were not kept. These Puritan marriage ways were unique to New England in the seventeenth century."[23]

To what extent and in what ways did the people of this society sometimes drift outside the aforementioned clearly defined boundaries of what was considered appropriate behavior between the sexes? In order to discover this, it is first necessary to understand New England's Puritan culture and the perceived pervasiveness of Satan and his influence as an omnipresent force acting upon the daily behavior of all citizens, both men and women, constantly striving with them to give into temptation and commit sin. Puritan theology understood that even depraved and corrupt humankind would ultimately follow the dictates of God's grand design, but during one's own lifetime there were many opportunities to stray from the "narrow way" and into evil practices and sinful behavior displeasing to God and harmful to the spiritual health of the soul and more importantly, to the community in general.

Were there known persons who regularly and openly violated the accepted standards of sexual morality living in Massachusetts Bay Colony? Without doubt, a distinct minority of such persons made no attempt to hide their sin, and indeed lived under the constant condemnation of the local community. Consider, for example, the young widow, Sarah Stickney of Newbury, "who had more than one illegitimate child and little reputation to lose." According to the court record, she called out to Goodman Samuel Lowell as he passed, "Ay you rogue! Yonder is your child under the tree, go take it up and see it!" A suggestion made all the more curious by her later success in having the same court name Goodman John Atkinson as the father of another of her children when she successfully sued him for support. Upon this last occasion, Goodwife Atkinson, a mother of nine children herself, "railed at Sarah and called her 'an impudent bawd,' she (Sarah) spat in the wife's face."[24]

It should be noted that, unlike other colonies such as Maryland, Massachusetts prosecuted the crime of adultery in a very even-handed manner whereby both men and women convicted of the crime "commonly received similar punishments."[25] An excellent example of punishment parity involved the adulterous case of Philip Darland, a miller from the town of Beverly and Mary Knights. According to court testimony, this young couple was caught together in an orchard engaging in what was described by a witness as "vile, filthy, and abominably libidinous actions." Interestingly, no one claimed that they were actually engaging in sexual intercourse. Nevertheless, after his conviction Philip spent two nights in jail and was then placed for one hour upon the gallows wearing a noose about his neck. This was to remind him that technically his conviction of adultery carried with it a capital punishment. After his hour on the gallows, he was then tied to the rear of a cart and returned to jail while being whipped upon the bare back. His female accomplice, Mary, pled innocent of committing adultery, despite an earlier confession which she later denied. She was tried and convicted, held in prison, placed upon the gallows wearing a sign describing her behavior as "whorish," then whipped on the bare back behind a cart en route to her cell. Neither of these prisoners was allowed to be released until the jailer's bill and court costs were paid.[26]

Another case of adultery was handled by the well-known magistrate of the witch trials, Hon. John Hathorne involving

John Honiwell, a married fisherman from Marblehead and Elizabeth Gilligan, wife of Alexander Gilligan, also of Marblehead. Elizabeth was arrested for being seen in the company of Honiwell "conversing together with much familiarity," and for "absenting herself from her husband and keeping company with John Honiwell." In the course of their trial, it was discovered that they had traveled together to Black Point (present-day Scarborough), Maine, and during this journey had slept together for several nights, claiming to Maine authorities that they were married "about five or six weeks." Both were confined to jail, tried, and convicted with a severe whipping of twenty stripes to follow their period of imprisonment. Elizabeth was then told to return to her elderly husband in Marblehead.[27]

It should be noted that within the Puritan social order, ministers reminded their listeners that temptation was always a weapon Satan used to lure his followers away from the path of righteousness, but that every time they were tempted, every believer possessed the ability to resist the temptation to commit willful sin, even sexual sin. For this reason, persons caught in adultery and fornication were held, and usually held themselves, personally responsible for the sinfulness of their actions without offering an excuse for their behavior. Humankind was, after all, inherently corrupt and naturally tended to sin unless acted upon and delivered from corruption by the Holy Spirit, or as Rev. Samuel Willard warned, "The corruption that is in men makes them fit subjects for Satan to work on."[28]

Fornication as a sexual sin in Massachusetts was regarded as a somewhat lesser offence than adultery since it did not involve the violation of the marriage contract or the betrayal of a marriage partner. Fischer explains the distinctions and punishments for this more common criminal sexual activity: "For an act of coitus (sexual intercourse) with an unwed woman, the criminal laws of Puritan Massachusetts decreed that a man should be jailed, whipped, fined, disenfranchised, and forced to marry his partner. Even in betrothed couples, sexual intercourse before marriage was regarded as a pollution which had to be purged before they could take their place in society and—most importantly—before their children could be baptized."[29]

Concerning the sexual activities of engaged couples, the crime of fornication was applied to them whenever a child was born less than nine months following the marriage. This usually resulted in the couple being made to pay a fine, and presenting a public statement, often before the church, acknowledging their sin and asking the community's forgiveness for their transgression. After this, "In both courts and churches, the Puritans created an elaborate public ritual by which fornicators were cleansed of their sin, so that they could be speedily admitted to full moral fellowship."[30]

On the other hand, the crime of rape was virtually unforgivable and according to English common law, punishable by death. Rape was defined in Massachusetts law as "a sexual act performed with a girl under the age of ten with or without her consent, or with a girl over ten without her consent." In one case, the nine-year-old daughter of a colonist, who was described in court as one who had "grown capable of man's fellowship and took pleasure in it" had been the object of the attentions of three of her father's male servants. Because the Puritans tended to give precedence to Old Testament law over English common law, the court decided that in view of the unique attitude of the victim, they would instead heavily fine the chief offender, slit and seared his nostrils, and for the next decade forced him to wear "an hempen rope about his neck." The two other less guilty parties were fined and whipped, but no one was executed.[31]

Suffice it to say that while sexual activity was perfectly acceptable in Puritan society within the context of marriage, in any other context it was repressed and punished severely whenever discovered. Adultery, rape, homosexuality, and bestiality were all regarded as crimes of so dark a hue that death was the penalty on the statute books, only occasionally tempered by special circumstances to lesser punishments. For most Puritans however, the sexual fulfillment of a happily married life was the hope and expectation of every engagement, while courtship was a carefully guarded intermediary step with an almost ritualized protocol involving gifts, permissions granted, courting sticks, and in some cases, bundling boards. What can be said is that Massachusetts in the late seventeenth century could still boast a population with almost no illegitimate births, and a community-wide surveillance system capable of spying upon and informing on the private lives of nearly every citizen.

NOTES

1. Leland Ryken, *Worldly Saints*, 55.
2. Anne Bradstreet, "To My Dear and Loving Husband," in *Seventeenth Century American Poetry*, ed., Harrison T. Meserole (New York: W. W. Norton and Company, 1968, rpt. 1972), 32.

3. Secker quoted in Laurel Thatcher Ulrich, *Good Wives*, 107.

4. Cotton Mather quoted in Ryken, *Wayward Puritans*, 39.

5. Hooker, in Ryken, *Wayward Puritans*, 40.

6. John Winthrop quoted in Ryken, *Worldly Saints*, 50–51.

7. Fischer, *Albion's Seed*, 76–77.

8. Ibid., 91.

9. Ulrich, *Good Wives*, 119.

10. Fischer, *Albion's Seed*, 78.

11. Ibid.

12. Ulrich, *Good Wives*, 121.

13. Ibid., 121–22.

14. Fischer, *Albion's Seed*, 79.

15. Henry R. Stiles, *Bundling: Its Origins, Progress and Decline* (Mt. Vernon, NY: Nabu Press, 1937); also Fischer, *Albion's Seed*, 79.

16. Quoted in Fischer, *Albion's Seed*, 78.

17. Ulrich, *Good Wives*, 122.

18. Fischer, *Albion's Seed*, 81.

19. Ibid.

20. George Francis Dow, *Everyday Life in Puritan Massachusetts*, 100.

21. Fischer, *Albion's Seed*, 81.

22. Ibid.

23. Ibid., 82.

24. Essex County Records, vol. 8, quoted in Ulrich, *Good Wives*, 96.

25. Fischer, *Albion's Seed*, 86.

26. Record of the Essex County Court of Assistants, quoted in Tom Juergens, *Wicked Puritans of Essex County*, 29–30.

27. Ibid., 30–33.

28. Reis, *Damned Women*, 49.

29. Fischer, *Albion's Seed*, 89.

30. Ibid.

31. David Freeman Hawke, *Everyday Life in Early American*, 106.

CONCLUSION: TRANSITION, TROUBLE, AND TRADE: THE EVOLUTION OF MASSACHUSETTS IN THE 1690s

The Salem witch trials themselves were a major turning point in the social history of Massachusetts, especially in the Essex County and Boston regions. Never again would the colonial population be overwhelmed by a pervasive sense of satanic power and imminent spiritual danger. To be sure, the belief in a spiritual Satan, and the "wonders of the invisible world" would continue to persist through the eighteenth century, but would never be seen as representing a tangible threat to entire communities of citizens.

Never again would the judicial system exercise such ruthless power, threatening and imprisoning dozens of innocent victims on the basis of circumstantial and in many cases, spectral evidence. Never again would the unregulated and random testimony of children bring and entire society to a point of crisis. Rather, in the years that followed, a profound sense of community guilt for the trials and their effect swept through the population prompting a colony-wide acceptance of the trials as both a travesty of justice and an offence against God, meriting a colony-wide day of fasting and prayer seeking God's forgiveness.

Finally, never again would the religious elite of Boston and the Puritan establishment possess the ability to exercise such unbridled authority and power in decision making, leaving the business of politics and policy in the hands of an evergrowing secular power base of merchants who would quickly rise to dominate Massachusetts social and political institutions. This growing secularization of Puritan society would continue through the eighteenth century as the ideas and writings of the Enlightenment would begin to take hold of the popular mind, while the writings of secular authors such as Benjamin Franklin would work help to dilute and subtly undermine the previously unquestioned authority of the religious elite.

The society that emerged from the crucible of the 1690s was therefore in many ways profoundly different from that which existed prior to the Glorious Revolution of 1688. The question of Massachusetts as a semi-autonomous political entity was answered. Ties to the mother country would be strengthened while the original motivational dream of Winthrop's "a city upon a hill"—the godly commonwealth of New Israel—would be forever abandoned in favor of a more pragmatic, secular vision.

THE POPULATION

But on a deeper level, the essential way of life of the Puritan population—both urban and rural—during the witch trial era, evidenced a surprising diversity. Urban dwellers lived a more sophisticated lifestyle and had a wider range of material culture available to them than their rural counterparts. Rural families were more given to providing the necessities of life for themselves, while urban families tended to purchase that which they needed. Farming was the dominant activity of most of the population and was more extensive in the countryside, yet practiced to a limited extent in the settled towns as well. As a result, no one was too far removed from an agricultural way of life.

The Puritan families of New England were patriarchal, but all household and domestic activities were closely controlled by the mother, or deputy husband. While it seems reasonable to assume that such clear occupational distinctions between genders were the norm in most cases, recent scholarship has discovered that there was significant crossover in tasks assigned to men and women in New England Puritan households, with few activities being exclusively given to one gender or the other.

Both parents assumed the responsibility for the training and education of their children and took responsibility for preparing them for their future life occupations. Children were closely controlled and educated at home, with both boys and girls learning to read in order to encourage the study of the Bible. As part of that training, sons and daughters were assigned specific tasks to assist the parents in farming activities and maintaining the household in general. Most importantly, family life was faith-centered with parents, especially the father, taking a leading role in the spiritual development of their children with daily periods devoted to collective prayer and Bible study at home, followed by regular, weekly attendance at Sunday service for both the morning and afternoon. This mandated practice had a profound effect upon societal mores and behavioral expectations on the part of the general population, underscoring the importance of Christian belief and values in virtually every aspect of daily life. This fact is perhaps no more evident than in the surprisingly uniform and effective attitude of Puritan society concerning courting practices involving parental approval and sexual behavior clearly proscribed by biblical expectations resulting in a stable family life and very low incidence of illegitimate births.

IMPACT OF SIR WILLIAM PHIPS

In the political and religious sphere, the time of the witchcraft trials was also a time of transition and trouble. In the wake of the Glorious Revolution of 1688–1689, the colonies were in the midst of a major political shift, most receiving new charters and royal governors, curtailing earlier tendencies toward autonomy and independent action. For Massachusetts, the arrival of Governor Sir William Phips in the spring of 1692 was, beyond all doubt, the single most significant political development of the year since he represented the newly crowned King William and Queen Mary, jointly appointed as the first constitutional monarchs in English history. He came with the primary intention of ending the long-standing dispute between New England and French Canada by conquering key fur trade and military bases while securing frontier boundaries against the attacks of the French and their native allies. This he only partially succeeded in doing.

What Governor Phips *did* achieve was to nearly bankrupt Massachusetts with an expensive war the colony was ill-prepared to fight, and alienate a significant portion of the colonial leadership through his heavy-handed tactics and his undiplomatic manner of dealing with people. Indeed, it might be argued that Governor Phips, while a fortunate treasure-hunter, was in many ways the wrong person to lead Massachusetts through its time of political and social crisis. He immediately demonstrated an unwillingness to involve himself directly in the witch trials which dominated the public's attention at the time of his arrival. For this reason, and perhaps because Phips felt, as an uneducated man, unqualified to take a prominent role in the proceedings, he created a special Court of Oyer and Terminer placing the entire crisis into the hands of Deputy Governor, Chief Justice William Stoughton—a man of harsh temperament who would turn the trials into a travesty of justice.

Added to this was Governor Phips's tendency to ignore and sometimes defy the wishes of his constituencies, creating an opposition faction within the colonial leadership openly critical of his handling of the frontier war and the witch trials, while implicating him in several economic controversies which would eventually result in his being recalled to London in 1694 for questioning. In light of this mismanagement of colonial affairs, not to mention the trials themselves, it is not surprising that the general population experienced a period of uneasiness and general anxiety during the years 1692 and 1693. Despite such anxiety, the colony of Massachusetts continued to prosper by expanding its maritime trade to an extent never before realized. By the early 1690s, regardless of the occasional forays of French privateers and the occasional pirate cruiser, the merchants of Massachusetts had created an Atlantic empire of commercial connections, firmly built upon a foundation of salt cod—linking them to the highly lucrative West Indies trade. In this regard, they were locked in direct competition with the merchants of England now beginning to view Massachusetts maritime trade as unfair and unwarranted competition.

By the 1690s also, the New England fishing industry, which had always maintained the region's economy was a dominant economic force. Recent historians have argued that without the "sacred cod" little economic achievement would have been possible for Massachusetts Bay Colony. By the late seventeenth century not only did Massachusetts produce more than a sufficient supply of salt cod for its own needs, but it became a major supplier to the world market including Catholic Europe, the British Isles, and the West Indies where "dun fish" were exchanged for vast amounts of molasses and sugar. Sugar and molasses now flowed to Boston and Salem in vast amounts. Some "sweet gold" would be sold at tidy profits in New England's seaports and market towns, while some would be reexported—the surplus molasses distilled into New England rum—to help maintain a vigorous and profitable triangle trade with Africa's western coast for slaves to be quickly transported and sold in the West Indies to serve as labor to produce yet more sugar.

In addition, by the 1690s Massachusetts merchants were selling their produce at ports along the entire length of the Atlantic seaboard. This colonial coastal trade in agricultural produce, lumber, and salt fish would continue to earn profits for the merchants of Salem and Boston until the outbreak of the Revolution, and well beyond. Beyond this, in the 1690s the merchants of Massachusetts still dealt in lumber and fur, always important commodities to a mother country that regarded its colonies as a source of raw materials for industry at home. To maintain this facet of the economy, New England Puritans needed to exploit the frontier for new sources of timber as virgin forests disappeared near the coast. Added to this demand was the ever-growing demand for domestically produced vessels, which in order to meet the increasing demands of both the fishing and maritime trading industries, was growing rapidly in every coastal village and town. This era marks the beginning of the legendary New England shipbuilding industry which would continue to prosper and expand, finally reaching its height during the age of sail in the 1850s with the clipper ships of Donald McKay.

In order to meet the growing demand for the fur trade, it was also necessary to maintain treaties and friendships with some Native American tribes who would serve as suppliers of fur from the forests of interior New England. These trade alliances with Native Americans frequently also served a military purpose when occasional frontier wars with the French and their Native American allies would break out. For many, this represented the most constant danger to the lives of Massachusetts colonists during the witch trial era which revolved around this aspect of daily life— the possible threat of native attacks, especially along the rural frontiers bordering New Hampshire, Maine, and the Hudson River Valley.

Recent scholarship in the area of the Salem witch trials has convincingly demonstrated that not only were some of the afflicted children refugees from areas recently attacked and devastated by hostile Native American war parties, but that the trauma experienced with the loss of home and parents helped precondition some of the afflicted to their outbreaks of hysteria and fear when presented with yet another potential threat. In this regard, the impact of the Salem witch trials upon the lives of all people living in

Eastern Massachusetts was significant. The trials not only created a climate of pervasive fear and suspicion, but also an everyday sense of community guilt no better expressed than by Boston merchant Thomas Brattle where he states: "I am afraid that ages will not wear off that reproach and those stains which these things will leave behind them upon our land."

APPENDIX

First Massachusetts Charter (March 4, 1629)

The "errand in the wilderness" would not have been possible for the Massachusetts Bay Company without the permission of King Charles I providing the colonists access to the area between three miles north of the Merrimack River and three miles south of the Charles River. This geographic area would remain the region known as Massachusetts Bay Colony until the arrival of Sir Edmund Andros and the creation of the Dominion of New England. The First Massachusetts Bay Charter outlines not only the boundaries of the colony, but also the government responsibilities of the Massachusetts Bay Company in establishing their "city upon a hill."

Charles, by the grace of god . . . [does] give and graunte unto . . . Sir Henry Rosewell, Sir John Younge, Sir Richard Saltonstall, Thomas Southcott, John Humfrey, John Endecott, Symon Whetcombe, Isaack Johnson, Samuell Aldersey, John Ven, Mathewe Cradock, George Harwood, Increase Nowell, Richard Pery, Richard Bellingham, Nathaniel Wright, Samuell Vassall, Theophius Eaton, Thomas Goffe, Thomas Adams, John Browne, Thomas Hutchins, William Vassall, William Pinchion, and George Foxcrofte, their Heires and Assignes, all that Parte of Newe England in America, which lyes and extendes between a great River there, comonlie

called Monomack River, alias Merrimack River, and a certain other
River there, called Charles River, being in the Bottome of a certain
Bay there, commonly called Massachusetts, alias Mattachusetts, alias
Massatusetts Bay: And also all those Landes and Hereditaments
whatsoever, which lye and be within the Space of Three English
Myles to the Northward of the saide River, called Monomack, alias
Merrymack, or to the Norward of any and every Parte thereof, and
all Landes and Hereditaments whatsoever, lying within the Lymitts
aforesaid, North and South in Latitude and Bredth, and in Length
and Longitude, of and within all the Bredth aforesaid, throughout
the mayne Landes there, from the Atlantick and Westerne Sea and
Ocean on the east Parte, to the South Sea on the West Parte; and all
Landes and Groundes, Place and Places, Soyles, Woodes, and
Wood Groundes, Havens, Portes, Rivers, Waters, and Hereditaments whatsoever, lyeing within the said Boundes and
Lymytts, and every Parte and Parcel l thereof; and also all Islandes
in America aforesaid, in the saide Seas, or either of them, on the
Westerne or Easterne Coastes, or Partes of the saide Tracks of
Landes hereby mentioned to be given and graunted, or any of them;
and all Mynes and Mynerals as well Royal mynes of Gold and Silver
and other mynes and minerals, whatsoever, in the said Landes and
Premisses, or any parte thereof, and free Libertie of fishing in or
within any the Rivers or Waters within the Boundes and Lymytts
aforesaid, and the Seas therevnto adjoining; and all Fishes, Royal
Fishes, Whales, Balan, Sturgions, and other Fishes of what Kinde or
Nature soever. . . . To be holdes of Vs our Heires and Successors, as
of our Manor of Eastgreenwich in our Countie of Kent, within our
Realme of England, in free and common Soccage, and not in
Capite, nor by Knights Service; and also teilding and paying therefor, to Vs, our Heires and Successors, the fifte Parte onlie of all Oare
of Gould and Silver, which from tyme to tyme, and at all tymes hereafter, shall be there gotten, had, or obteyned, for all Services,
Exactions, and Demaundes whatsoever. . . . Wee have further hereby
of our especial Grace, [&] certain Knowledge . . . Given, graunted
and confirmed . . . vnto our said trustie and welbeloved subjects . . .
and all such others as shall hereafter be admitted and made free of
the Company and Society hereafter mentioned, shall from tyme to
tyme, and att al tymes forever hereafter be, by Vertue of theis
presents, on Body corporate and politique in Face and Name, by
the Name of the Governor and Company of the Mattachusetts Bay
in Newe-England, and them by the Name of the Governour and
Company of the Mattachusetts Bay in Newe-England, one Bodie

politique and corporate, in Deede, Fact, and Name; Wee doe for vs, our Heires and Successors, make, ordeyne, constitute, and confirme by theis Presents, and that by that name they shall have perpetuall Succession, and by that Name they and their Successors shall and maie be capeable and enabled aswell to implead, and to be impleaded, and to prosecute, demaund, and aunswere, and be aunsweared vnto, in all and singular Suites, Causes, Quarrells, and Actions, of what kinde or nature soever. And also to have, take, possesse, acquire, and purchase and Landes, Tenements, or Hereditaments, or any Goodes or Chattells, and the same to lease, graunte, demise, alien, bargaine, sell, and dispose of, as other our liege People of this our Realme of England, or any other corporacon or Body politique of the same may lawfully doe.

AND FURTHER, That the said Governour and Companye, and thier Successors, maie have forever one comon Seal, to be vsed in all Causes and Occasions of the said Company, and the same Seale may alter, chaunge, breake, and newe make, from tyme to tyme, at their pleasures. And our Will and Pleasure is, and Wee doe hereby for Vs, our Heires and Successors, ordeyne and graunte, That from henceforth for ever, there shalbe on Governor, one Deputy Governor, and eighteene Assistants of the same Company, to be from tyme to tyme constituted, elected and chosen out of the Freemen of the saide Company, for the twyme being, in such Manner and Forme as hereafter in theis Presents is expressed, which said Officers shall applie themselves to take Care for the best disposeing and ordering of the generall buysines and Affaires of, for, and concerning the said Landes and Premisses hereby mentioned, to be graunted, and the Planticion thereof, and the Government of the People there. AND FOR the better Execution of our Royall Pleasure and Graunte in this Behalf, Wee doe, bu theis presents, for Vs, our Heires and Successors, nominate, ordeyne, make, & constitute; our welbeleved the saide Mathewe Cradocke, to be the first and present Governor of the said Company, and the saide Thomas Goffe, to be Deputy Governor of the saide Company, and the saide Sir Richard Saltonstall, Isaack Johnson, Samuell Aldersey, John Ven, John Humfrey, John Endecott, Simon Whetcombe, Increase Noell, Richard Pery, Nathaniel Wright, Samuell Vassall, Theophilus Eaton, Thomas Adams, Thomas Hutchins, John Browne, George Foxcrofte, William Vassall, and William Pinchion, to be the present Assistants of the saide Company, to continue in the saide several Offices respectivelie for such tyme, and in such manner, as in and by theis Presents is hereafter declared and appointed. AND FURTHER, Wee . . . doe ordeyne and graunte, That the Governor of the saide Company . . . shall have Authoritie from tyme to tyme vpon all Occasions, to give order for the assembling of the saide Company, and calling them together to consult and advise of the Bussinesses and Affaires of the saide Company, and that the said Governor, Deputie Governor and Assistants of the saide Company, for the tyme being, shall or maie once every Moneth, or oftener at their Pleasures, assemble and houlde and keepe a Courte or Assemblie of themselves, for the better ordering and directing of their Affaires, and that any seaven or more persons of the Assistants, togither with the Governor, or Deputie Governor soe assembled, shalbe saide, taken, held and reputed to be, and shalbe a full and sufficient Courte or Assemblie of the said Company, for the handling, ordering and dispatching of all such Buysinesses and Occurrents as shall from tyme to tyme happen, touching or concerning the said Company or Planation; and that there shall or maie be held and kept by the Governor, or Deputie Governor of the said Company, and seaven or more of the said Assistants for the tyme being, vpon every last Wednesday in Hillary, Easter, Trinity and Michas Termes respectivelie forever, one greate generall and solempe assemblie, which foure generall assemblies shalbe stiled and called the foure greate and generall Courts of the saide Company; IN all and every, of any of which saide greate and generall Courts soe assembled, WEE DOE . . . give and graunte to the saide Governor and Company, and their Sucessors, That the Governor, or in his absence the Deputie Governor of the saide Company for the tyme being, and such of the Assistants and Freeman of the saide Company as shall be present, or the greater nomber of them so assembled, whereof the Governor or Deputie Governor and six of the Assistants at the least to be seaven, shall have full Power and authoritie to choose, nominate, and appointe, such and soe many others as they shall thinke fitt, and that shall be willing to accept the same, to be free of the said Company and Body, and them into the same to admitt; and to elect and constitute such Officers as they shaall thinke fitt and requisite, for the ordering, mannaging, and dispatching of the Affaires of the saide Govenor and Company, and their Successors; And to make Lawes and Ordinances for the Good and Welfare of the saide Company, and for the Government and ordering of the saide Landes and Plantation, and the People inhabiting and to inhabite the same, as to them from tyme to tyme shalbe thought meete, soe as such Lawes and Ordinances be not contrarie or repugnant to the Lawes and Statuts of this our

Realme of England. AND, our Will and Pleasure is ... That yearely once in the yeare, for ever hereafter, namely, the last Wednesday in Easter Tearme, yearely, The Governor, Deputy-Governor, and Assistants of the said Company and all other officers of the saide Company shalbe in the Generall Court or Assembly to be held for that Day or Tyme, newly chosen for the Yeare ensueing by such greater parte of the said Comapany, for the Tyme being, then and there present as is aforesaide. ... And, Wee doe further ... give and graunte to the said Governor and Company, and their Successors for ever by theis Presents, That it shalbe lawfull and free for them and their Assignes, at all and every Tyme and Tymes hereafter, out of any our Realmes or Domynions whatsoever, to take, leade, carry, and transport, for in and into their Voyages, and for and towardes the said Plantation in Newe England, all such and soe many of our loving Subjects, or any other strangers that will become our loving Subjects, and live under our Allegiance, as shall willinglie accompany them in the same Voyages and Plantation; and also Shipping, Armour, Weapons, Ordinance, Municon, Powder, Shott, Corne, Victualls, and all Manner of Clothing, Implements, Furniture, Beastes, Cattle, Horses, Mares, Merchandizes, and all other Thinges necessarie for the said Plantation, and for their Vse and Defence, and for Trade with the People there, and in passing and returning to and fro, any Lawe or Statute to the contrarie hereof in any wise notwithstanding; and without payeing or yeilding any Custome or Subsidie, either inward or outward, to Vs, our Heires or Successors, for the same, by the Space of seaven Yeares from the Day of the Date of theis Presents. Provided, that none of the saide Persons be such as shalbe hereafter by especiall Name restrayned by Vs, our Heires or Successors. And, for their further Encouragement of our especiall Grace and Favor, Wee ... yeild and graunt to the saide Governor and Company, and their Successors, and every of them, their Factors and Assignes, That they and every of them shalbe free and quitt from all Taxes, Subsidies, and Customes, in Newe England, for the like Space of seaven Yeares, and from all Taxes and Imposicons for the Space of twenty and one Yeares, vpon all Goodes and Merchandizes at any Tyme or Tymes hereafter, either vpon Importation thither, or Exportation from thence into our Realme of England, or into any other our Domynions by the said Governor and Company, and their Successors, their Deputies, Factors, and Assignes, or any of them; Except onlie the five Pounds per Centum due for Custome vpon all such Goodes and Merchandizes as after the saide seaven Yeares shalbe expired, shalbe brought or imported into our Realme of England, or any other of our Dominions, according to the auncient Trade of Merchants. . . .

And, further our Will and Pleasure is . . . That all and every the Subiects of Vs, our Heires or Successors, which shall goe to and inhabits within the saide Landes and Premisses hereby mentioned to be graunted, and every of their Children which shall happen to be borne there, or on the Seas in goeing thither, or retorning from thence, shall have and enjoy all liberties and Immunities of free and naturall Subiects within any of the Domynions of Vs, our Heires or Successors, to all Intents, Constructions, and Purposes whatsoever, as yf they and everie of them were borne within the Realme of England. And that the Governor and Deputie Governor of the said Company for the Tyme being, or either of them, and any two or more of such of the saide Assistants as shalbe therevnto appointed by the saide Governor and Company at any of their Courts or Assemblies to be held as aforesaide, shall and maie at all Tymes, and from tyme to tyme hereafter, have full Power and Authoritie to minister and give the Oathe and Oathes of Supremacie and Allegiance, or either of them, to all and everie Person and Persons, which shall at any Tyme or Tymes hereafter goe or passe to the Landes and Premisses hereby mentioned to be graunted to inhabite in the same. And, Wee doe of our further Grace, certen Knowledg and meere Motion, give and graunte to the saide Governor and Company, and their Successors, That it shall and maie be lawfull, to and for the Governor or Deputie Governor, and such of the Assistants and Freemen of the said Company for the Tyme being as shalbe assembled in any of their generall Courts aforesaide, or in any other Courtes to be specially sumoned and assembled for that Purpose, or the greater Parte of them (whereof the Governor or Deputie Governor, and six of the Assistants to be alwaies seaven) from tyme to tyme, to make, ordeine, and establishe all Manner of wholesome and reasonable Orders, Lawes, Statutes, and Ordinances, Directions, and Instructions, not contrairie to the Lawes of this our Realme of England, aswell for setling of the Formes and Ceremonies of Government and Magistracy, fitt and necessary for the said Plantation, and the Inhabitants there, and for nameing and setting of all sorts of Officers, both superior and inferior, which they shall finde needefull for that Government and Plantation, and the distinguishing and setting forth of the severall duties, Powers, and Lymytts of every such Office and Place, and the Formes of such Oathes warrantable by the Lawes and Statutes of this our Realme of England, as shalbe respectivelie ministered vnto them for the Execution of the said severall Offices and Places; as also, for the disposing and ordering of the Elections of such of the said Officers as shalbe annuall, and of such others as shalbe to succeede in Case of Death or Removeall, and ministring the said Oathes to the newe elected Officers, and for Imposicons of lawfull Fynes, Mulcts, Imprisonment, or other lawfull Correction, according to the Course of other Corporacons in this our Realme of England, and for the directing, ruling, and disposeing of all other Matters and Thinges, whereby our said People, Inhabitants there, may be soe religiously, peaceablie, and civilly governed, as their good Life and orderlie Conversacon, maie wynn and incite the Natives of Country, to the Knowledg and Obedience of the onlie true God and Sauior of Mankinde, and the Christian Fayth, which in our Royall Intention, and the Adventurers free Profession, is the principall Ende of this Plantation. Willing, commanding, and requiring, and by theis Presents for Vs, our Heires, and Successors, ordeyning and appointing, that all such Orders, Lawes, Statuts and Ordinances, Instructions and Directions, as shal be soe made by the Governor, or Deputie Governor of the said Company, and such of the Assistants and Freemen as aforesaide, and published in Writing, vnder their comon Seale, shal be carefullie and dulie observed, kept, performed, and putt in Execution, according to the true Intent and Meaning of the same; and theis our Letters-patents, or the Duplicate or exemplification thereof, shal be to all and everie such Officers, superior and inferior, from Tyme to Tyme, for the putting of the same Orders, Lawes, Statutes, and Ordinances, Instructions, and Directions, in due Execution against Vs, our Heires and Successors, a sufficient Warrant and Discharge.

Source: Thorpe, Francis Newton. *The Federal and State Constitutions, Colonial Charters, and Other Organic Laws of the States, Territories, and Colonies Now or Heretofore Forming the United States of America*. Vol. III. Washington: GPO, 1909.

King Philip's War: The Puritan Explanation (November 3, 1675)

Without doubt one of the most devastating conflicts ever to take place in colonial New England, the King Philip's War (1675–1676) resulted in a near disaster for the Puritans of the region, destroying several towns and villages, driving back the English population

toward the coast and resulting in the deaths and captivity of thou-
sands. It set the stage for social tensions leading to the Salem witch
trials. The following is a brief interpretation of the events which
brought the conflict upon the colony. Following this explanation of
the war are a series of resolutions designed to correct behavior and
new customs which, in the opinion of the General Court, need to be
addressed.

Whereas the most wise and holy God for several years past, hath
not only warned us by his word, but chastised us with his rods,
inflicting upon us many general (through lesser) judgments, but
we have neither heard the word nor rod as we aught, so as to be
effectually humbled for our sins to repent of them, reform, and
amend our ways; hence it is the righteous God hath heightened
our calamity and given commission to the barbarous heathen to
rise up against us, and to become a smart rod and sure scourge to
us, in burning and depopulating several hopeful plantations, mur-
dering many of our people of all sorts and seeming as it were to cast
us off, and putting us to shame, and not going forth with our
armies, hereby speaking aloud to us to search and try our ways,
and turn again unto the Lord our God, from whome we have
departed with a great backsliding.

1. The Court, apprehending there is too great a neglect of discipline in the churches, and especially respecting those that are their
children, through the non acknowledgement of them according to
the order of the gospel; and watching over them, as well as chastis-
ing of them, inquiring into their spiritual estates, that, being
brought to take hold of the covenant, they may acknowledge and
be acknowledged according to their relations to God and to His
church, and their obligations to be the Lord's, and to approve themselves so to be by a suitable profession and conuersation; and does
therefore does solemnly recommended it unto the respective elders
and brethren of the several churches throughout this jurisdictions
to take effectual course for reformation herein.

2. Whereas there is manifest pride openly appearing amongst us
in that long hair, like women's hair, is worn by some men either
their own or others hair made into peerwigs, and by some women
wearing borders of hair, and their cutting curly & immodest laying
out their hair, which practice doth prevail and increase, especially
among the younger sort, —

This Court doth declare against this ill custom as offensive to
them, and diuers sober Christians amongst us, and therefor do

hereby exhort and advise all persons to use moderation in this respect; and further, do empower all grand juries to present to the County Court such persons, whither male of female whom they shall judge to exceed in the premises; and the County Courts are hereby authorized to proceed against such delinquents either by admonition, fined, or correction, according to their good discretion.

3. Not withstanding the wholesome laws already made by this Court for restraining excess in apparel, yet through corruption in many and neglect of due execution of those laws, the euill of pride in apparel, both for costjnes in the poorer sort, and vajne, new, strange fashions, both in port and rich with naked breast and arms, or, as it were, pinioned with the addition of superstitious ribbons on hair and apparel; for redress whereof, it is ordered by this Court that the County Courts from time to time, do give strict charge to present all such persons as they shall judge to exceed in that kind, and if the grand jury shall neglect their duty herein, the County Court shall impose a fine upon them at their discretion.

And it is further ordered, that the County Court, single magistrate, Commissioners' Court in Boston, have hereby power to summon all such persons so offending before them, and for each offence of that kind afterwards to impose a fine of 10 shillings upon them, or, if unable to pay, to inflict such punishment as shall be by them thought most suitable to the nature of the offense; in the same judges above named are hereby empowered to judge of and execute the laws already extant against such excess.

Whereas it may be found amongst us that men's thresholds are set up by God's thresholds, and man's posts besides God's posts, especially in the open meetings of Quakers, who's damnedable heresies, abominable idolatries, are hereby promoted, embraced, and practiced, to the scandal of religion, scandal of souls, and provocation of Divine jealousy against this people, for prevention and reformation whereof it is ordered by this Court and the authority thereof that every person found at a Quaker's meeting shall be apprehended, ex officio, by the constable, and by warrant from a magistrate or commissioner shall be committed to the house of correction and there to have the discipline of the house applied to them, and to be kept to work, with bread and water, for three days and then released or else shall pay 5 pounds in money as a fine to the county for such offense; and all constables neglecting their duty in not faithfully executing this order shall incur the penalty of 4 pounds upon conviction, one third thereof to the informer.

And touching the law of importation of Quakers, that it may be more strictly executed, and none transgressing to escape punishment —

It is hereby ordered, that the penalty to that law averred be in no case abated to less than 20 pounds.

5. Whereas there is so much profanes amongst us in persons turning their backs upon the public worship before it be finished and the blessing pronounced, —

It is ordered by this Court that the officers of the churches, or the selectmen, shall take care to prevent such disorders, by appointing persons to shut the meeting house doors or, or any other meet way to attain the end.

6. Whereas there is much disorder and rudeness in youth in many congregations in time of the worship of God, whereby sin and profaneness is greatly increased, for reformation whereof, —

It is ordered by this Court, that the selectmen do appoint such place or places in the meetinghouse for children or youth to sit in where they may be most together and in public view, and that the officers of the churches, or selectmen, do appoint some grave and sober person or persons to take a particular care and inspection over them, who are hereby required to present a list of the names of such, who, by their own observance or the information of other, shall be found delinquent, to the next magistrate or court, who are empowered for the first offence to admonish them, for the second offence to impose a fine of 5 shillings on their parents or governors, or order the children to be whipped, and if incorrigible to be whipped with ten stripes, or sent to a house of correction for three days.

7. Whereas the name of God is prophaned by common swearing and cursing in ordinary communication, which is a sin that grows amongst us, and many hear such oathes and curses, and conceals the same from authority, for reformation whereof, it is ordered by this Court, that the laws already in force against this sin be vigorously prosecuted; and, as addition thereunto, it is further ordered, that all such persons who shall at any time hear prophane oathes and curses spoken by any person or persons, and shall neglect to disclose the same to some magistrate, commissioner, or constable, such persons shall incur the same penalty provided in that law against swearers.

8. Whereas the shameful and scandalous sin of excessive drinking, tipling, & company keeping in taverns, &c, ordinaries, grows upon us, for reformation whereof, —

It is commended to the care of the respective County Courts not to license any more public houses then are absolutely necessary in any town, and to take care that none be licensed but persons of approved sobriety and fidelity to law and good order; and that licensed houses be regulated in their improvement for the refreshing & entertainment of travelers & strangers only, and all town dwellers are hereby strictly enjoyned & required to forbear spending their time or estates in such common houses of entertainment, to drink & tiple, upon penalty of five shillings for every offence, or, if poor, to be whipt, at the discretion of the judge, not exceeding five stripes; and every ordinary keeper, permitting persons to transgress as above said, shall incur the penalty of five shillings for each offence in that kind; and any magistrate, commissioner, or selectmen are empowered & required vigorously to put the abovesaid law in execution.

And, further, it is ordered, that all private, unlicensed houses of entertainment be diligently searched out, and the penalty of this law strictly imposed; and that all such houses may be the better discovered, the selectmen of every town shall choose some sober and discrete persons, to be authorized from the County Court, each of whom shall take the charge of ten or twelve families of his neighborhood, and shall diligently inspect them, and present the names of such persons so transgressing to the magistrate, commissioners, or selectmen of the town, who shall return the same to be proceeded with by the next County Court as the law directs; and the persons so chosen and authorized, and attending their duty faithfully therein, shall have one third of the fines allowed them; but, if neglect of their duty, and shall be so judged by authority, they shall incur the same penalty provided against unlicensed houses.

9. Whereas there is a wofull breach of the fifth commandment to be found amongst us, in contempt of authority, civil, ecclesiastical, and domesticall, this Court doeth declare, that sin is highly provoking to the Lord, against which he hath borne sure testimony in his word, especially in that remarkable judgments Upon Chorah and his company, and therefore doe strictly require & command all persons under this government to reform so great an evil, least God from heaven punish offenders heerin by some remarkable judgments. And it is further ordered, that all County Courts, magistrates, commissioners, selectmen, and grand jurors, according to their several capacities, do take strict care that the laws already made & provided in this case be duely executed, and particularly that evil of inferiors absenting themselves out of the families whereunto they belong in the night, and meeting with corrupt

company without leave, and against the mind & to the great grief of their superiors, which evil practice is of a very perilous nature, and the root of much disorder.

It is therefore ordered by this Court, that whatever inferior shallbe legally convicted of such an evil practice, such persons shall be punished with admonition for the first offence, with fine not exceeding ten shillings, or whipping not exceeding five stripes, for all offences of like nature afterwards.

10. Whereas the sin of idleness (which is a sin of Sodom) doeth greatly increase, notwithstanding the wholesome laws in force against the same, as an addition to that law, —

This Court doeth order, that the constable, with such other person or persons whom the selectmen shall appoint, shall inspect particular families, and present a list of the names of all idle persons to the selectmen, who are hereby strictly required to proceed with them as already the law directs, and in case of obstinacy, by charging the constable with them, who shall convey them to some magistrate, by him to be committed to the house of correction.

11. Whereas there is oppression in the midst of us, not only by such shopkeepers and merchants who set excessive prizes on their goods, also by mechanicks but *also by mechanicks* and day laborers, who are daily guilty of that evil, for redress whereof, & as an addition to ye law, title Oppression, it is ordered by this Court, that any person that judgeth himself oppressed by shopkeepers or merchants in setting excessive prizes on their goods, have hereby liberty to make their complaint to the grand jurors, or otherwise by petition to the County Court immediately, who shall send to the person accused, and if the Court, upon examination, judge the person complaining injured, they shall cause the offender to return double the overplus, or more then the equal price, to the injured person, and also impose a fine on the offenders at the discretion of the Court; and if any person judge himself oppressed by mechanicks or day laborers, they may make complaint thereof to the selectmen of the town, who if upon the examination doe find such complaint just, having respect to the quality of the pay, and the length or shortness of ye day labor, they shall cause the offender to make double restitution to the party injured, and pay a fine of double the value exceeding the due price.

12. Whereas there is a loose & sinful custom of going or riding from town to town, and that oft times men & women together, upon pretence of going to lecture, but it appears to be merely to drink & revel in ordinarys & taverns, which is in itself scandalous,

and it is to be feared a notable means to debauch our youth and hazard the chastity of such as are drawn forth thereunto, for prevention whereof, —

It is ordered by this Court, that all single persons who, merely for their pleasure, take such journeys, & frequent such ordinaryes, shall be reputed and accounted riotous & unsober persons, and of ill behavior, and shall be liable to be summoned to appear before any County Court, magistrate, or commissioner, & being thereof convicted, shall give bond & sufficient sureties for the good behavior in twenty pounds, and upon refusal so to doe, shall be committed to prison for ten days, or pay a fine of forty shillings for each offence.

It is ordered by this Court, that every town in this jurisdiction shall provide, as an addition to their town stock of ammunition, six hundred of flints for one hundred of listed soldiers, and so proportionally for a lesser or greater number, to be constantly maintained & fitted for public service.

14. This Court, considering the great abuse & scandal that hath arisen by the license of trading houses with the Indians, whereby drunkenness and other crimes have been, as it were, sold unto them, —

It is ordered by this Court, that all such trading houses, from the publication hereof, shall wholly cease, and none to presume to make any sale unto them, except in open shops and towns where goods are sold unto the English, upon the penalty of ten pounds for every conviction before lawful authority, one third to the informers, the remainder to the country, any law, usage, or custom to the contrary notwithstanding.

This Court, having ordered two watchmen from Dorchester and Milton to watch at Dorchester mill, and understanding the undertakers of the powder mill, for better defense thereof, are erecting a small stone watch erecting a small stone watch house at their own charges, on their request, as being of public concernment, this Court declares, that the undertakers of the powder mill may repair to any one magistrate, who, by the law, are empowered to give warrant to impress workmen to carry on public works, of which sort this is.

This Court, considering the inconvenience & damage that may arise to particular towns by such as, being forced from their habitations through the present calamity of the war, do repair unto them for succor, do order and declare, that such persons (being inhabitants of this jurisdiction) who are so forced from their habitations & repair to other plantations for relief, shall not, by virtue of their residence in said plantations they repair unto, be accounted or reputed inhabitants thereof, or imposed on them, according to law, title Poor; but in such case, and where necessity requires, (by reason of inability of relations, &c,) they shall be supplied out of the public treasury; and that the selectmen of each town inspect this matter; and do likewise carefully provide, that such men or women may be so employed, and children disposed of, that, as much as may be, public charge may be avoided.

Whereas this Court have, for weighty reasons, placed sundry Indians (that have subjected to our government) upon some islands for their and our security, —

It is ordered, that none of the said Indians shall presume to go off the said islands voluntarily, upon pain of death; and it shall be lawful for the English to destroy those that they shall find straggling off from the said places of their confinement, unless taken of by order from authority, and under an English guard. And it is further ordered, that if any person or persons shall presume to take, steal, or carry away either man, woman, or child of the said Indians, off from any the said islands where they are placed, without order from the General Court or council, he or they shall be accounted breakers of the capital law printed & published against man stealing; and this order to be forthwith posted and published.

The whole Court being met, it is ordered, that the country Treasurer take care for ye provision of those Indians that are sent down to Deare Island, so as to prevent their perishing by any extremity that they may be put unto for want of absolute necessaries, and for that end he is to appoint meet persons to visit them from time to time.

Source: Laws of Massachusetts, 1675, p. 32.

No document better provides a more accurate picture of everyday life at an earlier time than a household inventory. The following two inventories illustrate what sorts of material culture might be found in the houses and storehouses of two prosperous Salem merchants of the late seventeenth century.

Inventory of the Estate of Edward Wharton of Salem,
Deceased, and What Goods were in His Possession,
Consigned to Him by Several, Taken 12:I: 1677–8

By Hillard Veren, SR., John Hathorne and,
John Higginson

Valued in England as By Invoyce

1 plaine cloath cloake, 1Li. 5s.;

1 boys worsted cloake, 1li. 5s.;

1 heare camlet cloake, 2 li. 18s.;

5 cloathe cloakes, 28s. p., 7Li.;

1 cloathe cloake, 1 li. 8s.;

1 fine cloath cloake, 1 Li. 1 5s.;

1 cloath cloake, 1 li, 12s.;

6 cloathe cloake, 28s. p., 8 li, 8s.;

1 childs stuff coates st 9s. 1li. 7s.;

1 yeolow Tamy, 10s.;

1 ditto, 13s.;

1 boyes coate. 13s.;

1 doz. Home made wooll hose, 1 li. 14s.;

1 doz. Ditto, 1 li. 10s.;

8 pr. Of youths ditto, 14s.;

10 pr. Of woemens home made wooll Stockens, 1 li. 2s.;

7 pr. Of sale wooll hoase, 10s. 6d.;

17 pr. Of womens & youths stockens 14s. 10d.;

7 pr. Of home made woemans 4 thrid, 3s. 2d p., 4 pr. Ditto sale 4 third, 3s. 4d. p., 1li. 10s. 10d.;

4 pr, youths 4 thrid ditto, 3s.4d. p., 3 pr. Youths ditto, 3s. 1li. 2s. 4d.;

4 pr of wooll home made hose, 14s.;

1 pr. Mens worsted made stock-Ens 5s.;

8 pr. Of home made worsted 4 thrid, 1 li. 14s.;

6pr. Sale ditto, 18s.;

2pr. Of fine home made. 10s.;

1 childes coate, 7s.;

1 greene say frock, 5s.;

9 childs wascoates, 5d. p., 3s. 9d.;

6 Ditto. 7d. p., 3s. 6d.;

5 ditto, 9d p., 3s. 9d.;

4 Ditto, 10d.p., 3s. 4d.;

2 Keasey ditto, 2s. 6d., 5s.;

1Ditto, 2s. 8d.;

2 ditto, 3s. p., 6s.;

6 childrens, 12d. p., 6s.;

4 woemens yeolow wascoate, 22d.; p., 7s. 4d.;

1 Cloake of lite collrd, haire cmlett, 3li.7s.;

4 coates of the same cmlett, 36s., p., 7li. 4s.;

1 cloath collrd, haire cmlett cloake, 35s.;

2 worsted camlet cloakes, 34s., 3li., 8s.;

1 fine haire camlet cloake, 5 li.;

2 trunks, 16s.;

3 ditto, 1li. 1s.;

1 ditto, 6s.;

2 dittos, 5s.p., 10s.;

2 boxes or little red trunks, s. 2d. p., 6s. 4d.;

1 ditto, 2s. 8d.;

3 silk say under pettecoates lite colLrd, at 12s. 6d. p., 1li. 17s. 6d.;

2 Ditto, 1li. 8s.;

Cloath woemans wascoats, 8s., 7 ditto, worth each 8s., 10s., 8s., 10s., 6s., 13., 15s.;

1 cheny sad. Collrd. Upper woemans Coate, 7s.;

1 sad collrd. Woemans searge coate, 17s., 6d;

1 black fine searge upper pettecoate, 19s.;

1 stuff cloake for woeman, 10s.;

1 ditto for a girle, 7s.;

1 large worsted rug lite collrd 1li. 14s.;

1 large sad collrd. Ditto, worsted, 18s.;

1 ditto worsted sad cold, 1li.;

6 greene & blew paine Rugge, 8s.
p., 2li. 8s.;

1 sad callrd thrum Rugg, 11s. 6d.;

1 cabbin Rugg, 4s. 8d.;

1 cource 8-4 Rugg, 10s.;

3 coverleds, ordinary, 6s., p., 18s.;

2 ditto at 5s., 10s.;

2 coverleds, large at 7s. 6d., p., 15s.;

1 smale one, 6s. 6d.;

1 red plaine rug. 8s.;

1 peece wt. cotton, 19s.;

1 darnex carpet, 5s. 6d.;

1 ditto greene, 6s. 6d.;

4 pr. Wt. drawers, 10s.;

6 peeces of searge at 40s., 12li.;

7 peeces narrow searge at 25s.,
8li. 15s.;

1 peece padaway searge, 2li. 15s.;

13 yds. Claret collrd. Tamy at 19d.
p., 1li. 1s. 1d.;

1 large draft lite collrd, 14s.;

1 2d sort. 12.;

1 small ditto, 10s.;

1 doble 10 qtr. Coverled. 1li. 4s.;

1 ditto 9 qrts. 1li.;

2 dittos, 8 qrts., 15s. 6d., p. 1li. 11s.;

8 yrds. ¾ striped Tamarene at 18d.
p., 13s. 1 1/2d.;

12 yrds. ¾ Turkey mohair, 2s. 10d.
p., 1li. 16s. 1 ½.;

6 yrds. ¼ of striped stuffe at 22d.
p., 11s. 51/2.;

9 yrds. Striped camlet, 2s. 4d. p.,
1li. 1s.;

1 peece orange collrd worsted
draft, 2li. 5s.;

4 yrds. Haire camlet, 3s. p, 2li. 2s;

10 yrdes. Of ash collrd, silk
moheare, 4s. p, 2li.;

6 yrds. ½ of ash collrd silk
farrendine, 4s. 6d. p, 1li. 9s. 3d.;

12 yrds. Ash collrd. Haire camlet
at 3s. p., 1li, 16s.;

1 peece sad collrd. Stuff, mixt with
Gold collrd, 2li. 10s.;

24 yrds. Flowered silk draft, 2s.
2li. 8s.;

13 yrds. Striped vest at 22d. p., 1li.
3s., 10d.;

18 yrds. Scotch Tabby at 16s. p.,
1li. 4s.;

16 yrds., Scotch Tabby at 16s, p.,
1li. 1s. 4d.;

10 yrds. Tiking at 15d. p., 12s., 6d.;

8 yrds. Padaway at 2s.6d. p., 1li.;

7 yrds. Of Linsy at 12d. 1/2p,
7s. 6d.;

2 pr. Boyes cotton drawers, at
2s.p., 4s.;

3 cotton wascoate at 2s. 10d. 6d.;

2 pr. Blew drawers, 2s, 5d. p., 4s.
10d.;

1 boyes haire sad coll. Camlet
cloake, 1li. 15s.;

1 large flanders like & bolster, 1li.
9s. 6d.;

30 yrds. Of upper Tiking, at 18d.
p, 2li. 5s.;

42 yrds. Diaper at 15d. p, 2li.
12s. 6d.;

12 yrds. Of Tabling, 2s. 6d.
p, 1li. 10s.;

21 yrds. of diaper for napkins,
18d., P, 1li. 11s.6d.;

2 pillow Tikins, at 2s. 2d. 4s. 4d.;

1 light coll. Boyes cloake, 1li. 12s.;

2 yrds. ¼ of plush at 8s. p., 9d.;

20 tobaco boxes at 1d. 1/2p,
2s. 6d.;

3 ditto at 2d. p. doz., 33/4 d.;

4 brass roles for chalk lines, 5s. 6d.
p. doz., 1s. 10d.;

8 ditto large at 6s. 6d., p. goz.
4s. 4d.;

8 chalk lines at 18d. p. doz., 1s.;

Tinware, 4 Cullenders, 5s. 4d.:

6 ditto, 5s. 6d.;

2 doz. Wood save-alls, 3d 1/2p,
7d.;

1 large kettle, 2s. 3d.;

1 next size, 2s.;

8 6qty. Ketles, 14d. p., 9s 2d.;

3 gallon Kettles, 12d. p., 3s.;

5 3qrt. Kettles, 9d. p., 3s. 9d.;

2 3pt. Kittles, 7d. p. 1s. 9d.;

5 best save-alls, 2s. 4d. p doz., 111/2 d.;

11 second sort at 8d. p. doz., 71/4.;

3 extinguishers, 8d. per doz., 2 ¾.;

3 doble plate pans, 18d., p., 4s. 6d.;

A doble puden pan, 9d.;

2 middle sised lanthornes, 18d. p., 3s.;

4 band candlesticks, 5d. ½ p, 1s. 10d.;

5 tinder boxes & steele, 7d. p., 2s 11d.;

4 writing candlesticks, 2d 1/2p 10d.;

2 pt sace pans, 3s. 8d. p doz., 7d.;

3 bread or flower boxes, 3d. 1/2dp., 10 1/2d.;

4 casters, 2d p., 8d.;

1 peper box, 2d., 1 fish plate, 8d., 10d.;

6 smale bread graters, 8d. p. doz., 4d.;

2 pts. At 3d ¾ p., 1 funnell, 4d., 2 covers, 8d, p., 2s. 3 1/2d.;

3 brass save-alls, 7d. p., 3 larger graters, 3d. 1/2p., 2s. 7d.;

2 egg slices. 2d. ½ p. 5d.;

2 whip saws & tillers 5s. 6d. p., 16s. 6d.;

2 marking irons, 2s., 1 cloase stoole &pan, 8s, 9d., 10s. 9d.;

2 steele handsawes with scres, 3s. p., 6s.;

1 large steele hand saw, 2s. 2d.;

8 hand sawes at 14d.p., 9s.4d.;

1 handsaw, 10d.;

2 faling axes, 1s. 5d., 2s. 10d.;

8 bright smale Hamers, 6d.p. 4s.;

9 Rivited hanars at 10d. p., 7s.6d.;

2 hamers, 4d. p. 8d.;

5 hamers, steele heads, 10s. p. doz., 4s. 2d.;

4 choppers at 15s. p. doz., 3s. 8d.;

2 mincing knives, 12d. p., 2s.;

7 small ditto, 13s. p doz., 7s. 7d.;

9 hatchetts, 12d, p., 9s.;

7 smale mincing knives, 9s. p. doz., 5s. 9d.;

3 steele saws & screws, 3s. p., 9s.;

5 doz. 8 gimletts at 12d. p doz., 5s. 8d.;

27 pensills at 8d. p doz., 1s 6d.;

10 percer bitts at 2d. p. 1s. 8d.;

1 large pincers to shooe horses, 1s.;

3 curry combs, 10d.;

2 large ditto, 6d. p. 1s.;

1 pr spincers for shoomakers, 1s.;

5 pr nippers, 4d. p. 1s. 8d.;

2 bundles of files, 20d. p. bundles, 3s. 3d.;

12 doz. Of straite all blades, 5d. p. doz., 5s.;

7 doz crooked blades at 5d. p. doz., 2s. 11d.;

14 doz. Of fire steeles at 6s. per grosse, 7s.;

21 pr. Of spurs at 7s. p doz., 12s. 3d.;

8 pr. Dove tailes at 2 1/2d. p, 1s. 8d.;

22 pr. sid hinges, 3d.p., 5s. 6d.;

6 pr. Esses at 8d. p, 4s.;

1 smooth Iron , 1s. 4d.;

3 doble spring lockes at 20d. p, 5s.;

1 single ditto, 9d.;

2 doz. Trunk lockes at 6s. p doz., 12s.;

1 doz. Of single ditto, 3s.p, 3s.;

½ doz. Large ditto, 4s.;

2 ship scrapers, 2s.;

6pr. Coll. Yarne mens hose, 12s.;

6pr. Worsted ditto at 3s. 4d., 1li.;

12 pr. Stockens, 7d.p. 7s.;

7 pr ditto, 9d.p, 5s. 3d.;

6 pr. Ditto 8d. p., 4s.;
6 pr. Ditto. At 5d., 2s., 6d.;
10 pr. Ditto at 6d. p, 5s.;
6 pr. Ditto at 13d.p., 6s. 6d., 5pr.
   Ditto at 18d. p, 7s. 6d.;

1 pr. Fine woemens red worsted,
   3s.;
2 pr. Mens worsted, 3s.;
2 pr. Mens worsted black & cold,
   & 1 pr. White, 7s. 6d.

Valued heare as money in New England:

2 linsy Woolsey pettecoates, 6s. p.,
   12s.;
1 little boyes coate of camlet
   worSted, 6s.;
2 linsey Woolsey & 1 pr. Of
   Fustian Draws, 9s.;
1 pr linen drawers, more, 3s.;
1 boyes coat, 4s.;
2 red childs blankets bound with
   ferret, 4s. p, 8s.;
1 smale childs camlet petticoat, 3s.;
9 sashes at 12d., 9s.;
50 yrds. of Irish searge at 2s. 2d.
   p, 5li. 8s. 4d.;
10 yrds. ½ broad worsted
   camletduble, 2s. 6d. p, 1li. 6s. 3d.;
16 ¼ yrds. narrow camlet, 1li. 12s.
   6d.;
20 ¼ yrds. mixt stuff, very bad,
   12d. p. 1li. 3d.;
14 yrdes, new Coll. Stuff at 2s.
   p., 1li. 8s.;
1 ell of farrindine, 2s. 4d. p yd, 2s.
   11d.;
6 yrds. coll fustian, 14d. p. 7s.;
3 yrds. red perpetuana at 2s. 6d.
   p, 7s.6d.;
6 yrds. ¼ greene say at 5 s.p, 1li
   11s. 3d.;
42 mens & woemens shifts, 4s. 9
   d.p, 9li. 19s. 6d.;
12 youth & girls ditto, 3s, 6d,
   p. 2li. 2s.;
8 finer mens, womens ditto, 6s. 6d.
   p., 2li. 12s.;

5 white dimity wascoates, 3s. 6d.
   p, 17s. 6d.;
1 yrd. ½ cambric, 4s. 6d. p, 6s. 9d.;
2 ends of fine wt. calico, 20s. p, 2li.;
2 peeces broade white calico, 40s.
   p. 4 li.;
2 peeces cource Holland, cont, 69
   yrds. 30s. p, 8li. 12s. 6d.;
5 1/4 yrds. fine dowlas at 2s. 6d.
   p, 13s. 1 ½ d.;
7 yrds. cource dowlas at 20d.
   p. 12s. 6d.;
1 ell cource Holland at 2s. 6d.
   p, 3s. 1 ½ d.;
9 yrds. scimity, 6s., 2 peeces of
   dimity, 6s. p. 18s.;
1 callico table cloath, 7s. 6d.;
2 callico shirts, 6s. p, 12s.;
2 calico painted table cloathes, 8s.
   p, 16s.;
1 large ditto, 14s.;
in English money, 2li. 7s.;
16 B. Indian corne, 2s. p, 1 barrell,
   2s., 1li. 14s.;
6 chests, 6s. p, about 13 C, Spanish
   Iron, 2s, p., C, 12 li. 16s.;
2 barrells of porke, 50 s., 5 li.;
Almost 2 barrekks of tarr, 7s. 6d.
   p. 15s.;
100 li. Tobacco at 3d p. 1 li. 5s.;
11 moose skins, 5li. 8d.;
2 Racoones, 12d. p, 2 sealls at 12d.
   P, 4s.;
1 hhd. ½ passader wine much
   deCaid, 4li.;
Pt. of 5 barrell very much decaid &
   Pricked madera, ——————;

2 hhd. Mallasses nott full, 5li. 10s.;

An old small catch exceeding out of repair almost worne out, both Hull & all appurtenances, valued By Mr. Bar. Gedney & John Norman, ship carpenters, 15 li.;

a dwelling house & land neere the meeting house & appurtenances, 8o li.;

A smale peece of land part of a frame For a warehouse & wharf, not finished & stones upon the ground, 14 li. 10s.;

A smale pcell of timber & old board, 10s.;

An old smale canoe, 10s.;

A horse running in the woods if alive ———;

A remnant of stuff, 2s.;

A peell of land at New Jersey but doe not know the quantity yet & some goods at some other places not yet knowne what they are ———; total, 630li. 6s. 5 3/4d.

Samll. Shattock's account of the debts: To several in England above, 300li.;

to several in New England which cannot yet be known how much, mincing knife, 6d., 2 curry combes, 2s.;

Glass redy made & som lead, 1li. 10s.;

nor Justly what yt is in England, but as himself said when he was sick & I ptly finde it by Invoys of Goods.

Appraised since the forgoing goods brought from the eastward as cost per invoice:

2 coates, 19s. p. coate, 1li. 18s.;

2 coats, 15s., p, 1li. 12s.;

3 white childs coates, 1 at 11s. & 2 at 14s., 1li. 19s.;

2 coates, 19s. p, 6 or 7 yeare old, 1li. 18s.;

1 Coat tamet, 16s.;

1 boyes coate, 13s.;

a flanders Tick & bolster, 1 li.; 9s. 6d.;

a draft, 8qrts., 14s.

Valued as cost here in New England

2 silk barateene undercoates, 1 li. 6s.;

1 large silk Rugg, 3li.;

1 calico India carpet, 4s.;

7 bushell & ½ malt, 1li. 2s. 6d.;

3 B. & ½ of Indian, 7s.;

1 B. wheate, 3s. 6d.;

a speckled pillow beere, 1s.;

to sugar sold at 5s. 3d.;

a gold ring, 7s. 6d.;

an Iron Casement, 5s.;

460 feet of board, 3s. p, 13s. 8d.;

8 narrow brimmed hats, 2s. p, 16.;

3 old rusty curry combs, 1s.;

2 old saws, 2s. 6d.;

4 pr. Sissers, 1 twissers, 1 gimlet punch, som ales & steeles, 4s. 6d.;

3 firkins of old butter, 3li.;

decayed wine, 1li, 15s.;

an old pr. Of hand screws, 1li. 10s.;

debt of 12s;

supposed 3 acres of land at merimake, to a silver seale, 2s.;

books, 12s; 2 chests & 1 trunke, 15s.;

8 & 2 yd. of narrow serge, at 2s. p, 17s.;

Debts, 40 li.;

total 69li. 6s. 11d.

Allowed in Salem court 27:4: 1678, Samuell Shattuck, sr., being a Friend affirming, and Samuell Shattock, jr. making oath to the truth of The inventory.

Source: *Essex County Probate Records, Vol. III*, pp. 203–208.

Inventory of the Estate of Capt. George Corwin of Salem, Taken by Barthl. Gedney, Benja. Browne, John Higgenson Junr. And Timo. Lindall on Jan. 30 and the Beginning of Feb., 1684–5

Dwelling house & land wheron it stands& adjoyneing to it wth. the out housing & fence, &c., 400li.;

the pastor, qt.* about 3 acres ½, considering a buriall place ther appointed, 90 li.;

the lower warhouse & wharfe, 110 li.;

the upper warhouse & land adjoining, 50li.;

About 8 acres Medow & upland by Ely Geoules, 45li.;

The farme on the plaines goeing to Lin bought of Trask, Pickering Adams, &c., qt. about 200 acres, 25p., 250li.;

The Farme now Reding bought of Burnap, qt. about 800 acres, aprized by Tho. Flint & Jos. Pope, 250li.;

the Farme bought of John Gold, qt. about 500 acres, 50li.;

60 acres of Land bought of GoodMan Dutton, 20li.;

15 acres of medow bought of Lt. Smith, 25 li.;

the houses & Land adjoyneing that was Wm. Godsoes & wharfe, 45 li.;

a pc, of land at the point nere Jer. Neales yt was _____, 10li.;

the Katch Swallow wth her apurtenancies, 130li.;

*Quantity

the Katch George with her aputtenancies, 65li.;

620 oz. 7/8 plate at 6s. 8d. 206 li. 19s. 2d.;

in New England mony, 47li. 1s.;

in English mony, 37li. 15s., advance 7li.11s., 45li. 6s.;

in pieces of Eight, 1519 li. 1s. 8d.;

72 oz. ¼ gold at 5li., 361li. 5s.;

1 Silver hat band & 6 Spones, qt. 4 oz. 9/13, 1li. 10s. 4d.;

1 watch wth. a stard case, 1 watch wth. a Silver case, 5li.;

1 Silver case & doctors Instruments, 5li.;

more in New England mony, 2li. 18s. 6d.;

1 Plate hilt rapier, 4li. 10s.;

1 Two edged Sword, 1li.;

1 Silver headed cane, 5s.

In the Shope

2 yd. broadcl(oth) at 8s., 16s.;

1 yd. ¾ ditto at 8s., 14.;

16yd. 3/8 Redcloth Rash at 6s. 6d., 5li. 6s. 5 1/4d.;

2yd, ¾ serge at 3s. 6d.; 9s. 7 1/2d.;

6 yd, perpcheana at 18d., 9s.;

7 yd. ¼ percheana at 18d., 10s. 101/2d.;

11 yd, ditto at 18d., 16s. 6d.;

20 yd. ½ ell French Stufe at 2s., 2li. 1s. 3d.;

36 yd. ½ ditto at 2s., 2li. 10s.;

1 Sad colerd Ruge, 18s.;

1 Grene ditto, 18s.;

9 yd. ½ Stript Stufe at 18d., 14s. 8d.;

1 yd. ¼ Grene Say, damaged, 2s.,

19 yd. ¾ Grene tamey at 10d., 16s. 25 1/2d.;

1 yd. ¾ bl. Calico at 18d., 2s 71/2 d.;

4 yd. 1.2 crape at 18d., 6s. 9d.;

11 yd. ¾ Crape at 18d., 17s. 7 ½.;

2 yd 1,s Stript Stufe at 18d., 3s. 9d.;

2 yd 1.2 ell Curle deroy at 18d., 3s. 11d.;

4 yd. ¾ prunella at 22d., 8s. 8 1/ 2d.;

10 yd. ¼ Silk baronet at 2s. 6d., 1li. 5s. 7 1/2d.;

7 yd. buckram at 18., 10s. 6d.;

10 yd. bla Cloth rash at 6s., 3li. 4s 6d.;

6yd. ¾ Sad Colerd ditto at 6s., 2li. 6s.;

14 yd. ½ Gr. Tamey at 10d., 12s. 1d.;

6 yd. flanell at 18d., 9s. 4 1/2d.;

2 pr. White blankets, 14s.;

(2) 1yd. ¾ Red cotton at 20d., 1li. 16s. 3d.;

14 yd. peniston————————, 1li. 8s.;

11 yd, ½ Carsey in Remnts. At 4s., 2li; 6s.;

1 yd. ½ Red buckron at 18d., 2s. 3d.;

2 Sutes Curtains & calients at 4li., 8li.;

2 yd ¼ Flanell at 18., 3s. 4 ½ d.;

28 yd 1/2 ell persian silkeat 5s. 6d., 7li. 17s. 5d.;

6 yd ¾ wosted Farenden at 20d., 11s. 3d.;

5 yd ¾ camlet at 20d., 9s 7d.;

16 yd. ¾ ticking at 20d., 1li. 7s. 11d.;

20 yd. ½ ditto, at 20d. 1 li. 14s. 2d.;

3 yd ¼ ditto at 20d., 5s. 5d.;

11 yd. ½ ditto at 17s., 16s. 3 1/2d.;

17 yd. bengall at 18d., 1li. 5s. 6d.;

24 yd. ½ St Petters canis at 16d., 1li. 12s. 8d.;

10 yd. 1.4 hall cloth at 15d., 12s. 9 3/4d.;

5 yd. ½ canvas at 16d., 7s. 4d.;

14 yds. Ditto damaged ay 12d., 16s. 4d.;

29 yds. Ditto damaged ay 12d., 1li. 9s.;

12 yd. 1.2 fugeres at 15d., 15s. 7 1/ 2d.;

22 yd. ¾ Vittery at 13d., 1 li. 4s. 7 ¾ d.;

19 yd. ¾ ditto at 12d., 1li. 1s. 4 ¾ d.;

24 yd. 1.4 fine canvas at 18d., 1li. 16s. 41/2d.;

3 pcs. Broad linon, qt. 309 yd., at 20d., 25li. 15s.;

32 yd. ¾ blu linon at 9d., 1li. 4s. 6 ¾ d.;

10 yd. ¾ pillow Ticking at 18d. 16s. 1 2/3 d.;

5 yd. wte. Fustian at 15d., 6s. 3d.;

18 yd. course Holland at 2s., 1li. 16s.;

7 yd. Slesy Holland at 21 d., 12s. 3d.;

10 yd. ½ Scotch cloth at 16d., 14s.;

25 yd. ¾ locrom at 15d., 1li. 12s. 2 1/4d.;

61 yd 2/3 doulas at 16d., 4li. 2s. 4d.;

2 halfe peces of 2/3 doulas, 9li.;

26 yd. browne diaper at 14d., 1li.
  10s. 4d.;

55 yd Vittery at 12d., 2li. 15s.;

12 yd high Brene at 22d., 1li. 2s.;

1 bolt Noyles, qt 140 yd., at 16d.,
  9li. 6s. 8d., 2 pcs. Course ticing
  at 35d., 3 li. 10s.;

12 pr. Weo. Hose, 18s.;

12 pr. mixed Stockrs. Smll. &
  Great, 14s.;

13 pr. bodys at 4s., 2li. 12s.;

4 pr. Paragon bodys & Stomachers
  At 8s., 1li. 12s.;

11 pr. Small bodys at 20d., 18s. 4d.

1 doz large Combes, 4s 6d.;

3 doz ditto at 3s. – dz., 9s.;

5 doz. Ditto at 2s. – dz, 10s.;

8 combes at 3d. ½ , 2s. 4d.;

23 wte. Haft knives at 8d., 15s. 4d.;

3 thousd, pins, 2s. 6d.;

17 long bla. Haft knives without
  sheaths at 3d., 4s. 3d.;

2 dz. Bl. Haft knives at 2s.
  6d., 5s.;

3 papers manchrs. & pt. of a piece,
  12s., 49 pcs. Colerd tapes at
  12d., 2li. 9s.;

3 papers colered Filiting, 9s.;

40 pcs. Wte. Tape at 12d. 3li.;

23 pcs. nar tape at 8d., 17s. 4d.;

17 doz. thred laces, 4s. 11d.;

A percell of broken tape, 5s.;

4 pcs. ½ diaper Filiting, 6s.;

41 Smll. Pcs. Colerd tape at 3d. ½,
  11s. 11 1/2d.;

A percell of broken colerd tape,
  1s. 6d.;

21 cards old fashioned silke lace &
  5 cards Gimp Lace, 4 li.;

1li. 2 oz. fine thred at 10 s., 11s. 3d.;

5 pr. Gloves, 2s.;

6 doz. ½ Sisers at 2s., 13s.;

½ doz. Barbers Sisers at 6d., 3s.;

A box nedles, qt. about 3
  thousand, 1li. 10s.;

44 doz. yds. Floerd & Plain Ribin
  At 12s., 26li. 8s.;

20 yd. flowred Ribin at 5d., 8s, 4d.;

22 yd ¾ ferit Ribin at 4d., 7s. 7d.;

1 pc. ½ Cotton Ribin, 4s. 6d.;

2 yd ¼ Ribin at 6d., 1s. 1d.;

12 li. Knitting nedles at 12d., 12s.;

1 pr. Fishing boots, 12s.;

4 pr. Fr. Held shouse & 2 pr.
  Galotias 1li.;

6 flower boxes, 4 tin porringers, 1
  candle box, 1 Tinder box, 1
  Calender, 4 Candlesticks, 7
  driping pans, 4 fish plates, 1li.;

1 brase Skilit, 4s.;

27 m. 4d. Nayles at 2s. 6d., 3li. 7s.
  6d.;

4m. 6d. nayles at 3s. 8d., 14s. 8d.;

226 macherell lines at 9d., 8li. 9s. 6d.;

Erthen ware & wooden ware 3s.;

4m., 2ct. 12d. Nayles at 10s. ——m.,
  2 li. 2s.;

5 ct: 1: 14 li. Shot at 20s. –ct. 5li. 7s.
  6d.;

147li. French lines at 10d., 6li. 2s.
  6d.;

8 yd. ½ yellow Ribin at 6d., 4s. 3d.;

15 yd. bone lace at 4d., 5s.;

a percell of hat bands, ili. 15s.;

24m. ½ hobs at 21d. ——m., 24li. 2s.
  10 1/2d.;

11 Grose buttens at 21d., a percell
  loose buttons, 1li. 3s. 3d.;

1 ct. Suger, 1li.;

1li. ¼ Silke at 22s., 1li. 7s. 6d.;

3 Iron morters & 2 Iron pots, qt. 95
  li. At 3d., 1li. 3s. 9d.;

a parcel of Ginger in a Caske, 6s.;

1 brase morter, 9s.;

9 Cow bells at 8d., 2 pr. Pattens at
  12d., 8s.;

10 Chalke lines, 1s. 8d.;

7 doz. ½ Capl. Hooks at 18d., 11s.
  3d.;

2 Reme paper, 8s.;

a percell of white beades, 1s.;
34 li. Puder blue at 14d., 1li. 19s. 8d.;
114 li. Allspice at 21s., 9li. 19s. 6d.;
1 pr. Cards, 1s. 6d.;
33 li. Shott, 6s.;
4 large, 3 Smll. Salt Sellers, 8d.;
A bundle of Galome, 15s.;
3 Combs, 2s.;

10 Catticises at 12d., 3s.;
2 pr. Blu Stockins, 2s. 6d.;
A percell of Red filit & tape, 2s.;
1 qut. Pot, 1 pt. pot, 1 Gill pott, 4s.;
4 pr. Seales & waites, 37., 1 pr. Stiliards, 3s., 2 li.;
Cloves, mace, Cinomon & Nutmegs, 10s.;
3 black Silk Caps for men, 3s.

In the Shop Chamber

21 Stock locks at 8d. 1.4, 14s. 5 1/4d.,
30 ditto at 11d. 1/4., 1 li. 8s. 1 1/4d.;
42 ditto at 15d. ¾, 2li. 15s. 1 1/2d.;
9 ditto at 6d. ½, 14s. 7 1/2d.;
11 ditto at 22d. ½, 1li. 71/2 d.;
14 ditto at 25d. ½, 1 li. 9s. 9d.;
6 ditto at 31d. ½, 15s. 9d.;
45 Smll. Lines at 6d., 1 li. 2s. 6s.;
5 M. brase nayles at 9s. 9d., 2li. 8s. 9d.;
5 Candlesticks at 10d. ½, 4s. 4 ½ d.;
2 doz. Augers at 7s. 6d., 15s.;
13 carveing Tooles at 3d., 3s. 3d.;
5 paring Chisells at 6d. ¾, 2s. 9 ¾ d.;
19 Gouges & Chisells at 7d. ½, 11s. 10 1/2d.;
6 doz & 3 plaining Irons at 5s. Doz., 1li. 11s. 3d.;
Oct:2: 5li. Hooks & Twists at 48s., Ili. 6s 2d.;
18 Spring locks at 2s. 3d., 2li. 6d.;
3 Spring locks with. Screws at 2s. 9d., 8s. 3d.;
3 best ditto at 3s. 6d., 10s. 6d.;
6 Single Spr. Locks at 13d., 6s. 6d.;
12 warded outside chist lockes, 15s. 9d.;
155 li. Frying panes at 6d., 3li. 17s. 6d.;

23 outsid box locks at 6d.,
17 Reape hooks at 9d., 12s. 9d.;
10 ward cuberd locks at 9d. ¾. 8s. 1 ½ d.;
1 doz latches & Hatches, 6s. 6d.;
26 plaine cuberd locks at 6s., 13s.;
3 pr. Pinchers at 11d., 2s. 9d.;
8 pr. Nipers at 4d. ½, 3s.;
10 pr. Marking Irons at 15 d., 12s. 6s.;
2 doz. & tacks at d. —dz., 9d.;
½ doz. Shepe sheres at 19d. ½, 9s. 9d.;
1 doz. Shepe sheres, 16s. 6d.;
13 doz. ½ all Blades at 6d. —doz., 6s. 9d;
3 best box Irons at 3s. 6d., 10s. 6d.;
2 plaine box Irons at 18s., 3s.;
6 Stell Sawes at 3s. 3d., 19s. 6d.;
20 Sawes at 18d., 10s.;
7 doz. & 2 wte. haft knives at 8s., 2li. 17s. 4d.;
1 pr. Tongs & fire pan, 5s. 6d.;
2 doz. ½ horne haft knives at 4s., 10s.;
5 tilers hamers at 22de. ½, 9s. 4 1/2d.;
7 pr. Barbers Sisers at 6d., 3s. 6.;
4 doz. & 5 pr. Large Sisers at 3s., 13s. 3d.;
2 doz. 11 Glase bottles at 3s., 8s. 9d.;

4 doz. 3 Sorted hamers at 12s., 2li.
11s.;

3 doz. Speke Gimlets at 4s. 3d.,
12s. 9d.;

6 doz. 9 Small Gimlets at 12s., 13s.
6d.;

15 pr. Buttons at 19d. 1/2, 1li. 4s. 4
½ d.

4 Stared bridles at 3s. 3d., 13s.;

7 chafeing dishes at 12d., 7s.;

1 doz. Best wte. bridles 14s., 3d.;

½ doz. Ordinary ditto, 6s.;

11 bolls, 6d. ¾, 6s. 2¼ d.;

5 bl. Paline bridles at 14s. ¼, 5s. 11
½ d.;

11 dutch bridles at 25d. ½, 1li. 3s. 4
½ d.,

2 French ditto at 22d. ½, 3s. 9d.;

1 doz. Best Stirop leathers at 18s.
18s.;

8 Stirop leathers at 10d. ½, 7s.;

1 Grose of diaper Girt web, 1li. 2s.
6d.;

1 Grose fine paine ditto,
1li.3s. 3d.;

1 Grose ¼ ditto at 15s., 18s. 9d.;

7 pr. Swevell Stirop Irons at 16d.
½, 9s. 7 1/2d.;

1 doz. Boxhorse combes, 5s.;

11 horse combes at 2s. 9d. —doz.,
2s. 6 1/4d.;

3 pr. Plaine Stirop Irons at 10d. ½,
2s, 7 1/2d.;

11 horse brushes at 12d. ½, 11s. 5
1/2d.;

2 Grose Girt buckles at 8s. 3d., 16s.
6d.;

4 papers wte. buckles at 18d., 6s.;

11 curry combes at at 5d. ½, 5s. 1/
2d.;

4 best wte. Cury combes at 18d.
6s.;

5 wte. ditto at 15d., 6s. 3d.;

14 Files at 8d. ¼, 9s. 7 ½d.;

4 horse locks at 14d. ½, 4s. 10d.;

6 Twisted Snafells at 7d. ½, 3s.
9d.;

5 large plaine ditto at 6d., 2s. 6d.;

4 small ditto at 4d. ½, 1s. 6d.;

8 Smll. Padlocks at 9d., 6s.;

3 large ditto at 12d. ¾. 3s. 21/4d.;

4 tiling trowels at 12d., 4s.;

2 pointing trowels at 12d., 2s.;

45 pr. Plaine Soures at 6d. ¼, 1li.
3s. 5 ¼ d.;

3 pr. Joynted Spures at 7d. ½, 1s.
10 1/2d.;

287 Curtaine rings at 18d. — ct.,
4s. 4d.;

10 Curr Bitts at 22d. 1/2., 18s. 9d.;

12 pr. Bosses, 8s 3d.;

2 drawing knives at 14d., 2s., 4d.;

3 doz. 1 Shoue Spurs at 2s. 6d., 7s.
8 1/2d.;

3 shoue knives at 2d. ½, 7d. ½;

4 wimble bits & 1 Gimlet, 1s.;

1 brick Joynter, 4d.;

4 outside Chist lock at 10d.——, 3s.
4d.;

1 Chist lock, 10d.;

12 li. Pack thred at 12d.——, 14s.;

1 Cutting Knife, 6d.;

2 X Gernels at 8d., 1s. 4d.;

1 cow bell, 8d.;

1 halfe pt. pott, 1s.

14 yd ¾ Carsey at 3s. 6d., 2 li. 11s.
7 ½ yd.;

8 pcs. Blu linon, qt. 233 yd. ¾, at
9d., 8li. 15s. 3 ¾ d.;

37 yd ticking at 2d., 3 li. 14s.;

25 yd. ¾ yellow flanell at 18d., 1li
18s. 7 1/2d.;

61 yd ¾ fine doulas, and ½ pc. fine
Doulas, 13li.;

1 pc. Course Ticking, qt. 35 yds., at
12d., 1li. 15s.;

171 yd. Genting in 20 pls. &
Severll. Remnts. At 18d., 12li.
16s.

4 yd. ¾ peniston at 2s., 9s. 6d.;

45 yd. ¾ St. Petters linin at 15d., 2li. 17s. 2 1/4d.;

16 yd. ¼ Red flannell at 20d., 1 li., 7s. 1d.;

½ doz. Chusians at 2s., 12s.;

35 yd. Small Noyles at 9d., 1 li. 6s. 3d.;

18 yd. ¼ medrinix damaged at 4d., 6s. li.;

1 pc. Red Cotton, qi. 72 yd., at 21d., 6li. 6s.;

1 pc. Ditto, qt. 76 yd., at 21d., 6li. 13s.;

42 yd. medrinix at 9d., 1li. 11s. 6d.;

33 yd. St Petters Linon at 14d., 1li. 18s 6d.;

59 yd. ½ medriniz at 9d., 2li. 4s 7 ½ d.;

45 yd. ¾ broad linon at 18d., 3li. 8s. 7 ½ d.;

26 yd broad Linon at 15d., 1li. 12s 6d.;

94 yd Narow Brene at 15d., 5li. 17s. 6d.;

32 yd ¾ Longloses at 16d., 2 li. 3s. 8d.;

115 yd Vittery at 13d., 6li. 4s 7d.;

107 yds ditto damaged at 6d., 3 li. 11s. 4d.;

1 Ruge Eaten, 20s. 1 li.;

1 ditto, 1li. 4s.;

1 ditto, 16.;

1 ditto, 1li. 3s.;

70 yd Smll. Noyles at 9d., 2li. 12s. 6d.;

35 yd ½ Red Cotton at 2s., 3li. 11s.;

45 yd ½ St Petters linon at 16d., 3li. 8d.;

1 bolt Ranletts, qt. 70 yd., at 12d., 3li. 10s.;

62 yd Lockrom at 12d., 3li. 2s.;

1 pc. Course Ticking, qt. 35 yd., at 12d., 1li. 15s.;

16 yd ½ Medrinix at 9d., 12s. 4 ½ d.;

59 yd. Vittery damaged at 6d., 1 li. 9s. 6d.;

63 yd fine hall cloth at 16d., 4 li. 4s.;

13 doz. & 8 pr. Large Sisters at 3s., 2 li. 1s.;

4 doz. Smll. Sisters at 2s., 8s.;

4 doz. Large Combes at 4s. 6d., 18s.;

16 doz. Ditto at 3s. 6d., 2li. 16s.;

12 doz. ditto at 3s., 1 li. 16d.;

4 doz. ditto at 2s., 8s.;

9 white haft knives at 8d., 6s.;

6 bl. Haft knives at 4d., 2s.;

16 bl. Woden haft case knives at 4d., 5s. 4d.;

2 ct. ½ Clabords at 4s., 10s.;

20 barells Tarr at 4s. 6d., 4li. 10s.;

5 barells Oyle at 25s., 6li. 5s.;

1 Cask Nayles, qt. 0:0:25, ditto Qt. 1:1:34, 1 ditto, qt. 2:0:01 1 ditto, qt. 0:3:00, 1 ditto, qt. 1: 0:09, 1 ditto, qt. 1:0:05, 1 ditto Qt. 1:3:15, total 8:3:23, deDuct Tare, 0:3:23, Rest, 8:0: 00 at 46 s. 8d., 18li. 13s. 4d.;

1 Caske hobs, 6li.;

1 Cable, qt. 3ct: 3: 2li. At 25s., 4 li. 14s. 2d.;

48 ct: 0: 13li. Spas Iron at 20s. 48li. 2s. 4 ½ d.;

26:0:00 Lead at 20s., 25 li.;

2 doz. 3 Rubstones at 18d. — doz., 3s., 4 ½ d.;

35 doz. Erthen ware, 3li.;

1 barll. Yellow Oaker, qt, neat 2 ct: 0:17li. At 10s., 1 li. 1s. 6s.;

a percell of old Junke, 10li.;

1 Great beame Scales & 1 halfe hunDrd., 1li. 15s.;

1 Smll. Beame & 2 morters, 10s.;

2 netts damaged, 10s.;

Old rey in ye Garret, 3s.;

5 m. Red Oak hogshead staves at 25s., 6li. 5s.;

1 pr. Old hand screws, 10s.;
2pr. Stilliards, 1li. 5s.;
A percell of Rozin, 10s.;
1 longe Oare, 5s.;
Shod shoule, 1s. 6d.;

Old cask, 10s.;
1 Suger drawer, 1s. 6d.;
A percell Limestones on the
  wharfe, 8li.;

In the Uper Warehouse

3 ketles 95 li. 1.2, 15 potts 550 li. At
  25s. —ct., 7li. 4s.;
9 ct:2:2 li. Lead at 20s. — 9li. 10s.
  4d.;
1 Smll. Table. 1 Red carpet,
  10s.;
2 Curtaine rods & window
  Curtaines, 7s.;
1 Scritore & frame, 1li. 10s.;
2 Trunks, 15.;
1 old Cuberd & Red cloth, 6s.;
1 pr. Brase Andirons, 1 back, 1 pr.
  Tongs, 13s.;
1 looking glase, 6s.;
1 large white Quilt, 2li.;
1 ditto, 1li. 10s.;
1 ditto, 1 li.;
1 pr, Shetts, 1li.;
1 pr. ditto, 1li.;
1 pr. ditto, 1li.2s.;
1 pr. ditto, 18s.;
1 pr. ditto, 1li. 2s.;
1 pr. ditto, 1li. 2s.;
1 pr. ditto, 1li. 5s.;
1 pr. ditto, 1li. 2s.;
1 pr. ditto, 1li. 2s.;
1 pr. ditto, 1li. 2s.;
1 pr. ditto, 1li.;
1 pr. ditto, 1li.;
1 pr. ditto, 18s.;
1 pr. ditto, 12s.;
1 pr. ditto, 18s.;
1 pr. ditto, 18s.;
1 pr. ditto, 1li 4s.;
1 pr. ditto, 16s.;
½ pr. ditto, 8s.;
½ pr. ditto, 18s.;

17 Napkins, 1 large table cloth & a
  Towell all of Damaske, 4li.;
9 diaper Napkins & 1 Table Cloth,
  15s.;
1 doz. Ditto & 1 Table Cloth, 1li.
  2s.;
1 doz. Ditto & 1 Table Cloth, 1li.
  2s.;
1 doz. Ditto & 1 Table Cloth, 18,
  18.s.;
1 doz. Diaper Napkins & a Table
  Cloth, 17s.;
1 Table Cloth, 8s.;
2 pillowbers at 2s. 6d.—, 5s.;
86 hower Glases at 6d., 2li. 3s.;
7 papers Manchester at 4s. 1li. 8d.;
1 pc. Filiting, 2s.;
½ li. Fine thred at 10 s., 5s.;
128 li. Colered & browne thread at
  2s. 8d., 17 li. 1s. 4d.;
25 Grose & 8 doz. Gimp coat
  buttons at 21d., 2li. 4s 11d.;
2 Grose brest dotto at 16d., 2s 8d.;
1 pc. Slesy Holland, 15s.;
1 pr. Gerles Gren Stockings, 1s.
  2d.;
A percell of hat bands & linings,
  5s.;
1 pr. Bandelers, 6s.;
31 old fashioned high Crowned
  hats at 18d., 2li. 6s. 6d.;
1 low ditto, 1s. 6d.;1 ditto, 1li. 2s.; 2
  yd ½ Curle at 2s. 5d., 6s ½d.;
28 wooden blocks at 4d., 9s. 4d.
1 Ruge, 18s.;
2 Red Cushian, 5s.;
1 Red Ruge, 10.;
old Curtaines, &c.. in a Chist, 10s.;

1 Silke cradle ruge, 12s.;

1 Canvis Sute, 2s. 6d.;

1 large wainscot chist, 18d.;

1 old chist 7 two old Trunks, 8s.;

1 Chaire & 1 Table, 6s.;

1 pr. Weo. Black shouse, 3s. 6d.;

4 tin pans, 3s.;

1 watch Glase, 1s.;

3 Sase pans, 2 tunells & 2 peper boxes, 1s.6d.;

1 bed, bolster & pillow, 2li. 15s.;

1 bedsted & matt, 10s.;

1 pr. Grene Curtains & valients, 1 li.;

2 Red Fethers, 5s.;

1 cod line, 1s. 3d.;

1 Cloake bage, 3s.;

oatmell, 6s.

In the Lower Warehouse

120 hh. Or thereabouts of salt at 8s., 48li.;

17 m. shingle at 5s. ——, 4li. 5s.;

4:1:9 Stelle att 50s. ——, 10li. 16s. 6d.;

1:2:8 of Old Iron at 12s.——, 19s.; neat 20s. 6li. 8s.;

1 Cask Starch, qt. 159 li. Neate at 3d., 1li. 6d.;

7 doz, 2/3 Glase botles at 2s. 9d., 1li. 1s. 1d.;

2 barll. Mattasows at 30s. 3li.;

1 pr. Great hand screw, 3li.;

12 whip Sawes at 9s., 5li. 8s.;

Beans, 3s;

1 Chist drawers, 1li. 10s.;

Wheate, 6s.;

1 pr. Great Stilliards, li. 5s.;

1 pr. Smll. Stilliards defective, 5s.;

219 fot Bords, 3s. ——, 2 harpn. Irons 12d. ——, 8s. 7d.;

olde caske, 10s.;

Graine, the Sweeping of the Chamber, 3s.;

part of an old Clock, 10s.

In the Old Hall

9 turkey worke chaires without. backs, 5s. ——, 2li. 5s.;

4 ditto wth. Backs at 8s. ——, 1li. 12s.;

6 low Turky worke ditto wth. Backs, 8s.——, 2li. 8s.;

1 Tables, 20s ——, 1 ditto, 5s., 2li. 5s.;

1 Carpet, 15.;

1 pr. Large brase Andirons, 1li. 10s.;

1 Large looking Glase & brases, 2li. 5s.;

3 Curtaine rods & Curtains for windows, 15s.;

2 Cadlesticks, 5s.;

1 Glase Globe, 1s.

In the Red Bedchamber

8 Red branched chaires wth Covers, 16s. ——, 6li. 8s.;

1 Table Cloth, 5s.;

1 diaper Table Cloth, 8s.;

1 ditto, 8s.;

1 Cuberd Cloth, 5s.;

1 ditto, 3s.;

1 Calico Counter pain, 8s.;

18 pilobers & napkins;

4 towells & a Cuberd Cloth, 10s.;
1 Child's Bed, 1s.;

1 Red Cushion, 1s.

In the Two Closets Adjoyning

10 doz. Erth. Ware, 15 large, 33

Small tins pans for Sugar Cakes, 16 qt. botles, 3 Erthen pots, 3 long mum Glases, 2li. 10s.

In the Glase Chamber

1 bed sted & appurtenances, 1li.;
1 fether bed, bolster 7 2 pillows, 4 li. 10s.;
1 pr. Curtains & Valients, 2li. 10s.;
1 Red Ruge, 8s.;
1 large white blanket, 8s.;
1 Stript blanket, 3s.;
1 Silke blanket, 12s.;
1 large Striped blanket, 8s.;
1 Smll. Blanket, 4s.;
1 pr. shettes, 14.;
2 pillowbers, 2s.;
6 parogon Chaires at 10s.——, 3li.;

2 longe Stooles, at 10s.,——, 1li.;
2 stands at 4s., 8s.;
1 Table, 1 linsy carpet, 10s.;
1 Calico Carpet, 3s.;
1 looking Glase, 7s.;
1 pomander basket, 10s.;
1 Ouall fine wicker basket, 3s.;
1 painted Couberd Cloth, 3s.;
1 Glase frame for Glase worke, 1li.;
3 Curtain rods & window Curtains, 10s.;
1 pr. Andirons wtj. Brases, 12s.;
1 pr. brasse fire pan & Tongs, 8s

In the Corner Chamber

1 bedsted, 10s.;
2 Ruges, 1li. 12s.;
1 pr. Curtains & Valients & Rods, 2li.;
1 Grene Counter paine, 5s.;
1 pr. Sheets, 12s.;
1 bolster & pillow, 1li.;
1 wainscot Chist, 10s.;
1 Table & Grene Carpet, 12s.;
8 yd bengall at 9d., 6s.;
7 yd doulas at 20d., 11s. 8d.;
4 yd ½ Stript linin at 16d., 6s.;
1 yd 1.2 Serge at 3s., 4s. 6d.;
7 yd Narr. Brene at 15d., 8s. 9d.;
1 yd 3/8 Grene Say at 3s. 6d., 4s 9 3/4d.;
8 pcs. Tape at 9d., 6s.;
3 yd Lockrom at 9d., 2s.;

1 yd ¾ ticking at 20d., 2s. 11s.;
A Remnant of Holland, 1s.;
19 yd high brene at 2s., 1li. 18s.;
1 yd Red Cotton, 1s. 9d.;
3 yd course Holland at 18d., 4s. 6d.;
3 yd 1.2 narr Cloth at 8d., 2s. 4d.;
7/8 yd Linon at 18d., 1s. 3 3/4d.;
2 yd ¾ fustian at 12d., 2s. 9d.;
A Remt. Fine Canvis, 7d.;
1 yd ½ Linon at 18d. ——, 2s. 3d.;
1 yd wte Calico, 1s.;
1 yd ½ linon at 18s., 2s. 3d.;
1 yd ½ Slesy at 12d., 1s. 6d.;
1 yd colerd Fustian, 1s;
1 pr. Red. Weo. Stockings, 1s. 6d.;
2 old Chaires at 2s., 4s.;
1 bundle of Remnants, 1s.

In the Counting House & Entery

1 dozn, pins. 9s.;
1 dozn. Ditto, 10s.;
2 li. Colerd thread at 2s. 8d., 5s. 4d.;
3 li. ½ wormseed at 4s. 6d.——, 15s. 9d.;
¼ Grose Girt web at 22s. —— Grose,
12 books Carell upon Jobe, 1 Grt. bible & Psalme Booke, 3li.;
1 booke Markham's Gramer, 2s.;
3 pls. Turtle Shell, 1s. 6d.;
1 Snafle bitt, 1 pr. Spures, 1s.;

2 pr. Dtirop Irons, 2s.;
1 Inkhorne, 6d.;
1 Caine, 3s.;
1 Turned Stick, 2s. 5s.;
1 Rapier Tipt wth Silver, 15s., 1 ditto, 5s. 1li.;
4 musketts, 2li.;
1 pr. pistols & holsters, 1 plush Sadlelayed wth. Silver lace & SadleCloth, 5li.;
1 Caduco box, 2s.;
1 buff belt wth. Silver buckles, 1li.;
2 old bells, 2s.

In the Hall Chamber

1 bed Sted, 5s.;
1 pr. Red Curtaines & Valients, 2li. 10s.;
1 Ruges, 16s.;
1 pr. Shetts, 10s., 1 pillow, 5s., 15s.;
1 flock bed & fether bolster, 16s.;
2 Ruges, 12s.;
1 Trundle bedsted & Curtaine rods, 7s.;
4 Trunks, 1 li.;
1 Chist drawers & Carpet, 10s.;
1 Table & 1 Carpet, 8s.;
1 looking Glase, 5s.;
1 Curtain Rod & window Curtaine, 3s.;

2 pr. white Calico Curtaines, Valients, tester Clothes & 6 Covers for Chaires, 2li. 5s.;
14 old Napkins at 9d., 10s. 6d.;
19 new diaper small ditto at 9d. 14s. 3d.;
2 Calico Side bord Clothes, 6s.;
3 Calico ditto, 6s.;
12 towells at 6d., 6s.;
More 35 diaper & other Napkins at 9d., 1li. 6s. 3d.;
7 Table Clothes at 5s., 1li. 15s.;
8 ditto at 2s. 6d., 1li.;
15 ditto, 18s.

Wareing Clothes

1 Tropeing Scarfe & hat band, 1 li. 10s.;
1 Cloake, 2li.;
1 Cloth Coat wth. Silver lace, 2li.;
1 Camlet Coate, 15.;
1 old bla. Farendin Sute, 1li.;
1 black Cloake, 2li.;
1 velvet Coate, 2li. 10s.;
1 old Tabey dublet, 5s.;
1 old fashioned duch Sattin dublet, 15s.;
1 black Grogrin Cloake, 1 li. 10s.;
3 Quilts, 3s.;

1 hatt, 15s.;
1 pr. Goldn Topt. Gloues, 10s.;
1 pr. Imbroiderd ditto, 8s.;
1 pr. bl. Fringed Gloues, 3s.;
1 pr. bl. & Gold fringed ditto, 3s.;
1 pr. new Gloves, 2s.;
2 pr. Gloves, 2s.;
3 pr. old Silke Stockings, 8s.;
2 belts and 1 Girdle, 2li.;
1 Sattin Imbroidred wascot wth. Gold, 7c., 3li.;
1 yd. ¾ Persian Silke at 5s. 6d., 9s. 7 1/2d.

In the Counting House & Entry More

1 Table, 5s.;
1 Carpet, 10s.;
1 Chaire, 4s.;
1 desk & Cuberd, 5s.;

In the Hall

1 Looking Glase, 7s.;
3 tables, 1li. 2s.;
1 Turky worke Carpet, 1li. 5s.;
8 leather Chaires at 5s., 2li.;
5 Stra bottomed Chaires, 5s.;
1 old wicker Chaire, 2s.;
1 napkin presse, 1li. 10s.;
1 Glase Case, 6s.;
1 Clocke, 2li.;
1 Scritore or Spice box, 6s.;
1 Screne wth. 5 leaves & Covering, 15s.;

In the Maides Chamber

1 bed 7 bolster, 3li.;
1 bedsted, 2s.;
1 new Bed & Case, 5li.;
1 Cushian 7 s 2 Stoole Covers, 3s.;
1 pillion & Cloth, 1li.;
1 pr old Shetts, 4s.;
3 pr. Shetts, 4s. 2li. 8s.;
1 pr. new Shetts, 1li. 2s.;
5 Shetts at 8s., 2li.;
3 Shetts at 4s., 12s.;
1 Table Cloth, 3s.;
1 old Sheet, 2s.;
1 wainscott chist, 5s.;

In the Garretts

12 Reame ½ paper at 4s., 2li. 10s.;
1 bolt Noyles, qt. 89 @ ¼ is 130 Yd. ¾ at 16d.—, 8li. 14s. 4d.;
1 Sadle, bridle & brest plate, 1li. 5S.;

1 pr. bandelers, 3s.;
Seling wax, 3s.;
1 Cushian, 6d.;
3 flasketts & to baskets, 5s.;
1 Iron bound Chist, 5s.;

1 old Smll. Turky worke Carpet, 3s.;
1 Armed Chaire, 2s.;
1 Stand, 1s 6d.;
1 Great Candlestick, 1li.;
1 pr. Grt. Dogs & 1 Iron Back, 2li. 5s.;
5 Cushians at 4s. pr, 1li.;
1 window Curtaine & rod, 6s.;
1 pr. Tongs, Shoule fire & Smll. Tongs & Toster, 7s.;
Glases in the Glase case, 5s.

2 Cotton Ironning Clothes, 3s.;
1 Calico Cuberd Cloth, 1s. 6d.;
Starch & a bage, 2s.;
2 boxes, 2s.;
1 Rat eaten Carpet, 5s.;
1 old Bed Tick, 7s.;
1 pr. old Stript Curtains & CarPets, 8s.;
1 Chist, 4s.;
1 Small. Brase Ketle tine, 6s.;
1 lanthorne, 5s.;
1 Calender & 1 plate
1 Wooden Voider, 1s. 6d.;
1 bird Cage, 2s.

2 pc, pole daine & a Rmnt, qt. 80 Yds., 4 li.;
150 li. Fr. Lines at 10d. —, 6li. 5s.;
1 pr. large brase Andions, 1li.;
1 Candlebox, &c., 2s.;

1 pillion & cloth, 5s.;
1 old port mantle, 1s.;
2 Childr. Blankets, 10s.;
1 Carpet, 8s.;
1 wainscot chist, 5s.;
1 pin Chest, 2s. 6d., 7s. 6d.;
Gloves 7 Some Lumber, 5s.;
2 old Ruge, 3s.;
1 hamaker, 5s.; 8s.;

1 Auger weges, & chisles, 5s.;
5 Shetts at 5s., 1li. 5s.;
1 fine Shett, 7s.;
19 napkins & towels, 12s.;
about 100li. Hogs & beffe Suet at
   2d., 16s. 8d.;
meale Troues, &c., 6s.;
old Bed steds, 10s.;
old cask, 5s.

In the Entry Below
1 Round table & 1 Gren Carpet,
   15s.;

2 Great Chaires & 4 high Chaires,
   15s.;
1 Cuberd & cuberd Cloth, 8s.

In the Closet
Erthen ware & a Glase bottle, 5s.;

a parcel of honey, 5s.

In the Peuter Rome
4 boles, 1 tray & Erth. Ware.
   10s.;
1 limeback & Iron pott, 2li.;
a percell of old Iron, 5s.;

1 large defective driping pan, 2s.
   6D.;
4 trayes, 1 platter, 2s., Erthen ware,
   18s., 3s. 6d.;
1 leather Jack.

In the Kitchin
7 Spitts, 1li. 5s.;
2 Racks, 1 li.;
1 Jack & waite, 12s.;
2 Iron potts & 2 pr. pot hooks, 1 li.;
4 Tramells & 1 Iron barr, 15s.;
1 pr. Iron doges, 10s.;
2 fenders, 4s.;
1 pr. la. Tonges, 4s.;
1 Iron driping pan, 3s.;
1 Iron back, 1li.;
1 Iron Ketle, 6s.;
4 box Irons, 8s.;
5 old Iron potts, 1li. 4s.;
1 pr. Fetters, 3s.;
2 Fring pans, 5s.;

3 Grid Irons, 1 pr. pot hookes &
   treuet, 7s.;
1 Slut or larance, 1s.;
1 Cleuer & a shredding knife, 4s.;
a hooke * Iron Squers, 2s.;
1 Chafeing Dish, 1s. 6d.;
1pr. bellows, 1s. 6d.;
1 warmeing pan, 2s.;
38 pls. Tin Ware, 1s. 4d.;
2 Iron Candlesticks & a toster, 5s.;
2 tables, 5s. 4 old Chaires, 6d., 7s.;
Erthen ware, 6s.;
453li. Peuter of all Sorts at 12d.,
   22li. 13s.;
24 li. Brase in Small ware at 20s.,
   2li.;

1 Coper Ketle, qt. 30 li. At 2s., 3li.;
2 brase Ketlesm qt. 57li. At 12d.,
   2li. 17s.;
1 brase Stew pan, 6s.;
3 bell mettle Skilets, qt. 25l., 1li.
   5s.;

1 payle, 1 bole & other wood.
   LumBer, 5s.; 2 Cases & 7 knives,
   12s.;
1 Slick Stone, 1s. 6d.

In the Wash House
1 Peuter Still, 10s.;
1 Coper, 4li.;

Tubes, a Table & Lumber, 5s.;
1 pr. Andirons 7 Iron eake,
   &c., 5s.

In the Stable
1 horse, 4li.;
1 Cow, 3li., wth. the hay, 7li.;

2 forks, 1 Tray, 2 Grain payles, 6s.;
1 axe, 3s.;
1 Cow at Is. Williams, 2li. 10s.

In the Seller Under the House
Old Caske, 1li.;
24 qt. Jugs, 4s.;
24 Glase botles, 5s. 6d.;

4 Jares, 4s.;
1 Ert. Pot. 1s.;
44li. Castle Sope at 6d., 1li. 2s.

In the Closet of the Kitchin Chamber
43 pls. Erthen ware at 2s. —doz.,
   7s., 2d.;
19 Glase cups & Smll. Botles, 2s.;
1 pr. Shouse, 4s.;

5 qt. botles, 15d.;
1 Stone Juge, 2s., 3s. 3d.;
3 woden boxes, 1s.;
1 Tin Candlestick, 1s.;
1 Cap for a Clock of belmetle, 2s.

In the Ktichin Chamber
1 large Scritore, 5li.;
1 bedsted & Teaster, 1li.;
1 fether bed & bolster cased & 2
   pillows, 6li. 10s.;
1 pr. Sad Colerd Curtaines &
   valients & counter paine &
   rods, 3li.;
1 worsted Stript Ruge, 3li.;
2 pillobers, 2s.;
1 pr. Blanketts, 1li.;
1 pr. Shetts, 1li.;

1 bedsted & Teaser & head piece,
   1li.;
1 fether bed & bolster cased & 2
   pillows, 4li.;
1 pr. Red Serge Curtains valients
   & Rods , 3li. 10s.;
1 Quilt of Calico Colerd &
   flowred, 1li. 10s.;
1 Red Ruge, 10s.;
3 blanketts, 1li.;
1 Pallet bedsted, Teaser & hed
   Piece, 1li.;

1 fether bed & bolster, 1 pillow, 3li. 10s.;

2 Curtaines & smll. Valients, 15s.;

2 Coverleds, 1li. 12s.;

1 pr. blankets, 1li.;

1 Shett, 5s.;

1 Stoole, 1s.;

7 Chaires Sad Colerd & 1 Grt. Chaire, 4s, 1li. 12s.;

1 Table wth. a drawer, 8s.;

2 Stands, 4s.;

1 Close Stoole, 6s.;

8 window Curtains & 4 Rods, 16s.;

1 looking Glases & brases, 1li. 5s.

1 Chist of Drawers, 25s. & Cloth, 4s., 1li. 9s.;

2 pr. bla., 1pr. Speckled Stockings, 12s.;

4 pr. old Stockings, 4s.;

1 pr. andirons wth brases, 10s.;

1 pr. tongs & fire pan, 4s.;

1 back, 12s.;

1 Round fender, 5s.;

1pr. bellows, 1s 6d.;

1 Japan Trunkw, 8d.;

5 neckclothes at 9d., 3s.;

4 night caps at 15., 5s.;

17 bands at 6d., 8s. 6d.;

2 pockets hanchesters, 1s.;

1 pr. Gloves, 1s.;

3 fustian wescoats, 6s.;

3 pr. ditto drawers, 8s.; 10s.;

6 Shirts, 1li.12s.

Goods that Came From England From Mre. John Iues

Pr. Capt. Gener. 6 pls. penistonamo. To wth. charges, 18li. 17s. 7d., wth. advance, 50li. —-Ct., 28li. 6s.4d.

Pr. Capr. Edwards. 20 pls. blue linon & a percell of Spice amounting to wth. Charges, 48li. 17s. 6d., wth. adva. At 50li. —- Ct.,73 li. 6s. 3d.

In the Closet in Kitchin Chamber

18 Glass botles, 4s., 6d.;

10 pls. Erthen ware, 2s. 6d.

2 haire bromes, 2s 6d.;

1 knife tipt wth. Silver, 1s 3d.;

1 woden Screne, 3s.;

3 yd. bla. Broadcloth at 10s., 1li. 10s.;

35 Qn.* mercht. Fishat 9s., 15li. 15.;

½ QN. Pollack at 5s. 6d.;

22 barlls. Porke at 43., 47li. 6s.;

2 laced bands, 19s.;

2 pich pots, 8s.;

1 warehouse at Winter Island, 6li.;

1 Great Beame Scales & 1/2ct. waites, 1li. 10s.;

112li. Lead & 98 li. Spa Iron, 1li. 17s. 6d.;

137 li. Hide, gamages at 2d., 1li. 2s 10d.;

1780 fot Bords at 2s. 6d.—-ct. 2li. 4s. 5d.;

1 heffer, 1 Stere & a Cow aprized by Edward & Jno. Richards, 5li. 5s.

THE HOUSE & LAND yt was Jno. Gatchells wth. the appurtenances, 115li.;

the house & land yt was Jno. GatchElls now Wm. Furners, 60li.;

the dwelling house & land nere Micall Coas, 40li.;

2 oxe Yaokes wth. bowes, 4s.;
2 hows, 1peak ax & forks, 5s.;
1 barr Iron, 5s.;
1 load hay, 20s., 1li. 5s.;

1 old house & land formerly
   Hudsons according to Towne
   Grant,
aprized by Jno. Lege & Ambrise
   Gayle, 2li.;
total, 219li. 14s.

At Boston: The Warhouse & Ground

200li.;
1056 ounces ½ pcs. of eight, 6s.
   8d., 352 li. 3s.4d.;
2 Cloakes, 2li.;
an old Trunke, a hat & wax, &c.,
   6s. 8d.;
aprized by Eliak. Huchenson &
   Jer. Dumer, 554li. 10s.;
3 pipes Madara Wine at 11li., not
   being filled up, 33li.;*Quintal
In mony of Petter Millers freight,
   2li. 16s.
Brought home in Katch Jno. &
   William: 130 bushells Indian
   corne, At 18d., 9li. 15s.;
33 bushells Rey at 3s., 4li. 19s.;
25 bushells ½ wheate at 4s., 5li. 2s.;
1 barll. Porke, 2li.;
3 barells Beffe at 25s., 3li. 15s.;
1 plaine Ruge, 10s.;
15 hower Glases, bad, 5s.;
4 pr. Stirop Irons & Lethers, 7s.;
3 locks at 25d., 6s. 4 1/2d.;
6 ditto at 11d. 1/4d. 1/4., 5s. 1 1/
   2d.;
4 ditto at 8d. ¼, 2s. 9d.;
6 hand saws at 18d., 9s.;
11 trunk locks at 10d., 9s. 2d.;
6 box outsid locks, 6d., 3s.;
4 Cuberd locks at 6d., 2s.;
1 doz. Combs at 2s., 2s.;

1 doz. Ditto at 3s., 3s.;
1 doz. Ditto at 3s. 6d., 3s 6d.;
3 pr. paragon bodys at 8s., 1li. 4s.;
2 doz. Reap hooks at 9s., 18.;
12 duble Girts, 9s.;
1 pr. Shetts a 16s., 16s.; 2li. 16s.
1 pr. Shetts at 10s., 10s.;
1 pr. ditto at 36s. 2 bredths ½, 1li.
1 pr. ditto at 30s., 3 bredths, 1li.
   10s.;
1 pr. ditto at 30s., 3 bredths, 1li.
   10s.;

The land whereon the house
   commonly called Capt. Jno.
   Corwins stands, 35li.

The Katch John & William wth.
   her appurtenances, 80li.;
1 old Mainsayle of Katch
   Penelopy, 1li. 10s.

This Inventory amounting to five
   thousand nine hundred Sixty
   foure pounds nineteen shillgs,
   & one peny 4/4d. aprized as
   money by us.

   Barthl. Gedney
   Benja. Browne
   John Higginson, Junr,
   Timo. Lindall.

Source: *Essex County Quarterly Court Files*, Vol. XLIV, leaf 95.

Gov. Sir William Phips brought with him a new Massachusetts Charter upon his arrival in May 1692. This charter redefined the government and responsibilities of the Colony of Massachusetts and the new nature of its relationship with the Crown as a royal colony. From the arrival of this charter in 1692 until the American Revolution, Massachusetts operated according to the guidelines and conditions herein described.

Second Massachusetts Bay Charter (Oct. 7, 1691)

... And Wee doe further for Vs Our Heires and Successors Will Establish and ordeyne that from henceforth for ever there shall be one Governour One Leivtenent or Deputy Governour and One Secretary of Our said Province or Territory to be from time to time appointed and Commissionated by Vs Our Heires and Successors and Eight and Twenty Assistants or Councillors to be advising and assisting to the Governour of Our said Province or Territory for the time being as by these presents is hereafter directed and appointed which said Councillors or Assistants are to be Constituted Elected and Chosen in such forme and manner as hereafter in these presents is expressed. ... *And Our* Will and Pleasure is that the Governour of Our said Province from the time being shall have Authority from time to time at his discretion to assemble and call together the Councillors or Assistants of Our said Province for the time being and that the said Governour with the said Assistants or Councillors or Seaven of them at the least shall and may from time to time hold and keep a Council for the ordering and directing the Affaires of Our said Province *And further* Wee Will and by these presents for Vs Our Heires and Successors doe ordeyne and Grant that there shall and may be convened held and kept by the Governour for the time being vpon every last Wednesday in the Moneth of May every yeare for ever and at all such other times as the Governour of Our said Province shall think fitt and appoint a great and Generall Court of Assembly Which said Great and Generall Court of Assembly shall consist of the Governour and Councill or Assistants for the time being and of such Freeholders of Our said Province or Territory as shall be from time to time elected or deputed by the Major parte of the Freeholders and other Inhabitants of the respective Townes or Places who shall be present at such Elections Each of the said Townes and Places being hereby impowered to Elect and Depute Two Persons and noe more to serve for and represent them respectively in the said Great and Generall Court or Assembly To which

Great and Generall Court or Assembly to be held as aforesaid Wee
do hereby for Vs Our Heires and Successors give and grant full
power and authority from time to time to direct appoint and
declare what Number each County Towne and Place shall Elect
and Depute to serve for and represent them respectively in the said
Great and Generall Court or Assembly *Provided* alwayes that noe
Freeholder or other Person shall have a Vote in the Election of
Members to serve in any Greate and Generall Court or Assembly
to be held as. aforesaid who at the time of such Election shall not
have an estate of Freehold in Land within Our said Province or
Territory to the value of Forty Shillings per Annum at the least or
other estate to the value of Forty pounds Sterl' And that every
Person who shall be soe elected shall before he sitt or Act in the said
Great and Generall Court or Assembly take the Oaths mentioned in
an Act of Parliament made in the first yeare of Our Reigne
Entituled an Act for abrogateing of the Oaths of Allegiance and
Supremacy and appointing other Oaths and thereby appointed to
be taken instead of the Oaths of Allegiance and Supremacy and
shall make Repeat and Subscribe the Declaration mentioned in the
said Act before the Governour and Lievtenant or Deputy
Governour or any two of the Assistants for the time being who
shall be therevnto authorized and Appointed by Our said
Governour and that the Governour for the time being shall have
full power and Authority from time to time as he shall Judge neces-
sary to adjourne Prorogue and dissolve all Great and Generall
Courts or Assemblyes met and convened as aforesaid And Our
Will and Pleasure is and Wee doe hereby for Vs Our Heires and
Successors Grant Establish and Ordeyne that yearly once in every
yeare for ever hereafter the aforesaid Number of Eight and
Twenty Councillors or Assistants shall be by the Generall Court or
Assembly newly chosen that is to say Eighteen at least of the
Inhabitants of or Proprietors of Lands within the Territory formerly
called the Collony of the Massachusetts Bay and four at the least of
the Inhabitants of or Proprietors of Lands within the Territory formerly called New Plymouth and three at the least of the
Inhabitants of or Proprietors of Land within the Territory formerly
called the Province of Main and one at the least of the Inhabitants
of or Proprietors of Land any of them shall or may at any time hereafter be removed or displaced from their respective Places or Trust
of Councillors or Assistants by any Great or Generall Court or
Assembly And that if any of the said Councillors or Assistants shall
happen to dye or be removed as aforesaid before the Generall day

of Election That then and in every such Case the Great and Generall Court or Assembly at their first sitting may proceed to a New Election of one or more Councillors or Assistants in the roome or place of such Councillors or Assistants soe dying or removed And Wee doe further Grant and Ordeyne that it shall and may be lawfull for the said Governour with the advice and consent of the Councill or Assistants from time to time to nominate and appoint Judges Commissioners of Oyer and Terminer Sheriffs Provosts Marshalls Justices of the Peace and other Officers to Our Council and Courts of Justice belonging *Provided* alwaves that noe such Nomination or Appointment of Officers be made without notice first given or summons yssued out seaven dayes before such Nomination or Appointment vnto such of the said Councillors or Assistants as shall be at that time resideing within Our said Province *And Our Will and Pleasure* is that the Governour and Leivtenant or Deputy Governour and Councillors or Assistants for the time being and all other Officers to be appointed or chosen as aforesaid shall before the Vndertaking the Execution of their Offices and Places respectively take their severall and respective. Oaths for the due and faithfull perforrnance of their duties in their severall and respective Offices and Places and alsoe the Oaths appointed by the, said Act of Parliament made in the first yeare of Our Reigne to be taken instead of the Oathes of Allegiance and Supremacy and shall make repeate and subscribe the Declaration mentioned in the said Act before such Person or Persons as are by these presents herein after appointed. . . . *And further* Our Will and Pleasure is and Wee doe hereby for Vs Our Heires and Successors Grant Establish and Ordaine That all and every of the Subjects of Vs Our Heires and Successors which shall goe to and Inhabit within Our said Province and Territory and every of their Children which shall happen to be born there or on the Seas in goeing thither or returning from thence shall have and enjoy all Libertyes and Immunities of Free and naturall Subjects within any of the Dominions of Vs Our Heires and Successors to all Intents Constructions and purposes whatsoever as if they and every of them were borne within this Our *Realme* of England and for the greater Ease and Encouragement of Our Loveing Subjects Inhabiting our said Province or Territory of the Massachusetts Bay and of such as shall come to Inhabit there Wee doe by these presents for vs Our heires and Successors Grant Establish and Ordaine that for ever hereafter there shall be a liberty of Conscience allowed in the Worshipp of God to all Christians (Except Papists) Inhabiting or which shall

Inhabit or be Resident within our said Province or Territory ... *And whereas* Wee judge it necessary that all our Subjects should have liberty to Appeale to vs our heires and Successors in Cases that may deserve the same Wee doe by these presents Ordaine that incase either party shall not rest satisfied with the Judgement or Sentence of any Judicatories or Courts within our said Province or Territory in any Personall Action wherein the matter in difference doth exceed the value of three hundred Pounds Sterling that then he or they may appeale to vs Our heires and Successors in our or their Privy Councill Provided such Appeale be made within Fourteen dayes after the Sentence or Judgement given and that before such Appeale be allowed Security be given by the party or parties appealing in the value of the matter in Difference to pay or Answer the Debt or Damages for the which Judgement or Sentence is given With such Costs and Damages as shall be Awarded by vs Our Heires or Successors incase the Judgement or Sentence be affirmed ... *And* wee doe for vs our Heires and Successors Giue and grant that the said Generall Court or Assembly shall have full power and Authority to name and settle annually all Civill Officers within the said Province such Officers Excepted the Election and Constitution of whome wee have by these presents reserved to vs Our Heires and Successors or to the Governor of our said Province for the time being and to Settforth the severall Duties Powers and Lymitts of every such Officer to be appointed by the said Generall Court or Assembly and the formes of such Oathes not repugnant to the Lawes and Statutes of this our Realme of England as shall be respectiuely Administered vnto them for the Execution of their severall Offices and places And alsoe to impose Fines mulcts Imprisonments and other Punishments And to impose and leavy proportionable and reasonable Assessments Rates and Taxes vpon the Estates and Persons of all and every the Proprietors and Inhabitants of our said Province or Territory to be Issued and disposed of by Warrant vnder the hand of the Governor of our said Province for the time being with the advice and Consent of the Councill for Our service in the necessary defence and support of our Government of our said Province or Territory and the Protection and Preservation of the Inhabitants there according to such Acts as are or shall be in force within our said Province and to dispose of matters and things whereby our Subjects inhabitants of our said Province may be Religously peaceably and Civilly Governed Protected and Defended soe as their good life and orderly Conversation may win the Indians Natives of the Country to the knowledge and obedience of the onely true God and Saviour of Mankinde and the Christian Faith which his Royall Majestie our Royall Grandfather king Charles the first in his said Letters Patents declared was his Royall Intentions And the Adventurers free Possession to be the Princepall end of the said Plantation And for the better secureing and maintaining Liberty of Conscience hereby granted to all persons at any time being and resideing within our said Province or Territory as aforesaid *Willing* Commanding and Requireing and by these presents for vs Our heires and Successors Ordaining and appointing that all such Orders Lawes Statutes and Ordinances Instructions and Directions as shall be soe made and published vnder our Seale of our said Province or Territory shall be Carefully and duely observed kept and performed and put in Execution according to the true intent and meaning of these presents *Provided* alwaies and Wee doe by these presents for vs Our Heires and Successors Establish and Ordaine that in the frameing and passing of all such Orders Laws Statutes and Ordinances and in all Elections and Acts of Government whatsoever lo be passed or done by the said Generall Court or Assembly or in Councill the Governor of our said Province or Territory of the Massachusetts Bay in New England for the time being shall have the Negative voice and that without his consent or Approbation sig-nified and declared in Writeing no such Orders Laws Statutes Ordinances Elections or other Acts of Government whatsoever soe to be made passed or done by the said Generall Assembly or in Councill shall be of any Force effect or validity anything herein con-tained to the contrary in anywise notwithstanding *And* wee doe for vs Our Heires and Successors Establish and Ordaine that the said Orders Laws Statutes and Ordinances be by the first opportunity after the makeing thereof sent or Transmitted vnto vs Our Heires and Successors vnder the Publique Seale to be appointed by vs for Our or their approbation or Disallowance And that incase all or any of them shall at any time within the space of three years next after the same shall have presented to vs our Heires and Successors in Our or their Privy Council be disallowed and rejected and soe signi-fied by vs Our Heires and Successors vnder our or their Signe Manuall and Signett or by or in our or their Privy Councill vnto the Governor for the time being then such and soe many of them as shall be soe disallowed and riected shall thenceforth cease and determine and become vtterly void and of none effect *Provided* alwais that incase Wee our Heires or Successors shall not within the Terme of Three Yeares after the presenting of such Orders Lawes Statutes or

Ordinances as aforesaid signifie our or their Disallowance of the same Then the said orders Lawes Statutes or Ordinances shall be and continue in full force and effect according to the true Intent and meaneing of the same vntill the Expiracon thereof or that the same shall be Repealed by the Generali Assembly of our said Province for the time being. . . .

Source: *The Charters and General Laws of the Colony and Province of Massachusetts Bay,* Published by order of the General Court, Boston, T.B. Wait and Co., 1814, pp. 18–37.

Arrest Warrant

> *Arrest warrants were issued throughout the Salem episode when evidence was presented to a magistrate sufficient to convince him of the likelihood of criminal behavior on the part of an individual. The arrest warrant authorized a court-appointed law enforcement official—usually a marshal or sheriff—to locate, apprehend, and bring the suspected witch to the Court for questioning. The next step would be a pretrial examination to determine if sufficient evidence of wrongdoing existed to warrant a trial of the suspected witch.*

Warrant for Arrest of Rebecca Nurse

To: To the Marshall of Essex or his deputie
There Being Complaint this day made (before us by Edward putnam and Jonathan Putnam Yeomen both of Salem Village, Against Rebeca Nurce the wife of franc's Nurce of Salem Village for vehement Suspition, of haveing Committed Sundry acts of Witchcraft and thereby haveing donne much Hurt and Injury to the Bodys of Ann putnam the wife of Thomas putnam of Salem Village Anna puttnam the dauter of Said Thomas putnam and Abigail Williams &c

You are therefore in theire Majesties names hereby required to apprehend and bring before us Rebeca Nurce the wife of franc's Nurce of Salem Village, to Morrow aboute Eight of the Clock in the forenoon at the house of Lt Nathaniell Ingersoll in Salem Village in order to her ExaminatioN Relateing to the aboves'd premises and hereof you are not to faile Salem March the 23'd 1691/2

p us *John Hathorne [unclear:] Assists
*Jonathan Corwin
March 24'th 1691/2 I have apprehended the body of Rebeca Nurse and brought her to the house of Le't Nath. Ingersal where shee is in Costody
p'r *George Herrkick Marshall of Essex
(reverse) in the meeting house (be) Mary Walkott Marcy Lewis Eliz: Hubberd
all these accused goody Nurce then to her face that she then hurt them &c and they saw besides the others on Contra Side

Source: Peabody Essex Museum, Salem, MA.

Confession

Nearly 50 individuals confessed to the crime of witchcraft after being accused. The Salem Court followed the policy of allowing self-confessed witches to live, but they were expected to cooperate with the Court in providing evidence to identify other witches. Confessions were written and submitted to the Court often implicating others while expressing remorse.

Confession of Sarah Churchill

Sarah Churchwell confesseth that Goody pudeator brought the book to this Examin't and she signed it, but did not know her at that tyme but when she saw her she knew her to be the same and that Goody Bishop als Olliver appeared to this Examinant & told her she had killed John Trask's Child, (whose Child dyed about that tyme) & said Bishop als Olliver afflicted her as alsoe did old George Jacobs, and before that time this Examin't being afflicted could not doe her service as formerly and her s'd Master Jacobs called her bitch witch & ill names & then afflicted her as [before] above and that putEater brought 3: Images like Mercy Lewis, Ann putnam, Eliza' Hubbard & they brought her thornes & she stuck them in the Images & told her the person whose likeness they were, would be afflicted & the other day saw Goody Olliver [sitt] sate upon her knee,
Jurat in Curia by
Sarah Churchill

This Confession was taken before John Hathorne and Jonathan Corwin Esq'rs l'o Juny 1692, as attests
*Tho Newton

Source: Essex County Court Archives, *Salem Witchcraft Papers*, Vol. 1, p. 110.

Death Warrant

Death warrants were handed down by the Salem Court of Oyer and Terminer on 19 occasions. These documents were issued by Chief Justice William Stoughton to George Corwin, high sheriff of Essex County. They explain the details surrounding the indictment, conviction, and execution of the criminal including details concerning those who claimed to be victims of his/her acts of witchcraft. Each warrant provides exact instructions as to where the criminal is being imprisoned, as well as how, when, and where they are to be executed. In all cases the law enforcement official in charge of the execution is required to report back to the court when the orders of the death warrant have been successfully carried out.

Death Warrant for Bridget Bishop

To George Corwin Gent'm high Sherriffe of the County of Essex Greeting

Whereas Bridgett Bishop als Olliver the wife of Edward Bishop of [Salem] in the County of Essex Sawyer at a speciall Court of Oyer and Termin[er held at] Salem the second Day of this instant month of June for the Countyes of Esse[x] Middlesex and Suffolk before William Stoughton Esq'r and his Associates J[ustices] of the said Court was Indicted and arraigned upon five severall [Seal] I[ndictments] for useing practiseing and exercisein[g] [on the Nyneteenth day of April] last past and divers other days and times [before and after certain acts of] Witchcraft in and upon the bodyes of Abigail Williams, Ann puttnam J[un'r] Mercy Lewis, Mary Walcott and Elizabeth Hubbard of Salem village singlewomen, whereby their bodyes were hurt, afflicted pined, consu[med] Wasted and tormented contrary to the forme of the Statute in that Case [made and] provided To which Indictm'ts the said Bridgett Bishop pleaded no[t guilty] and for the Tryall thereof put her selfe upon

God and her Country, where [upon] she was found guilty of the fel-
onyes and Witchcrafts whereof she stood Indicted and sentence of
Death accordingly passed ag't her as the Law directs, Execution
whereof yet remaines to be done These and theref[ore] in the
Name of their Maj'ties William and Mary now King & Queen [over]
England &c to will and Comand you That upon fryday next being
the Tenth day of this instant month of June between the houres of
Eight and twelve in the afternoon of the same day You safely conduct the s'd Bridgett Bishop als Olliver from their Maj'ties Gaol in
Salem afores'd to the place of Execution and there cause her to be
hanged by the neck untill she be de[ad] and of your doings herein
make returne to the Clerk of the s'd Court and pr'cept And here
of you are not to faile at your peril And this shall be [your]
Sufficient Warrant Given under my hand & Seal at Boston. the Eig
[hth day] of June in the fourth Year of the Reigne of our
Sovereigne Lord and [Lady] William & mary now King & Queen
over England &c Annoq'e Dm 1692;

*Wm Stoughton

June 10th-1692;

According to the Within Written precept I have taken the body of
the within named Brigett Bishop of their Majes'ts Goale in Salem
and Safely Conveighd her to the place provided for her Execution
and Caused the s'd Brigett to be hanged by the neck untill Shee
was dead [and buried in the place] all which was according to the
time within Required and So I make Returne by me

George Corwin Sheriff

Source: Peabody Essex Museum, Salem, MA.

Deposition

*A deposition is a verbatim statement of a witness—called a deponent
—made under oath and recorded by the court clerk. The following
deposition provides testimony against a suspected witch, Bridget
Bishop, in the Salem episode. After a sufficient number of such documents were gathered, court officials would issue an arrest warrant to
have the suspect brought to the court for further questioning and held
for possible trial. If a trial is determined by the court, deposition state-
ments may be used as evidence if the deponent is not available to serve
as a live witness. Witnesses during the witchcraft trials were usually*

brought back into court to provide verbal testimony confirming their deposition statement.

Deposition of John Bly, Sr. and Rebecca Bly v. Bridget Bishop

John Bly sen'r and Rebecka Bly his wife of salem, both Testifie and say that s'd Jno Bly Bough a Sow of Edw'd Bushop of Salem Sawyet and by agreement with s'd Bushop was to pay the price agreed upon, unto Lt Jeremiah Neale of Salem, and Bridgett the wife of Said Edward Bushop because she could not have the mony of vallue agreed for, payd unto her, she [came] to the house of the deponents in Salem and Quarrelled w'th them aboute it soon after which the sow haveing piged, she was taken with strange fitts Jumping up and knocking hir head against the fence and seemed blind and deafe and would not Eat neither Lett her pigs suck but foamed at the mouth, which goody hinderson hearing of sayd she beleived she was over-looked, and that thay had theire cattle ill in suck a manner at the Eastward when she lived there, and used to cure them by giveing of them Red Okar & Milk. which wee also gave the sow. Quickly after eating of which she grew Better. –and then for the spave of neere two howres togather she getting into the street did sett of Jumping & running betweene the house of s'd deponents and s'd Bushops as if she ware stark mad; and after that was well againe and wee did then Apprehend or Judge & doe still that s'd Bishop had bewitched s'd sow
  Jurat in Curia
  (Reverse) John Bly and wife

Source: Essex County Court Archives, *Salem Witchcraft Papers*, Vol. 1, p. 43.

Examination

Examinations were conducted for each individual accused of witch-craft. The purpose of such direct questioning was to ascertain the response of the alleged witch to the accusations of the victims, wit-nesses, and deponents.

   In all cases, the questions and responses as well as the occasional interruptions by people in the court were recorded by the court clerk. This verbatim record of court room testimony is critical evidence in understanding the trial process, as well as the positions taken by the accused when faced directly by their accusers.

Examination of Bridget Bishop, Second Version

The examination of Bridget Bishop before the Worshipful John Hathorne and Jonathan Corwen esq'rs

Bridget Bishop being now coming in to be examined relating to her accusation of Suspicon of sundry acts of witchcrafts and afflicted persons are now dreadfully afflicted by her as they doe say.

(Mr. Harthon)	Bishop what doe you say you here stand charged with sundry acts of witchcraft by you done or committed upon the bodyes of mercy Lews and An Putnam and others.
(Bishop)	I am innocent I know nothing of it I have done no witchcraft
(Mr. Harthon)	Looke upon this woman and see if this be the woman that you have seen hurting you. Mercy Lewes and An Putnam and others doe [doe] now charge her to her face with hurting of them.
(Mr Harthon)	What doe you say now you see they charge you to your face
(Bishop)	I never did hurt them in my life I did never see these persons before I am as innocent as the child unborn
(Mr. Harthon)	is not your coate cut

answers no but her garment being Looked upon they find it cut or toren two wayes Jonathan walcoate saith that the sword that he strucke at goode Bishup was not naked but was within the scabbord so that the rent may very probablie be the very same that mary walcoate did tell that she had in her coate by Jonathans striking at her apperance

The afflicted persons charge her, with having hurt them many wayes and by tempting them to sine the devils Booke at which charge she seemed to be very angrie and shaking her head at them saying it was false they are all greatly tormented (as I conceive) by the shaking of her head

(Mr. Harthon)	good Bishop what contract have you made with the devill

(Bishop)	I have made no contract with the devill I never saw him in my life.
	An Putnam sayeth that shee calls the devill her God
(Mr. Harthon)	what say you to all this that you are charged with can you not find in your heart to tell the truth
(Bishop)	I doe tell the truth I never hurt these persons in my life I never saw them before.
(Mercy Lewes)	oh goode Bishop did you not come to our house the Last night and did you not tell me that your master made you tell more than you were willing to tell
(Mr. Harthon)	tell us the truth in this matter how comes these persons to be thus tormented and to charge you with doing
(Bishop)	I am not come here to say I am a witch to take away my life
(Mr. Harthon)	who is it that doth it if you doe not they say it is your likenes that comes and torments them and tempts the to write in the book what Booke is that you tempt them with.
(Bishop)	I know nothing of it I am innocent
(Mr. Harthon)	doe you not see how they are tormented you are acting witchcraft before us what doe you say to this why have you not an heart to confese the truth
(Bishop)	I am innocent I know nothing of it I am no witch I know not what a witch is
(Mr. Harthon)	have you not given sonsent that some evill spirit should doe this in your likenes
(Bishop)	no I am innocent of being a witch I know no man woman or child here
(Marshall Herrik)	how came you into my bed chamber one morning then and asked me whether I had any curtains to sell shee is by some of the afflicted persons charged with murder
(Mr. Harthon)	what doe you say to these murders you are charged with
(Bishop)	I am innocent I know nothing of it now she lifts up her eyes and they are greatly tormented again

(Mr. Harthon)	what doe you say to these thing here horrible acts of witch craft.
(Bishop)	I know nothing of it I doe not know whither be any witches or no
(Mr. Harthon)	no have you not heard that some have confessed
(Bishop)	no I did not.
	two men tolder her to her face that they had told her here shee is taken in a plain lie now shee is going away they are dreadfully afflicted 5 afflicted persons doe charge this woman to be the very woman that hurts them

This is a true account of what I have taken down at her examination according to best understanding and observation I have also in her examination taken notice that all her actions have great influence upon the afflicted persons and that have been tortored by her

*Ezekiel Cheever.

(Reverse) Examination ag't Bishop

Source: Peabody Essex Museum, Salem, MA.

Letters

No other political figure played such a significant role in the life of the Massachusetts Bay Colony during the early to mid-1690s than did Governor Sir William Phips. These two letters by Phipps provide some keen insight into his unique perspective, and how he wished the British officials in England might view his activities during the Salem witch episode.

Two letters of Governor William Phips (1692–1693)

Letter One

When I first arrived I found this Province miserably harrassed with a most Horrible witchcraft or Possession of Devills which had broke in upon several Townes, some scores of poor people were taken with preternaturall torments some scalded with brimstone some had pins stuck in their flesh others hurried into the fire and water and some dragged out of their houses and carried over the tops of trees and hills for many Miles together; it hath been represented to mee much like that of Sweden about thirty years agoe, and there were many committed to prison upon suspicion of Witchcraft before my arrivall. The loud cries and clamours of the friends of the afflicted people with the advice of the Deputy Governor and many others prevailed with mee to give a Commission of Oyer and Terminer for discovering what witchcraft might be at the bottome or whether it were not a possession. The chief Judge in this Commission was the Deputy Governour and the rest were persons of the best prudence and figure that could then be pitched upon. When the Court came to sitt at Salem in the County of Essex they convicted more than twenty persons of being guilty of witchcraft, some of the convicted were such as confessed their Guilt, the Court as I understand began their proceedings with the accusations of the afflicted and then went upon other humane evidences to strengthen that. I was almost the whole time of the proceeding abroad in the service of Their Majesties in the Eastern part of the County and depended upon the Judgment of the Court as to a right method of proceeding in cases of Witchcraft but when I came home I found many persons in a strange ferment of dissatisfaction which was increased by some hott Spiritts that blew up the flame, but on enquiring into the matter I found that the Devill had taken upon him the name and shape of severall persons who were doubtless inocent and to my certain knowlege of good reputation for which cause I have now forbidden the committing of any more that shall be accused without unavoydable necessity, and those that have been committed I would shelter from any Proceedings against them wherein there may be the least suspition of any wrong to be done unto the Innocent. I would also wait for any particular directions of commands if their Majesties please to give mee any for the fuller ordering this perplexed affair. I have also put a stop to the printing of any discourses one way or the other, that may increase the needless disputes of people upon this occasion, because I saw a likelyhood of kindling an inextinguishable flame if I should admitt any publique and open Contests and I have grieved to see that some who should have done their Majesties and this Province better service have so far taken Councill of Passion as to desire the precipitancy of these matters, these things have been improved by some to give me many interuptions in their Majesties service and in truth none of my vexations have been greater than this, than that their majesties service has been hereby unhappily clogged, and the Persons who have made soe ill improvement of these matters here are seeking to turne it all upon mee, but I hereby declare that as soon as I came from fighting against their Majesties Enemyes and understood what danger some of their innocent subjects might be exposed to, if the evidence of the afflicted persons only did prevaile either to the committing or trying any of them, I did before any application was made unto me about it put a stop to the proceedings of the Court and they are now stopt till their Majesties pleasure be known. Sir I beg pardon for giving you all this trouble, the reason is because I know my enemies are seeking to turn it all upon me and I take this liberty because I depend upon your friendship, and desire you will please to give a true understanding of the matter if any thing of this kind be urged or made use of against mee. Because the justnesse of my proceeding herein will bee a sufficient defence. Sir

I am with all imaginable respect Your most humble Servt
*William Phips.

Dated at Boston on the 12'th of october 1692.

Mem'dm

That my Lord President be pleased to acquaint his Ma'ty in Councill with the account received from New England from Sir Wm. Phips the Governor there touching Proceedings against severall persons for Witchcraft as appears by the Governor's letter concerning those matters.

Source: George Lincoln Burr, ed., *Narrative of the Witchcraft Cases*, 1648–1706 (New York: Charles Scribner's Sons, 1914), 196–98. The letter was addressed to William Blathwayt, clerk of the Privy Council, and it is he who added the memorandum.

Letter Two

Boston in New England Febry 21st, 1692/3

May it please yor. Lordshp.

By the Capn. of the Samuell and Henry I gave an account that att my arrival here I found the Prisons full of people committed upon suspition of witchcraft and that continuall complaints were made to me that many persons were grievously tormented by witches and that they cryed out upon severall persons by name, as the cause of their torments. The number of these complaints increasing every day, by advice of the Lieut Govr. and the Councill I gave a Commission of Oyer and Terminer to try the suspected witches and at that time the generality of the people represented to me as reall witchcraft and gave very strange instances of the same. The first in Commission was the Lieut. Govr. and the rest persons of the best prudence and figure that could then be pitched upon and I depend upon the Court for a right method of proceeding in cases of witchcraft. At that time I went to command the army at the Eastern part of the Province, for the French and Indians had made an attack upon some of our Fronteer Towns. I continued there for some time but when I returned I found people much disatisfied at the proceedings of the Court, for about Twenty persons were condemned and executed of which number some were thought by many persons to be innocent. The Court still proceeded in the same method of trying them, which was by the evidence of the afflicted persons who when they were brought into the Court as soon as the suspected witches looked upon them instantly fell to the ground in strange agonies and grievous torments, but when touched by them upon the arme or some other part of their flesh they immediately revived and came to themselves, upon [which] they made oath that the Prisoner at the Bar did afflict them and that they saw their shape or spectre come from their bodies which put them to such paines and torments: When I enquired into the matter I was enformed by the Judges that they begun with this, but had humane testimony against such as were condemned and undoubted proof of their being witches, but at length I found that the Devill did take upon him the shape of Innocent persons and some were accused of whose innocency I was well assured and many considerable persons of unblameable life and conversation were cried out upon as witches and wizards. The Deputy Govr. notwithstanding persisted vigorously in the same method, to the great disatisfaction and disturbance of the people, untill I put an end to the Court and stopped the proceedings, which I did because I saw many innocent persons might otherwise perish and at that time I thought it my duty to give an account thereof that their Ma'ties pleasure might be signifyed, hoping that for the better ordering thereof the Judges learned in the law in England might give such rules and directions as have been practized in England for proceedings in so difficult and so nice a point; When I put an end to the Court there ware at least fifty persons in prison in great misery by reason of the extream cold and their poverty, most of them having only spectre evidence against them, and their mittimusses being defective, I caused some of them to be lett out upon bayle and put the Judges upon considering a way to reliefe others and prevent them from perishing in prison, upon which some of them were convinced and acknowledged that their former proceedings were too violent and not grounded upon a right foundations but that if they might sit againe, they would proceed after another method, and whereas Mr. Increase Mather and severall other Divines did give it as their Judgment that the Devill might afflict in the shape of an innocent person and that the look and touch of the suspected persons was not sufficient proofe against them, these things had not the same stress layd upon them as before, and upon this consideration I permitted a spetiall Superior Court to be held at Salem in the County of Essex on the third day of January, the Lieut. Govr. being Chief Judge. Their method of proceeding being altered, all that were brought to tryall to the number of fifety two, were cleared saving three, and I was enformed by the Kings Attorny Generall that some of the cleared and the condemned were under the same circumstances or that there was the same reason to clear the three condemned as the rest according to his Judgment. The Deputy Govr. signed a Warrant for their speedy execution and also of five others who were condemned at the former Court of Oyer and termined, but considering how the matter had been managed I sent a reprieve whereby the execution was stopped untill their Maj. pleasure be signified and declared. The Lieut. Gov. upon this occasion was inraged and filled with passionate anger and refused to sitt upon the bench in a Superior Court then held at Charles Towne, and indeed hath from the beginning hurried on these matters with great precipitancy and by his warrant hath cause the estates, goods and chattles of the executed to be seized and disposed of without my knowledge or consent. The stop put to the first method of proceedings hath dissipated the blak cloud that threatened this Province with destruccion; for whereas the delusion of the Devill did spread and its dismall effects touched the lives and estates of many of their Ma'ties Subjects and the reputation of some of the principall persons here, and indeed unhappily clogged and interrupted their Ma'ties affaires which hath been a great vexation to me, I have no new complaints but people minds before divided and distracted by differing opinions concerning this matter are now well composed.

    I am Yor. Lordships most faithfull humble Servant

*William Phips

To the Rt. Honble

The Earle of Nottingham att Whitehall London
R May 24, 93 abt. Witches

Source: George L. Burr, ed., *Narratives of the Witchcraft Cases*, 198–202.

Rev. Deodat Lawson was minister of Salem Village from 1684 to 1688 during which time he believed that he may have had some members of his family succumb to possible witchcraft. He returned to Salem Village and delivered the following sermon to the Salem Village congregation on March 24, 1692, less than a month after the first outcries of the afflicted girls. The sermon was later published in Boston in 1704. It provides the student with a vivid insight into the opinion of an eyewitness to the earliest chapter of the Salem witchcraft episode.

Deodat Lawson, "Christ's Fidelity: The Only Shield against Satan's Malignity" (1693)

1. Let *Regenerate Souls*, that are in good hope of their Interest in GOD, and his Covenant, stir up themselves to *Confirm* and *Improve, that Interest to the Utmost*. Under shaking Dispensations, we should take the faster hold of GOD by Faith, and cleave the closer to him, that *Satan* may not, by any of his Devices or Operations, draw us from our steadfastness of Hope, and Dependence on the GOD of our Salvation. We would hope we are Interested in the Everlasting Covenant of GOD, and Delivered from the *Raging* Tyranny of the *Rearing* Lyon. It is good to be sure, and too sure we cannot be at any time, much less at such a time as this: That it may appear before *Angels* and *Men*, that we are Chosen unto Salvation by the GOD of *Jerusalem*, and are accordingly *Devoted* to him and to his service in an *Unviolable Covenant* against which the Gates of *Hell* shall never have any power. And the clearing up that we are in Covenant with GOD, is a Sovereign *Antidote* against all Attempts of *Satan*, to bring us into Covenant *With* him or subjection *To* him. And in order to this, let us be Awakened.

First, *To put our selves upon Faithful and Thorow Tryal and* Examination, *what hath been amiss*. We all, even the Best of us, have by sin a hand and share, in *Provoking* GOD thus to let *Satan Loose*, in an unusual Manner, WHO *can say he is Clean?* This is a time then, for *Solemn-Self- Examination*. In this time of *Sore Affliction*, there should be great *Searchings of Heart*, as there was for the *Divisions of*

Reuben, Judg. 5. 19. GOD is a GOD of Wisdom, A *Righteous* and *Holy* GOD, and he never Afflicts the People of his Covenant without a *Cause*, and *that Cause* is always Just: We should go as far as we can in the Search, by the Light of Conscience, Conducted by the *Rule* of the Word, and when we can go no farther, we should Pray that Prayer of *Job.*, Chap. 10. 2. *Do not Condemn me; shew me wherefore thou Contendest with me.* Yet was he Upright, and (even in GOD's Account;) *One that Feared* GOD, *and Eschewed Evil* Chap. 1. 8. The like Prayer *David* makes, Psal. 139. 23, 24. *Search me Oh GOD, and know my Heart, try me and know my thoughts. And see if there be any wicked way in me*, &c. These malicious operations of *Satan*, are the sorest afflictions can befal a person or people: And if under the Consideration of *Grievous* Calamities, upon the People of GOD, the Nations round about, will *Inquire* with amazement *after the Cause:* Then surely the People themselves, ought strictly to Examine, as Deut. 29. 24. *What meaneth the heat of this Great Anger?* And to the making this improvement of remarkable Afflictions, we are *directed* by the Example of the *Church*, Lam. 3.40. *Let us Search and Try our ways, and Turn again unto the Lord.* Which leads to the second thing.

2. Add to the former, *True and Unfeigned Reformation, of whatsoever appears to be the Provoking Evils we fall into.* He or They that to *Serious Examination*, (which must be supposed to include *Hearty Confession* of what hath been done amiss) Adds *Thorow Reformation*, may only hope to obtain Pardoning Mercy at the Hands of God, *Prov.* 28. 13. And may it not be said, even to the *Purest Churches*, as he said to them, 2 Chron. 28. 10. *But are there not with You, even with You, Sins against the* LORD *your God.* And certainly, no *Provokings* are so Abhorred of the Lord, as those of *his Sons* and *Daughters, Deut.* 32. 19. This Returning and Reforming then, is the Duty *Required* of, and *Pressed* upon *Israel*, or the visible Covenant People of God, when by sin they had *departed from* him, Hosea 14. 1. O ISRAEL, *Return unto the Lord thy God, for thou hast fallen by thine Iniquity.* Hence the neglect of this Returning, in those that are under many and great Afflictions, is very displeasing unto God, Amos 4. 11. *And ye were as a Firebrand pluckt out of the Burning, yet have ye not returned unto me, saith the Lord.* Insomuch, that *obstinate persisting*, in the neglect of it after *Frequent Warnings*, provokes the Lord to punish those that are guilty thereof, *Seven and seven times more*, Lev. 26. 23, 24. If we would then, *avoid* the Displeasure, and *obtain* the Covenant Favour of GOD, we must both in Profession, and Practice, fall in with the Example, of the formerly Degenerous, but afterwards Reformed *Ephraim*, Jer. 31.

18, 19. *Turn thou me, and I shall be turned; for thou are the Lord my God.*
Surely after that I was turned, I Repented, and after that I was instructed,
I smote upon my Thigh, &c. Then, and not till then, will the *Bowels* of
the LORD, *be turned within him, and his Repentings kindled together* for
us. Now that our Reformation may be unto Divine Acceptation, it
must be,

First, *Personal* and particular. We commonly say, *that which is*
every Bodies work, is no Bodies work. Every one is Guilty, in the
Provocation, and therefore every one should apply themselves to
Reformation. Every one of us should set our selves to do our *Own*
Duty, and Repent of our *Own Sins.* There is an inclination in the
best, to Charge the *Sins of others*, as the procuring cause of GOD's
Judgments, and to reflect severely on the *Pride, Lukewarmness,*
Covetousness, Contention, Intemperance, and *Uneven Conversation* of
others; but we can hardly be brought, to smite upon our *own*
Breast, and say, *What have I done?* Unless we be, in particular
Charged, and *Convicted*, as *David* was by the Prophet *Nathan*, in 2
Sam. 12. 7. *Thou art the man.* Thou art he (q. d.) that art concerned
in this Povocation by thy Transgressions.

Secondly, *Reformation*, (by which we may clear up, that we are the
Covenant People of God) must be *Universal.* We must turn from *All*
and *Every* sin which hath been *committed*, and apply our selves to
the *discharge* of *Every* Duty, which hath been *neglected.* We must
have no sinful Reserves, as he, 2 Kings 5. 18. *In this thing pardon*
thy Servant, &c. He was Convicted it was a *Sin*, that needed
Pardon, and yet would fain be Excused in the Commission thereof.
Thus *Junius*, and *Trem.* and the *Dutch* Annotators translate it, and
Pise. Interprets it of his desire to continue in that Office, which he
could not with good Conscience discharge. Though some Learned
and Judicious understand it as a craving of pardon for what he
had therein done amiss in time past. In short, so far as we are guilty
of *Reservations* in our Reformation, so far will there remain a *Cloud*
upon the Evidences of our *Covenant Interest* in GOD *that hath*
Chosen Jerusalem. This to Regenerate Souls. Secondly then

Let *Unregenerate Sinners, be* warned *and* awakened, to *get out of*
that Miserable state of sin, and consequently of subjection to Satan,
(That Tyrannical, Implacable, and Indefatigable, Enemy of *Souls)*
in which you are. O break off your sins by Repentence, and your
Iniquities by a saving closure with the LORD JESUS CHRIST, for
Justification, Sanctification and *Salvation*, That ye may be delivered,
from the Power, and Dominion of *Satan*, under which you are
ensnared, to do his will, altho' utterly cross to the will of GOD,

and may be *Translated*, into the Kingdom of the Lord Jesus; the *Dear Son of God*, and Blessed Saviour of the Souls of men, *Col.* 1. 13. Being by infinite mercy, *Recovered* out of the snare of the Devil, who are (now) taken Captive by him at his will. 2 Tim. 2. 26. *Awake, Awake* then, I beseech you, and remain no longer under the Dominion of that *Prince of Cruelty* and Malice, whose Tyrannical Fury, we see thus exerted, against the *Bodies* and *Minds* of these afflicted persons. Surely no Sinner in this Congregation, who is *sensible* of his Bondage to *Satan*, that cruel (and worse than Egyptian) *Taskmaster*, and *Tyrant*, can be willing, to continue quietly, in subjection to him one day or hour longer. Thus much in respect of the Spiritual State of men.

Secondly, This *Warning* is directed to all *manner of persons*, according to their condition of life, both in *Civil* and *Sacred* Order: Both *High* and *Low, Rich* and *Poor, Old* and *Young, Bond* and *Free*. O let the observation of these amazing Dispensations of GOD's unusual and strange Providence, *quicken* us to our *Duty* at such a time as this, in our respective *Places* and *Stations, Relations*, and *Capacities*. The GREAT GOD, hath done such things amongst us, as *do make the Ears of those that hear them to Tingle;* JER. 1. 3. and serious Souls, are at a *loss* to what these things may *grow*; and what shall we find to be the end, of this dreadful visitation, in the permission whereof the *Provoked* GOD *as a Lyon hath Roared; who can but Fear? The* LORD *hath spoken, who can but Prophecy?* Amos 3. 8. The Loud *Trumpet* of God, in this Thundering Providence, is *Blown in the City*, and the Eccho of it, heard through the *Country*, surely then, the *People* must, and ought to be afraid, Amos 3. 6. ... Let it be for DEEP HUMILIATION, *to the people of this place, which is in special under the Influence of this Fearful Judgment of GOD. The* LORD doth at this day, manage a great controversy with You, to the astonishment of your selves and others, You are therefore to be deeply humbled, and sit in the dust Considering.

First, *The signal hand of God, in singling out this place, this poor Village, for the first seat of Satans Tyranny*, and to make it (as 'twere) the Rendezvous of Devils, where they *Muster* their infernal forces appearing to the afflicted, as coming Armed, to carry on their malicious designs, against the Bodies, and if God in mercy prevent not, against the Souls of many in this place. *Great Afflictions*, attended with Remarkable Circumstances, do surely call for more than ordinary degrees of Humiliation.

But Secondly be humbled also, *That so many Members of this Church, of the* LORD JESUS CHRIST, *should be under the Influences of Satans malice, in these his Operations;* some as the Objects of his Tyranny, on their Bodies to that degree of *Distress*, which none can be sensible of, but those that see and feel it, who are in the mean-time also, sorely distressed in their Minds, by frightful Representations, made by the *Devils* unto them. Other professors, and visible Members of this Church, are under the awful *Accusations*, and imputations of being the *Instruments* of *Satan* in his mischevious actings. It cannot but be matter of deep humilia-tion, to such as are Innocent, that the Righteous and Holy GOD, should permit them to be named, in such pernicious and unheard of practices, and not only so, but that HE who cannot but do right, should suffer the stain of suspected Guilt, to be as it were *Rubbed on*, and *Soaked in*, by many sore and amazing Circumstances; and it is matter of soul abasement, to all that are in the Bond of GOD's Holy Covenant in this place, that *Satans* seat should be amongst them, where he attempts to set up *his* Kingdom, in opposition to *Christ's* Kingdom, and to take some of the Visible Subjects of our LORD JESUS, and use at least their shapes and appearances, instru-mentally, to *Afflict* and *Torture, other* Visible Subjects of the same Kingdom. Surely his design is, that CHRIST'S Kingdom, may be *Divided against it self*, that being thereby weakened, he may the bet-ter take Opportunity to set up his own *Accursed powers* and Dominions. It calls aloud then, to all in this place, in the Name of the Blessed JESUS and words of his Holy Apostle; 1 Pet. 5. 6. *Humble your selves under the mighty hand of God*, thus thru up in the midst of you, *and he shall Exalt, Save, and Deliver you, in due time.*

To Conclude; The Lord is known by the Judgments which he Executes in the midst of us. The Dispensations of his Providence, appear to be unsearchable, and his Doings past finding out. He seems to have allowed *Satan*, to afflict many of our People, and that thereupon he is come down in *Great Wrath*, threatning the Destruction of the *Bodies*, (and if the Infinite Mercy of GOD prevent not) of the *Souls* of many in this place. Yet may we say, in the midst of all the *Terrible* things which he doth in Righteousness; He alone is the GOD of our Salvation, who represents himself, as the Saviour of all that are in a low and distressed Condition, because he is good, and *His Mercie endureth for ever.*

Let us then Return and Repent, rent our Hearts, and not our Garments. Who can tell if the LORD will *Return* in Mercy unto us? And by his Spirit lift up a Standard, against the GRAND *Enemy* who threatens to come in like a Flood, among us, and over-throw all that is *Holy*, and *Just*, and *Good.* It is no small comfort to consider, that *Job's* Exercise of Patience, had it's Beginning from the *Devil;* but we have seen the end to be from the LORD, *James* 5. 11. That We also, may find by experience, the same Blessed Issue, of our present Distress, by *Satan's* Malice. Let us repent of every Sin, that hath been Committed, and Labour to practice, every *Duty* which hath been Neglected. And when we are Humbled, and Proved for our good in the latter end: Then we shall assuredly, and speedily find, that the Kingly Power of Our LORD and SAVIOUR, shall be Magnifyed, in delivering his Poor Sheep and Lambs, out of the *Jaws* and *Paws* of the Roaring Lyon.

Then will JESUS the Blessed Antitype of *Joshua*, the Redeemer, and Chooser of *Jerusalem, Quell, Suppress*, and utterly *Vanquish*, this *Adversary* of ours, with *Irresistable* Power and Authority, according to our Text. *And the* LORD *said unto Satan, the* LORD *Rebuke thee O Satan, Even the* LORD *that hath Chosen Jerusalem, Rebuke thee: Is not this a Brand pluckt out of the* FIRE?

Source: *Christ's fidelity the only shield against Satan's malignity.* Asserted in a sermon deliver'd at Salem-village the 24th of March, 1692. Being lecture-day there, and a time of publick examination, of some suspected for witchcraft. By Deodat Lawson. Printed at Boston in New-England, and reprinted in London, by R. Tookey, for the author; and are to be sold by T. Parkhurst, at the Bible and Three Crowns in Cheapside; and J. Lawrence, at the Angel in the Poultry. 1704.

GLOSSARY OF KEY TERMS

Acadia—That part of French colonial Canada immediately to the north and east of New England encompassing the provinces of present-day New Brunswick and Nova Scotia.

Antinomian controversy—A dispute between the leaders of Boston and Anne Hutchinson resulting in her expulsion from Massachusetts Bay Colony in March 1638.

Apprenticeship—A contracted agreement between a parent and a skilled craftsperson agreeing to place a son in the care of the craftsperson for a specific number of years for the purpose of learning a skill such as blacksmithing or shoemaking.

Banns—A formal wedding announcement usually posted and read in a church no less than three weeks before a wedding notifying the local community of a couple's intention to get married.

"Bathsheba Model"—A Puritan ideal of womanhood as found in the book, Song of Solomon in the Old Testament of the Bible.

Blue laws—Laws which still remain in effect on the legal code reflecting the moral sensibilities of an earlier era, and often appear amusingly outdated to contemporary observers.

"Body of Christ"—In Christian theology, the belief that the members of the Christian church represent the spiritual body of Christ on Earth, acting on His behalf and working His will among the people of the Earth.

Carding—That part of the textile production process when the wool is combed between two paddles removing tangles and unwanted materials from the combed wool prior to spinning.

"City on a Hill"—The ideal, Puritan, Christian commonwealth envisioned by Gov. John Winthrop in his 1630 sermon, "A Model of Christian Charity," referring to the new Colony of Massachusetts Bay.

"Codfish aristocracy"—A phrase coined by Harvard historian, Samuel Eliot Morison, referring to those elite Puritan merchants who made their fortunes in the fishing and maritime trade exporting dried salt codfish.

Coif—A simple cloth headcovering worn by housewives at all times both to protect the head and hair as well as a symbol of domestic female modesty.

Contraction—A simple, premarital ceremony performed at the community meetinghouse to recognize the engagement of a couple.

Courting stick—A hollow tube from five to eight feet in length, used by courting couples to speak privately to each other when in the presence of friends and family.

Court of Oyer and Terminer—A specially appointed court whose primary purpose is to hear and determine the just verdict of a special series of cases based upon the evidence presented.

Covenant of Grace—In Puritan theology, the doctrine that God, through the sacrifice of His son, Jesus Christ, offers the free gift of forgiveness and salvation to His "elect" without the necessity of following a covenant of works.

Covenant of Salvation—In Puritan theology, the belief that God promises the free gift of salvation to His "elect" and in return expects faithfulness and obedience.

Covenant of Works—In Puritan theology, the belief that in the Old Testament the Children of Israel were promised salvation by God provided they kept all His commandments and laws.

Dalliance—An archaic term meaning a flirtatious exchange between a male and female having the appearance of a romantic interlude, but actually being of no serious meaning or value.

Deputy husband—A term describing the special legal status of a wife in relation to her husband, identifying her as the person who can legally act in her husband's place if he is not available.

Doctrine of grace—In Puritan theology, the belief that God offers to His "elect" the free gift of forgiveness for their sins. This gift may be received only from God and may not be won or deserved by any action on the part of the believer.

Dominion of New England—A political and geographical entity which lasted from 1686 to 1689, ruled by Sir Edmund Andros, and established by King James II for the purpose of placing the colonies of New England, New York , and New Jersey more firmly under royal control.

Elect—In Puritan theology, those people who God, for reasons known only to Himself, has given the free gift of salvation.

English common law—The law code of England developed over hundreds of years, forming the backbone of the British legal system.

First Massachusetts Charter—A charter issued in 1629 by King Charles I to the Massachusetts Bay Company authorizing them to colonize that portion of New England between three miles north of the Merrimack River and three miles south of the Charles River, extending west to the Pacific Ocean.

Fish flake—A wooden platform designed to support salted fish fillets allowing them to dry in the sun and open air.

Fishing bank—A shallow area in the open ocean where fish breed and feed in large numbers creating and ideal area for fishing.

Flummery—A soft, sweet pudding made from stewed fruit, oatmeal, and a sweetening agent such as molasses, often used as a dessert in colonial American homes.

Goodwin case—In 1689, a witchcraft case involving the Goodwin Family of Boston, and a servant woman, Goody Glover who allegedly bewitched the Goodwin children and was subsequently tried, condemned, and hanged for witchcraft.

Great Migration—A massive exodus of thousands of Puritans from England between the years 1630 and 1640, resulting in a dramatic population increase in New England, the British West Indies, and Ireland.

Great Swamp Fight, Kingston, RI—A battle between native Narragansett warriors and Massachusetts militia on December 19, 1675, during King Philip's War resulting in the loss of 300 Narragansett and more than 50 English colonists.

Halfway Covenant—In 1662, an agreement among New England Puritan congregations allowing partial church membership to the children and grandchildren of church members without the necessity of testifying to a conversion experience.

Joined-frame construction—A construction technique whereby a wooden frame is joined together with mortise-and-tenon joints held in place by wooden pegs or tree-nails (aka trunnels).

Justification—A theological doctrine, developed by reformer John Calvin, stating that those who are elected by God, upon receiving a conversion experience, are immediately made righteous by God and "justified" or cleansed of their sin.

Ketch—A two-mast sailing vessel used during the seventeenth century for fishing, the coastal trade, and the West Indies trade.

Naumkeag—The Native American name given by Roger Conant to the area now known as Salem, Massachusetts, meaning "the fishing place."

New Planters—That group of colonists to arrive in 1628 at Naumkeag (aka Salem) with Gov. John Endicott in 1628 as the vanguard of the Massachusetts Bay Company.

Old Planters—That group of colonists to arrive in 1626 at Naumkeag (aka Salem) with Roger Conant as the remnant of the Dorchester Company.

Original sin—The Judeo-Christian theological belief that from the first man, Adam, sin has been passed down to all succeeding generations of humankind, and are thus born corrupt and in need of the atonement of Christ's sacrifice to cleanse them of their sin.

Patriarch—The male head of a family, often the oldest male in the family.

Praying Indians—Native Americans in New England who had been converted to the Christian faith and often chose to live in Anglo-native villages near English colonial settlements.

Predestination—A theological doctrine developed by reformer, John Calvin, claiming that because God is omniscient (all-knowing), He knows in advance who will and who will not be saved, and nothing humankind may do will alter that predestined decision.

Privateer—A government-licensed, privately owned, and armed vessel whose purpose is to attack the merchant ships of an enemy county during a time of war.

Puritan—A member of a reformed Protestant sect within the Church of England which sought to completely cleanse or "purify" the English church from all vestiges of Roman Catholicism as well as all other immoral practices and doctrines.

Puritan oligarchy—The religious leaders and political rulers of the Puritan colony of Massachusetts Bay.

Rennet—A complex of enzymes found in the stomach of mammals to assist in the digestion of mother's milk. After extracted from an animal's stomach, it may be used to separate the curds from the whey in the cheesemaking process.

Sachem—A New England Native American tribal leader of either sex.

Saints—A term used by Separatists to refer to themselves as members of God's saved "elect."

Sanctification—A theological doctrine developed by reformer, John Calvin, claiming that those who are justified by God, immediately experience the indwelling of the Holy Spirit which positively transforms their personal behavior to that of a regenerated believer.

Second Massachusetts Charter—A revised royal charter issued by King William and Queen Mary to the Colony of Massachusetts in 1691 proclaiming the colony a royal colony, curtailing much of its autonomy, and merging Massachusetts with Plymouth Colony.

Separatists—A splinter-group of former Puritans who gave up attempting to purify the Church of England and broke away from that group to establish their own separate denomination in Holland, and finally at Plymouth, Massachusetts. They are commonly referred to as Pilgrims.

Shallop—A one-mast, open wooden vessel built with a shallow draft and designed for coasting and fishing.

Spectral evidence—Evidence presented to court in a witchcraft case testifying to the harm caused by a spirit or the spiritual likeness of an accused person.

Strangers—A term used by Separatists to refer to everyone other than themselves.

Sumptuary laws—Laws created to regulate and limit the wearing of extravagant apparel by individuals who are not of a high enough social or economic status to afford such clothing.

Thornback—A seventeenth-century slang term meaning an old, unmarried female.

Visible saints—In Puritan theology, these are the members of the elect, God's saved remnant, who may be readily identified by their testimony to having had a conversion experience.

Walking out—A betrothal ceremony between a bride and groom popular in Puritan New England whereby they officially announce in church their intention to get married.

Wattle and daub—In joined-frame house construction, a method of infilling spaces between vertical posts with green, interwoven saplings, then covering them with "daubing" or clay material containing straw, lime, and dung over which a coating of whitewash is painted.

BIBLIOGRAPHY

SECONDARY SOURCES

Anderson, Virginia DeJohn. *New England's Generations: The Great Migration and the Formation of Society and Culture in the Seventeenth Century.* Cambridge: Cambridge University Press, 1991.

Baker, Emerson W., and John G. Reid. *The New England Knight Sir William Phips, 1651–1695.* Toronto: University of Toronto Press, 1998.

Beyor, Paul, and Stephen Nissenbaum. *Salem Possessed: The Social Origins of Witchcraft.* Cambridge: Harvard University Press, 1974.

Bremer, Francis J. *The Puritan Experiment: New England Society from Bradford to Edwards.* Rev ed. 1976. Hanover and London: University Press of New England, 1995.

Collinson, Patrick. *The Elizabethan Puritan Movement.* Berkeley: University of California Press, 1967.

Crane, Elaine Forman. *Ebb Tide in New England: Women, Seaports, and Social Change, 1630–1800.* Boston: Northeastern University Press, 1998.

Craven, Wesley Frank. *The Colonies in Transition, 1660–1713.* New York: Harper and Row, 1968.

Crawford, Mary Caroline. *Social Life in Old New England.* New York: Grosset and Dunlap, 1914.

Davies, Horton. *Worship and Theology in England: From Andrews to Baxter and Fox, 1603–1690. Princeton*, NJ: Princeton University Press, 1975.

Davies, Horton. *Worship of the English Puritans.* Westminster: Dacre Press, 1948.

Demos, John Putnam. *The Enemy Within: Two Thousand Years of Witch-Hunting in the Western World*. New York: Viking Press, 2008.

Demos, John Putnam. *Entertaining Satan: Witchcraft and the Culture of Early New England*. Rev ed. 1982. Oxford University Press, 2004.

Demos, John Putnam. *A Little Commonwealth: Family Life in Plymouth Colony*. Oxford University Press, 2000.

Demos, John Putnam. *The Unredeemed Capture*. New York: Alfred A. Knopf, 1994.

Dow, George Francis. *Everyday Life in Massachusetts Bay Colony*. New York: Dover Publication, 1988.

Earle, Alice Morse. *Child Life in Colonial Days*. Stockbridge, MA: Berkshire House Publishers, 1993.

Erikson, Kai T. *Wayward Puritans: A Study in the Sociology of Deviance*. New York: John Wiley and Sons, 1966.

Ernst, James. *Roger Williams: New England Firebrand*. New York: Macmillan, 1932.

Gaustad, Edwen S. *Liberty of Conscience: Roger Williams in America*. Judson Press, 1999.

George, Charles H., and Katherine George. *The Protestant Mind of the English Reformation*. Princeton, NJ: Princeton University Press, 1961.

Godbeer, Richard. *The Salem Witch Hunt: A Brief History with Documents*. Boston and New York: St. Martin's Press, 2011.

Goss, K. David. *The Salem Witch Trials: A Reference Guide*. Westport, CT: Greenwood Press, 2008.

Greene, Jack P., ed. *Settlement to Society 1607–1763*. New York: W.W. Norton, 1975.

Greven, Philip J., Jr. *Four Generations: Population, Land, and Family in Colonial Andover*. Ithaca and London: Cornell University Press, 1970.

Halkett, John. *Milton and the Idea of Matrimony*. New Haven: Yale University Press, 1970.

Hall, David D. *Witch-Hunting in 17th Century New England*. Boston: Northwestern University Press, 1991.

Hall, Michael G. *The Last American Puritan: The Life of Lucrease Mather*. Middletown, CT: Wesleyan University Press, 1988.

Haller, William. *The Rise of Puritanism*. New York: Harper and Brothers, 1957.

Haskin, George L. *Law and Authority in Puritan Massachusetts*. New York: Macmillan, 1960.

Hawke, David Freeman. *Everyday Life in Early America*. New York: Harper and Row, 1988.

The Holy Bible. King James Version. Grand Rapids, MI: Zondervan Publishers, 1995.

Kaufmann, U. Milo. *The Pilgrim's Progress and Traditions in Puritan Meditation*. New Haven: Yale University Press, 1966.

Knappen, M. M., ed. *Two Elizabethan Puritan Diaries*. Gloucester, MA: Peter Smith Press, 1966.

Knox, Bernard, ed. *Essays Ancient and Modern*. New York: Harcourt, Brace and World, 1936.

Miller, Perry. *The New England Mind: From Colony to Province*. Cambridge: Harvard University Press, 1983.

Miller, Perry. Thos H. Johnson, ed. *The Puritans: A Sourcebook—Writings*. 1 and 2 vols. New York: Harper Torchbooks, 1938.

Miller, Perry, and Thomas H. Johnson, eds. *The American Puritans: Their Prose and Their Poetry*. New York: Double Day and Co., 1956.

Morgan, Edmund S., eds. *The Founding of Massachusetts: Historians and Their Sources*. Indianapolis: The Bobbs-Merril Company, Inc., 1964.

Morgan, Edmund S. *The Puritan Dilemma: The Story of John Winthrop*. New York: Addison, Wesley-Longman, 1999.

Morgan, Edmund S. *The Puritan Family: Religion and Domestic Relations in Seventeenth Country New England*. New York: Harper and Row, 1966.

Morgan, Edmund S., ed. *Puritan Political Ideas*. Indianapolis: The Bobbs-Merril Company, Inc., 1965.

Morison, Samuel Eliot. *Builders of the Bay Colony*. Oxford: Oxford University Press, 1930.

Norton, Mary Beth. *In The Devil's Snare: The Salem Witchcraft Crisis of 1692*. New York: Vintage Books, 2002.

Phillips, James Duncan. *Salem in the Seventeenth Century*. Boston: Houghton and Mifflin Co., 1933.

Risjord, Norman K. *The Colonists*. Lanham, MD: Rowman and Littlefield, 2001.

Rosenthal, Bernard. *Salem Story: Reading the Witch Trials of 1692*. Cambridge: Cambridge University Press, 1993.

Ryken, Leland. *Worldly Saints: The Puritans as They Really Were*. Grand Rapids, MI: Academic Books, 1986.

Smith, J. W. Ashley. *The Birth of Modern Education: The Contribution of the Dissenting Academies*. London: Independent Press, 1954.

Stannard, David E. *The Puritan Way of Death: A Study in Religion, Culture, and Social Clause*. New York: Oxford University Press, 1977.

Ulrich, Laurel Thatcher. *Good Wives*. New York: Alfred A. Knopf, 1982.

Upham, Charles W. *Salem Witchcraft*. 1867. Reprint, Mineola, NY: Dover Publishers, 2000.

Webster, John Clarence, ed. *Acadio at the End of the Seventeenth Century: Letters, Journals, and Memoirs of Joseph Robineau de Villebon*. Saint John N.B. Museum, 1934.

Wertenbaker, Thomas Jefferson. *The Puritan Oligarchy*. New York: Grosset and Dunlap, 1947.

ARTICLES

Bailyn, Bernard. "Communications and Trade: The Atlantic in the Seventeenth Century." *Essays on American Colonial History.* Ed. Paul Goodmen. New York: Holt, Rinehart, and Winston, Inc., 1972.

Demos, John. "Notes on Life in Plymouth Colony." *William and Mary Quarterly.* 3rd ser. vol 22 (1965): 264–86.

Hemphill, C. Dallett. "Age Relations and Social Order in New England." *Journal of Social History.* 8 vols. 1994.

PRIMARY SOURCES

Blathwayt, William. Letter to Francis Nicholson. *Blathwayt Papers.* Folder 2. 15 vol. Colonial Williamsburg.

Bradford, William. *Of Plymouth Plantation.* New York: Capricorn Books, 1962.

Bradstreet, Gov. Swion. Letter to Massachusetts agents in London. *Documentary History of the State of Maine.* 5 vol.

Essex County Records. 1 and 2 vols. Essex County Court.

Felt, Joseph B. *Annals of Salem.* 1 and 2 vol. Boston: W. and S.B. Ives., 1849.

Hale, John. *Modest Inquiry into the Nature and of Witchcraft.* Reprint by Beverly Historical Society. Beverly, MA, 1992.

"Massachusetts Bay Charter." *Documents for the Study of American History.*

Mather, Rev. Cotton. "Cares about Nurseries."

Mather, Rev. Cotton. *Magnolia Christi Americana.*

Mather, Rev. Cotton. *Memorable Providences Relating to Witchcrafts and Possessions.* Boston, 1692.

Mather, Richard. "Farewell to the Church and People of Dorchester in New England."

Records of the Admiralty Court. U.K.: Public Record Office.

Records of the Massachusetts Great and General Court. Massachusetts State Archives.

Shurtleff, Nathaniel B. ed. *Records of the Governor and Company of the Massachusetts Bay in New England, 1628–1686.* 1853–1854.

Winthrop, John. "A Model of Christian Charity." *The Papers of John Winthrop.* 2 vol. Ed. R.C. Winthrop.

INDEX

About the Author

K. DAVID GOSS is an assistant professor of history at Gordon College, Wenham, MA. He holds an MA from Tufts University and is currently a PhD candidate in American and New England Studies at Boston University. Among his publications are: *Officers and Soldiers of the French and Indian War*; *Maritime Salem in the Age of Sail*; *Treasures of a Seaport Town*; *Salem: Cornerstones of a Historic City*; and *The Salem Witch Trials: A Reference Guide* for Greenwood Press (2007).